A Working Lawyer's Life

The Letter Book of John Henry Senter 1879-1884

Karen S. Beck

Curator of Rare Books / Collection Development Librarian
Boston College Law Library

THE LAWBOOK EXCHANGE, LTD.
Clark, New Jersey
2008

ISBN-13: 978-1584779223 (cloth w/dust jacket)
ISBN-13: 978-15847779292 (paperback)

THE LAWBOOK EXCHANGE, LTD.
33 Terminal Avenue
Clark, New Jersey 07066-1321

Please see our website for a selection of our other publications and fine facsimile reprints of classic works of legal history:
www.lawbookexchange.com

Library of Congress Cataloging-in-Publication Data

Beck, Karen S.
A working lawyer's life : the letter book of John Henry Senter, 1879-1884 / by Karen S. Beck.
p. cm.
Includes bibliographical references and index.
ISBN 978-1-58477-922-3 (cloth with dust jacket : alk. paper) -- ISBN 978-1-58477-929-2 (pbk. : alk. paper)
1. Senter, John H. (John Henry), 1848-1916. 2. Lawyers--United States--Biography. I. Senter, John H. (John Henry), 1848-1916. II. Title.
KF373.S46B43 2008
340.092--dc22
[B]

2008031337

Printed in the United States of America on acid-free paper

For Paul

Acknowledgements

I would like to thank Mark Esser, Book Conservator at Boston College's John J. Burns Library, for providing me with much useful information about letterpress copying, and for allowing me to photograph the letterpress copier in his conservation lab. Reta Goss, Clerk for the Town of Warren, Vermont, searched through Warren's Registry of Deeds for me, for which I am very grateful. I am also grateful to Patrick Healy, Director of Green Mount Cemetery in Montpelier, Vermont, for providing me with John Senter's death certificate and information about his burial.

A project like this would not be possible without the resources of many libraries and the able assistance of the people who work in them. Special thanks to the librarians and staff at the Boston College Law Library (especially Helen Lacouture, Ann McDonald, Kerry Sloan and Katie Sosnoff); the Vermont Historical Society (Paul Carnahan and Marjorie Strong); the New England Historic Genealogical Society; the Warren (Vermont) Public Library (Deborah Kahn) and the Boston Public Library for their advice and assistance. I am also grateful to Filippa Marullo Anzalone and the Boston College Libraries for granting a summer research leave that enabled me to work on this project.

My editors Valerie L. Horowitz, Managing Editor of Publications at the Lawbook Exchange, and Frank Houdek, former Editor of the Law Library Journal, have my warmest thanks for providing me with expert editorial guidance and generous dollops of encouragement at many points along the way. It was an absolute pleasure to work with both of them.

At every phase of this project, Paul Baskett provided exactly what was needed in the way of editorial, photographic and artistic assistance. He also served as my all-around sounding board, always responding with wise advice and good humor. For this and much more, I dedicate this book to him.

And last but not least, a very special debt of gratitude to Professor Richard G. Huber; if not for his generous gift of Mr. Senter's copying book, this book could not have been written.

Contents

Part II

Part I

Introduction*

> I have in my hands for collection a note against you in favor of G. W. Cardell amounting to day to $6.50. An early settlement will save you costs.[1]

In April 1879, John Henry Senter of Warren, Vermont, penned these words in a letter to A.F. Martin, Esq. But before posting the letter, Senter carefully copied it into his brand new "Japanese Letter Copying Book." It was one of the first of some 326 letters he copied between April 1879 and December 1884. These letters document Senter's business dealings, which involved the areas of law, education, and politics. They reveal the daily details of five and a half years in Senter's life as he embarked upon a legal career at age thirty – what he did, what he hoped to accomplish, and what he thought about it all.

---

* A slightly different version of Part I was originally published as an article in 99 LAW LIBR. J. 471 (2007). The article published in *Law Library Journal* was a revised version of a winning entry in the Open division of the 2005 American Association of Law Libraries/Lexis Nexis Call for Papers Competition. The transcriptions of the letters appear for the first time here.

1. Letter from John Henry Senter to A.F. Martin (Apr. 14, 1879) *in* John Henry Senter, Letter Book 6 (1879-84) (available in the Daniel R. Coquillette Rare Book Room, Boston College Law Library, Newton, Massachusetts) [hereinafter Senter Letter Book]. A note about transcription: I have left all spelling, grammar, punctuation, and underlining exactly as Senter wrote them, without editorial comment. I have inserted square brackets to indicate completely illegible words or phrases, like so: [illegible]. I have placed square brackets around partially legible words to indicate my best guess at their meaning, and also when I have supplied context to fragments of letters by adding words to those that Senter wrote.

Eventually, through the generosity of Richard G. Huber, currently professor emeritus and formerly dean of the Boston College Law School from 1970 to 1985, Senter's copying book found its way to the Boston College Law Library.[2] Since 2001, it has been part of the rare book collection, housed inside the library's Daniel R. Coquillette Rare Book Room.

Ever since it arrived in our library, this humble volume has intrigued me for several reasons. It is a primary source – a record of what one nineteenth-century lawyer did on a daily basis, with his activities and thoughts set down at the time they occurred rather than being selectively reconstructed decades after the fact. I wanted to use Senter's letters as firsthand evidence to find out what his life was like. Of course, this single book of correspondence does not begin to provide a complete picture of a small-town lawyer's life in the 1880s. Senter may or may not have been a "typical" lawyer of the time, if indeed a "typical" lawyer even existed; his copying book contains baffling time gaps and a maddening lack of information about his personal life. Nevertheless, it is one piece of evidence that moves us many steps closer to understanding Senter's early life as a lawyer, and one step closer to understanding the lives of lawyers working in small New England towns during the late nineteenth century.

Besides wanting to learn what I could from the letters in Senter's copying book, I wished to bring the letters, and the copying book itself, into the light of day. Like most manuscripts, this copying book is unique – both as a physical object and in its content. Even a rare book usually exists in multiple copies, but a unique manuscript like this remains buried treasure until it is brought to light. By using the letters as a vehicle to write about John Senter, I wanted to highlight

---

2. According to Dick Huber, he got the book years ago while working at New England School of Law. He befriended a secretary there and, through her, got to know her father, then in his eighties. After several conversations, her father presented the book to Professor Huber. None of these people was related to John Henry Senter. Interview with Professor Emeritus Richard G. Huber, Boston College Law School, Newton, Massachusetts (June 20, 2001).

one special item in Boston College's rare book collection and give it the attention I believe it deserves. It is just one example of the kinds of unique resources in our libraries' rare book collections that librarians and scholars can use to engage in new research.

Part I begins with a brief biographical sketch of John Henry Senter compiled from published accounts and original source materials. It next examines Senter's copying book and provides a brief explanation of the lost art of letterpress copying. The heart of Part I contains a detailed analysis of Senter's correspondence, first presenting a summary of the letters, next reviewing Senter's education- and law-related correspondence at length, and finally noting themes and traits of character that seem to emerge from the letters.

Part II contains a full transcription of Senter's correspondence, followed by an index of people and place names.

Figure 1. John Henry Senter

Photograph courtesy of the Vermont Historical Society. On the back of this photograph of Senter, Dorman B.E. Kent identified him as "a lawyer of great ability." For more on Kent, *see infra* note 205.

CHAPTER 1

Who Was John Senter?

Biographical Sketch

John Henry Senter, son of Dearborn Bean and Susan Chase Lyford Senter, was born in Cabot, Vermont, on November 11, 1848, and, except for a few brief early interludes, remained a Vermonter for life.[3] He received his education in the Cabot public schools in Vermont and in high school at Concord, New Hampshire.[4] As a youth he also spent time in Montpelier and East Montpelier, Vermont.[5] Early on, he aspired to become a lawyer, and while studying his chosen profession he taught school for forty-three terms to support himself and his dependent mother.[6] Mrs. Senter was still alive at age seventy-three in 1882, so we can infer that her son supported her for years, even after becoming a lawyer and starting a family of his own.[7]

Senter studied law in the offices of Clarence H. Pitkin of Montpelier[8] and was admitted to the bar in the March term of

3. WALTER HILL CROCKETT, 5 VERMONT: THE GREEN MOUNTAIN STATE 410 (1923).
4. *Id.*
5. HAMILTON CHILD, PART FIRST: GAZETTEER OF WASHINGTON COUNTY, VT. 1783-1889, at 117 (William Adams ed., Syracuse, N.Y., Syracuse J. Co. 1889).
6. *The City of Montpelier*, 7 VERMONTER, Apr. 1902, at 153.
7. ABBY MARIA HEMENWAY, 4 PT. 2 VERMONT HISTORICAL GAZETTEER: THE TOWNS OF WASHINGTON COUNTY 810 (Montpelier, Vt., Vt. Watchman and St. J. Press 1882).
8. Clarence Pitkin appears as a frequent correspondent in Senter's copying book. Senter wrote twelve letters to him and mentioned him in several other letters as well. *See, e.g., infra* notes 147, 153, 162, and accompanying text.

1879.[9] He began his law practice in Warren, Vermont, and stayed there until 1885. His years in Warren are particularly interesting because they mark his transition from educator to lawyer. There was much overlap; even while getting his law practice off the ground, he continued to serve as Warren's Superintendent of Schools from 1879 through 1882.[10] The time period that marks the beginning of his law practice – 1879 through 1884 – is the focus of this project, and we shall return to John Senter's final five and a half years in Warren shortly.

In 1885, Senter left Warren for Montpelier and entered into a law partnership with Harlan W. Kemp, which lasted until 1891.[11] Jacks-of-all-trades in their offices at 47 State Street in downtown Montpelier, Senter and Kemp listed themselves in the 1889 Business Directory of Washington County, Vermont as "SENTER & KEMP, (John H.S. and Harlan W.K.) lawyers, fire, life and accident insurance and Remington typewriter agents, law reporters for Supreme Court of Vermont for Atlantic Reporter,[12] Langdon block, 47 State."[13] By 1889 Senter was living at 10 Winter Street at the corner of Summer

---

9. Jacob G. Ullery, Men of Vermont: An Illustrated Biographical History of Vermonters and Sons of Vermont 352 (Brattleboro, Vt., Transcript Publ'g Co. 1894).

10. The annual *Walton's Vermont Register* lists Senter as superintendent in 1880, 1881, and 1882. Walton's Vermont Register, Farmers' Almanac, and Business Directory for 1880, at 169 (Claremont, N.H., Claremont Mfg. Co. 1880) [hereinafter Walton's Vermont Register for 1880]; Walton's Vermont Register, Farmers' Almanac, and Business Directory for 1881, at 143 (Claremont, N.H., S.L. Farman 1881); Walton's Vermont Register, Farmers' Almanac, and Business Directory for 1882, at 143 (White River Junction, Vt., White River Paper Co. 1882). Before and after that time, the position was held by E.W. Slayton. Walton's Vermont Register, Farmers' Almanac, and Business Directory for 1879, at 169 (Claremont, N.H., Claremont Mfg. Co. 1879); Walton's Vermont Register, Farmers' Almanac, and Business Directory for 1883 at 147 (White River Junction, Vt., White River Paper Co. 1883).

11. Crockett, *supra* note 3, at 410.

12. Senter and Kemp served as Vermont reporters of decisions in 1887 and 1888. During this time, the two men reported 122 decisions that may be found in volumes 9 through 15 of the *Atlantic Reporter*, or in volumes 59 and 60 of

in downtown Montpelier, close to his office and the Washington County Court House.[14]

Senter repaid his debt to his former mentor Clarence Pitkin by mentoring at least one law student apprentice during his career. Twenty-one years Senter's junior, Edward M. Goddard clerked in Senter's office for one year, probably in 1897. He was admitted to the Vermont Bar in October 1898, and soon thereafter joined Senter as the junior partner in the firm of Senter & Goddard. Goddard was appointed assistant state librarian in 1901[15] and eventually became state librarian.

Always active in civic affairs, during his time in Montpelier Senter held "nearly all the municipal offices,"[16] including justice of the peace.[17] In 1898 and 1899, he served as Mayor of Montpelier, an office he won "unanimously" in both years.[18] In 1906, Senter represented Montpelier in the state legislature.[19] He remained involved with education throughout his career, serving for many years as Montpelier's superintendent of schools, just as he had done earlier in Warren.[20]

As is evident from his letters,[21] Senter was politically active from the very beginning of his career and remained so throughout his life. A lifelong Democrat, he served as chairman, secretary or assistant secretary of the Democratic State Committee for thirty years, and he frequently represented his party as a delegate at Democratic national

---

Vermont Reports. The 122 cases were retrieved by running the search **"reported by senter"** on Westlaw in the VT-CS database on Feb. 16, 2005.

13. Hamilton Child, Part Second: Business Directory of Washington County, Vt. 1889 at 135 (Syracuse, N.Y., Syracuse J. Co. 1889).

14. *Id.*

15. GeneaBios: Biographies for Genealogy, http://www.geneabios.com/vermont/executive3.htm [last visited Apr. 15, 2007].

16. *The City of Montpelier*, *supra* note 6, at 155.

17. Ullery, *supra* note 9, at 353.

18. *The City of Montpelier*, *supra* note 6, at 155.

19. Crockett, *supra* note 3, at 410.

20. *The City of Montpelier*, *supra* note 6, at 155.

21. *See infra* notes 202-204 and accompanying text.

conventions.[22] From 1900 through 1904, he also served as the Vermont representative of the Democratic National Committee.[23] One biography noted that "[a]lthough he resides in a state, county and town that are strongly Republican, he has been honored with public office when his party ticket as a whole was far in the minority."[24] Despite being in the minority party, Senter's Democratic affiliation occasionally paid off; during President Cleveland's first term of office, he appointed Senter to be National Bank Examiner from 1885 through 1889.[25] In 1894, Senter was appointed United States District Attorney for Vermont, a position he held through 1898.[26] During President Cleveland's second term in 1893-1897, he appointed Senter to be United States Attorney for the District of Vermont.[27]

From his early days in Warren, Senter was always a "joiner." At various points in his life he belonged to a host of fraternal organizations,[28] including the Masons, Knights Templars, Nobles of the Mystic Shrine,[29] and the International Order of Odd Fellows.[30] He founded The Club in 1899 or 1900, whose members met occasionally to discuss the works of Shakespeare,[31] and belonged to the Vermont Historical Society for at least the years 1905 through

22. CROCKETT, *supra* note 3, at 410.
23. 1 WHO WAS WHO IN AMERICA 1104 (1943).
24. *The City of Montpelier*, *supra* note 6, at 155.
25. CROCKETT, *supra* note 3, at 410.
26. *Id.*
27. *The City of Montpelier*, *supra* note 6, at 155.
28. *See, e.g.*, Letter from John Henry Senter to John H. Batchelder, Waterbury, Vt. (Aug. 29, 1881), *in* Senter Letter Book, *supra* note 1, at 158 (enclosing $3.12 for dues to the Grand Lodge, Mad River Lodge No. 91).
29. *The City of Montpelier*, *supra* note 6, at 155.
30. ULLERY, *supra* note 9, at 353.
31. PERRY H. MERRILL, MONTPELIER, THE CAPITAL CITY'S HISTORY, 1780-1976, at 110 (1976). According to Merrill, The Club was a successor to an earlier club, the Shakespeare Club. From its inception until 1902, The Club consisted of only twelve to fourteen members. It went dormant from 1902 to 1905, at which time it was revived with a membership of twenty-five and a mandate to discuss other topics in addition to Shakespeare. *Id.*

1910.[32] During this time he delivered at least two speeches that have been published, a funeral oration titled "An Address Delivered by John H. Senter Before Montpelier, Vt. Lodge, No. 924, B.P.O.E., on Elks Memorial Day, Sunday, December 6, 1908";[33] and a most intriguing address entitled "Was Shakespeare a Lawyer," [34] delivered on October 27, 1903, before the annual meeting of the Vermont Bar Association, of which he was president. In this long (sixty pages!) address, Senter dissected numerous authorities on both sides of the debate and analyzed many passages of Shakespeare's plays and sonnets before concluding that Shakespeare was not a lawyer. It is not a stretch to suppose that Senter joined all of these organizations to further his advancement in his own profession; certainly people still do that today. His correspondence does not reveal that he expressly relied upon his fraternal connections to gather business, advance himself, or otherwise curry favors. That said, he often addressed his intended recipient as "Brother X"[35] and closed his letters with "Yours fraternally, John H. Senter."[36]

During all his years of political activity Senter continued to practice law. A Westlaw search reveals that he appeared as attorney of record in forty-six reported cases in the thirty-two-year span between 1883 and 1915.[37] Thirty-six of these were decided in the Vermont Supreme

---

32. PROCEEDINGS OF THE VERMONT HISTORICAL SOCIETY 1905-1906, at 15 (1905); PROCEEDINGS OF THE VERMONT HISTORICAL SOCIETY FOR THE YEARS 1909-1910, at 14 (1910).

33. JOHN H. SENTER, AN ADDRESS DELIVERED BY JOHN H. SENTER BEFORE MONTPELIER, VT. LODGE, NO. 924, B.P.O.E., ON ELKS MEMORIAL DAY, SUNDAY, DECEMBER 6, 1908 (Montpelier, Vt., The Lodge[?] 1908).

34. JOHN H. SENTER, WAS SHAKESPEARE A LAWYER? AN ADDRESS BY JOHN H. SENTER, PRESIDENT OF THE VERMONT BAR ASSOCIATION: DELIVERED BEFORE THE ANNUAL MEETING, OCTOBER 27, 1903 (Montpelier, Vt., Argus and Patriot Press 1903).

35. The first example of this was a letter addressed to "Brother Durant." Letter from John Henry Senter to L.L. Durant, Montpelier, Vt. (Sept. 1, 1881), *in* Senter Letter Book, *supra* note 1, at 163.

36. The first instance of this was in Letter from John Henry Senter to "friend E.L.H." (May 7, 1879), *in* Senter Letter Book, *supra* note 1, at 41.

37. To find these cases, I searched on Westlaw in the ALLCASES-OLD database

Court, and ten in federal district court or the Second Circuit Court of Appeals. His win/loss record is close to fifty/fifty. He represented his clients in all capacities: plaintiffs, defendants, petitioners, respondents, appellants, and appellees.

The West Topics assigned to the cases show that he handled a wide variety of subject matters, from Abortion and Birth Control (once) to Waters and Water Courses (twice). Other topics that appeared in more than one case include Aliens, Banks & Banking, Breach of the Peace, Conspiracy, Criminal Law, Customs Duties, Eminent Domain, Insurance, Intoxicating Liquors, and Mortgages. Similarly, his letters reveal that even at the earliest stages of his career he handled a wide range of legal matters.[38]

Senter's private life remains quite private; published biographical sketches and his own letters provide very few glimpses into his home life. He was married in Plattsburgh, New York,[39] in November 1875 or 1876,[40] shortly before his twenty-seventh or twenty-eighth birthday, to Addie G. Martin of Warren.[41] Little is known of Addie, daughter of Carlos and Mary Ainsworth Martin.[42] John and Addie Senter raised five children – Frank Ginevra, Clarence Hiram,[43] Mabel Addie,

---

using the queries **"john henry senter," "john senter"** and **"j. h. senter"** on September 13, 2004. Naturally these searches do not capture all of the lower court and unreported cases in which Senter was involved. They also exclude the cases he reported during his 1887-88 stint as reporter of decisions. *See supra* note 12.

38. *See infra* pages 56-67 (describing "Senter's Diverse Law Practice").

39. ULLERY, *supra* note 9, at 353.

40. There is some confusion about the date of Senter's marriage. Some sources give the date as November 1, 1875. *See, e.g.*, WHO WAS WHO IN AMERICA, *supra* note 23, at 1104; CHILD, *supra* note 5, at 117. Another source gives the date as November 1, 1876. *The City of Montpelier, supra* note 6, at 155. Yet another source gives the date as November 30, 1876. ULLERY, *supra* note 9, at 353.

41. ULLERY, *supra* note 9, at 353.

42. *Id.*

43. John and Addie's second son was almost certainly named after two of John Senter's mentors, Clarence Pitkin and Hiram Atkins. Both of their names appear frequently in Senter's correspondence. *See, e.g., infra* notes 147, 153, 162, (Pitkin); 121, 181, 203, 206-08 (Atkins) and accompanying text.

Figure 2. John Henry Senter's death certificate

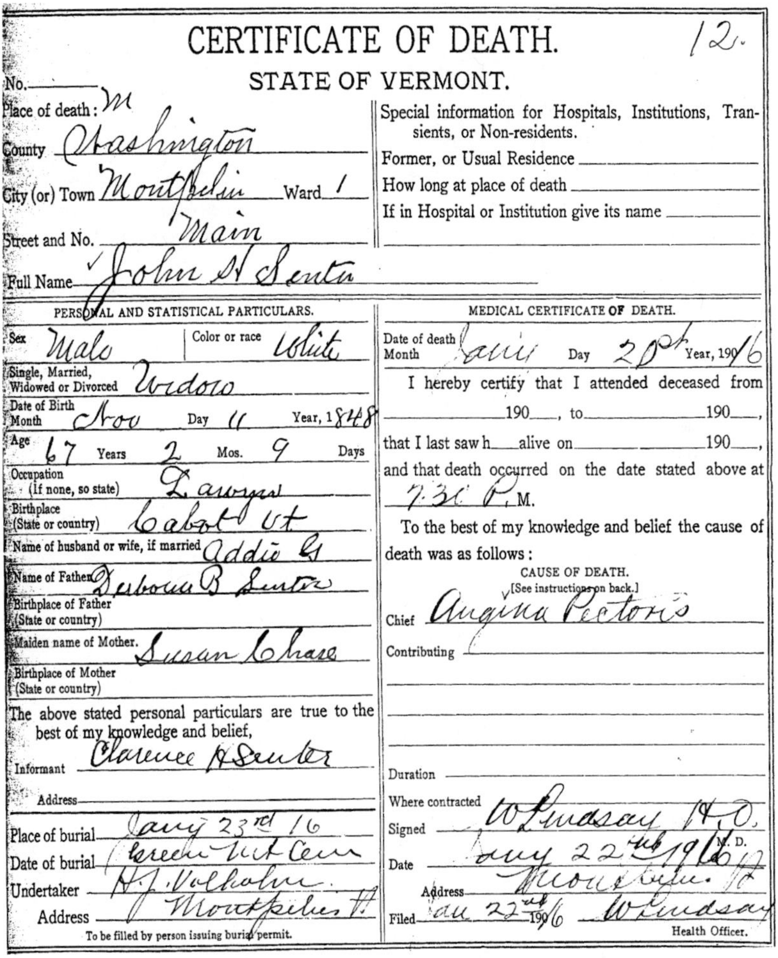

CERTIFICATE OF DEATH. 12.

STATE OF VERMONT.

No.——

Place of death: M

County Washington

City (or) Town Montpelier Ward 1

Street and No. Main

Full Name John H Senter

Special information for Hospitals, Institutions, Transients, or Non-residents.

Former, or Usual Residence

How long at place of death

If in Hospital or Institution give its name

PERSONAL AND STATISTICAL PARTICULARS.

Sex Male | Color or race White

Single, Married, Widowed or Divorced Widow

Date of Birth Month Nov Day 11 Year, 1848

Age 67 Years 2 Mos. 9 Days

Occupation (If none, so state) Lawyer

Birthplace (State or country) Cabot Vt

Name of husband or wife, if married Addie G

Name of Father Jerborne B Senter

Birthplace of Father (State or country)

Maiden name of Mother. Susan Chase

Birthplace of Mother (State or country)

The above stated personal particulars are true to the best of my knowledge and belief,

Informant Clarence H Senter

Address

Place of burial Jany 23rd 16

Date of burial Green Mt Cem

Undertaker H. J. Volholm

Address Montpelier Vt

To be filled by person issuing burial permit.

MEDICAL CERTIFICATE OF DEATH.

Date of death Month Jany Day 20th Year, 1916

I hereby certify that I attended deceased from ——190——, to——190——,

that I last saw h——alive on——190——,

and that death occurred on the date stated above at 7.30 P. M.

To the best of my knowledge and belief the cause of death was as follows:

CAUSE OF DEATH.

[See instructions on back.]

Chief Angina Pectoris

Contributing

Duration

Where contracted

Signed W Lindsay M.D.

Date Jany 22nd 1916

Address Montpelier Vt

Filed Jan 22nd 1916 W Lindsay Health Officer.

Courtesy of Patrick Healy, Director of Green Mount Cemetery. The likely cause of Senter's death was angina pectoris, heart disease.

John Henry, and Clara May[44] – and as of 1902 could boast of one granddaughter as well.[45]

After a very busy and productive life, John Henry Senter died suddenly of heart failure at age sixty-seven in his room at Montpelier on January 20, 1916.[46] He was buried in lot number 1807 in Montpelier's Green Mount Cemetery.[47]

Senter's Life in Warren, Vermont

Named for Dr. and General Joseph Warren, the town of Warren, Vermont was chartered in 1789, first settled in 1797, and organized in 1798.[48] It occupies 40.05 square miles, or 25,633 acres near the center of the state.[49] A mountainous area dominated by Lincoln Peak and Mt. Abraham,[50] Warren lies between the two ranges of the Green Mountains at the place where the ranges commence.[51] A second significant geological feature is the Mad River, which runs through Warren north into Waitsfield, "affording a splendid water power"[52] that supported many mills and abounded with trout as well.[53] Warren's

---

44. Ullery, *supra* note 9, at 353.
45. *The City of Montpelier, supra* note 6, at 155.
46. Crockett, *supra* note 3, at 410.
47. Telephone conversation with Patrick Healy, Director of Green Mount Cemetery (Oct. 18, 2005). I am grateful to Mr. Healy for providing me with information about Senter's burial, including a photocopy of an index card entitled "Green Mount Cemetery Interments" showing that Senter was buried in lot number 1807.
48. David Maunsell et al., Gazetteer of Vermont Heritage: A Concise Account of the Discovery, Settlement, and Progress of Interesting and Remarkable Events in the Green Mountain Country 86 (1976).
49. Virtual Vermont, Warren, http://www.virtualvermont.com/towns/warren.html#about (access link to About Warren) (last visited Apr. 15, 2007).
50. Maunsell et al., *supra* note 48, at 86.
51. Frederick W. Beers, County Atlas of Washington, Vermont 4 (New York, F.W. Beers, 1873).
52. *Id.*
53. Child, *supra* note 5, at 476. Senter himself mentions the splendid fishing

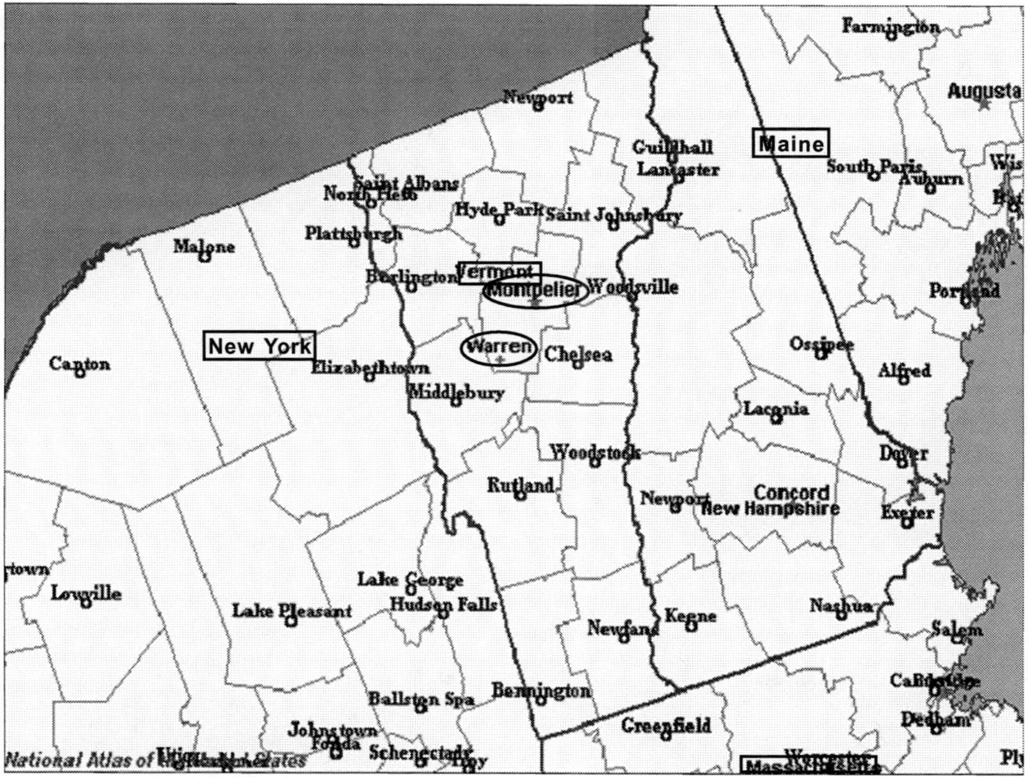

Figure 3. Map of Vermont and surrounding states. Warren and Montpelier are circled; state borders are drawn with bold lines, and county borders are drawn with faint lines. Map of Vermont was created by the author using the Map Maker function at the NATIONAL ATLAS OF THE UNITED STATES, http://nationalatlas.gov (created Jan. 27, 2005).

earliest claim to fame was as a lumber[54] and dairy farm town;[55] today it is a haven for skiers.[56] Lincoln Mountain Road, running east from the town into Lincoln, was an early gated toll road, built by William Cardell[57] for 50 cents a rod.[58] To pass through its gates, travelers paid 12 ½ cents for passing one-way with a team, 25 cents for a round trip.[59]

Within Warren, Warren Village was located near the town's center, where the Mad River joined with Bradley and Freeman brooks as seen in the center of Figure 4.[60] East Warren, seen at the right of Figure 4, was the first part of the town to be settled.[61]

---

opportunities near his hometown: "I should be happy to see you up here in Mad River Valley, we will find some fishing for you and try and make it pleasant." Letter from John Henry Senter to G.B. Damon (June 10, 1879), *in* Senter Letter Book, *supra* note 1, at 92-93. This letter contains a rare example of Senter's social chit-chat, which is quoted here in its entirety. In another letter, mostly about textbook business, Senter closes with an invitation: "I wish you could find time to spend a few days up here rusticating, if you like fishing we have plenty, and we have mountains to climb &c &c &c. . . ." Letter from John Henry Senter to Mr. McClintock (July 31, 1879), *in* Senter Letter Book, *supra* note 1, at 131.

54. FED. WRITERS' PROJECT, WORKS PROGRESS ADMIN. FOR THE STATE OF VT., VERMONT: A GUIDE TO THE GREEN MOUNTAIN STATE 251(1937). In an 1883 letter, Senter described the land as follows: "Mrs. Wallace has a farm, or rather William L. Wallace has, here in Warren. I don't know how many acres, enough any how, for the more land such as that is one owns the worse off they are. . . . There is quite a part of it timbered land, but it is hard wood timber, and hard wood timber in this town is not worth anything. The place is dear at $300.00, don't think you will be liable to find a customer." Letter from John Henry Senter to Osmand D. Clark (June 13, 1883), *in* Senter Letter Book, *supra* note 1, at 210.

55. CHILD, *supra* note 5, at 475.

56. MAUNSELL ET AL., *supra* note 48, at 86.

57. William Cardell's descendents figure prominently in the affairs of Warren, Vermont, and Senter mentions them in his correspondence as well. *See, e.g.*, text accompanying notes 1, 130, 185-86.

58. MAUNSELL ET AL., *supra* note 48, at 86.

59. 4 Pt. 2 HEMENWAY, *supra* note 7, at 811.

60. CHILD, *supra* note 5, at 478.

61. *Id.*

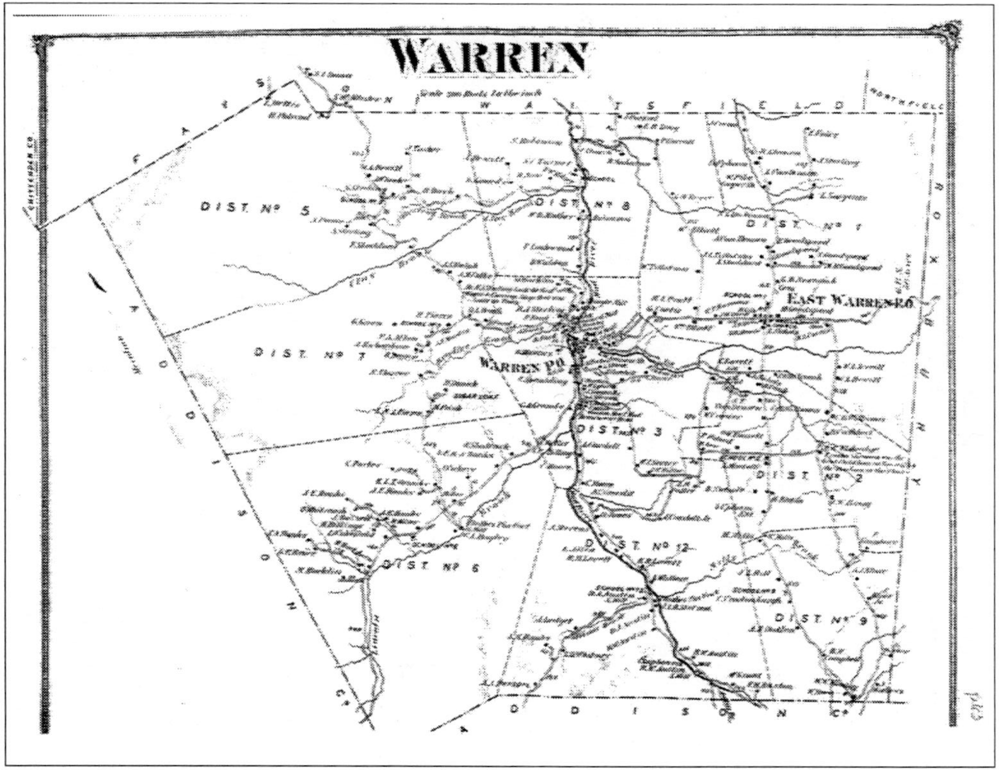

Figure 4. Map of Warren, Vermont. BEERS, COUNTY ATLAS OF WASHINGTON, *supra* note 51, at 63.

With a population numbering 951 in the 1880 census, by 1882 Warren was deemed "quite a village."[62] Its center, Warren Village, boasted

> some 50 dwelling-houses, 1 church, 1 school-house, a very good one; 3 stores, 2 boot and shoe shops, 1 tannery, 5 blacksmith shops, 2 clap-board mills, 2 sawmills, 1 grist-mill, 3 carriage shops, 1 harness-shop, 1 tin-shop, 2 cooper-shops, 2 clothes-pins shops, 1 gunsmith, 1 millinery shop, a tavern and post office.[63]

Being a rural area, residents got into scrapes with wolves and bears from time to time,[64] but readers will be relieved to learn that "Warren [could] boast of strong men" who no doubt were up to the challenge.[65]

In an 1873 atlas of Washington County, a "J.H. Sentre" was listed in the "Business Notices" for Warren as a "clerk" in Warren Village.[66] Unfortunately, a detailed map of residences and places of business in Warren Village (Figure 5) showed no home or office for John Senter, although the homes of many of Senter's correspon-

62. 4 Pt. 2 HEMENWAY, *supra* note 7, at 807.
63. *Id.* at 807.
64. *Id.* at 803.
65. *Id.*
66. BEERS, *supra* note 51, at 64. Although Senter never alluded to his work as a clerk in his letters, this description of a clerk's duties, taken from a sign on the walls of the New York Law Offices of James Moffett, June 5, 1884, might provide some idea of Senter's working life before he became a full-fledged lawyer:

> Office employees will daily sweep the floors, dust the furniture, shelves and show cases. Each day fill lamps, clean chimneys and trim wicks. Wash the windows once a week. Each clerk will bring in a bucket of water and a scuttle of coal for the day's business. Make your pens carefully. You may whittle to your individual taste. This office will open at 7 a.m. and close at 8 p.m. daily except on the Sabbath, on which it will remain closed. Each employee is expected to spend the Sabbath by attending Church and contributing liberally to the cause of our Lord.

Figure 5. Map of Warren Village

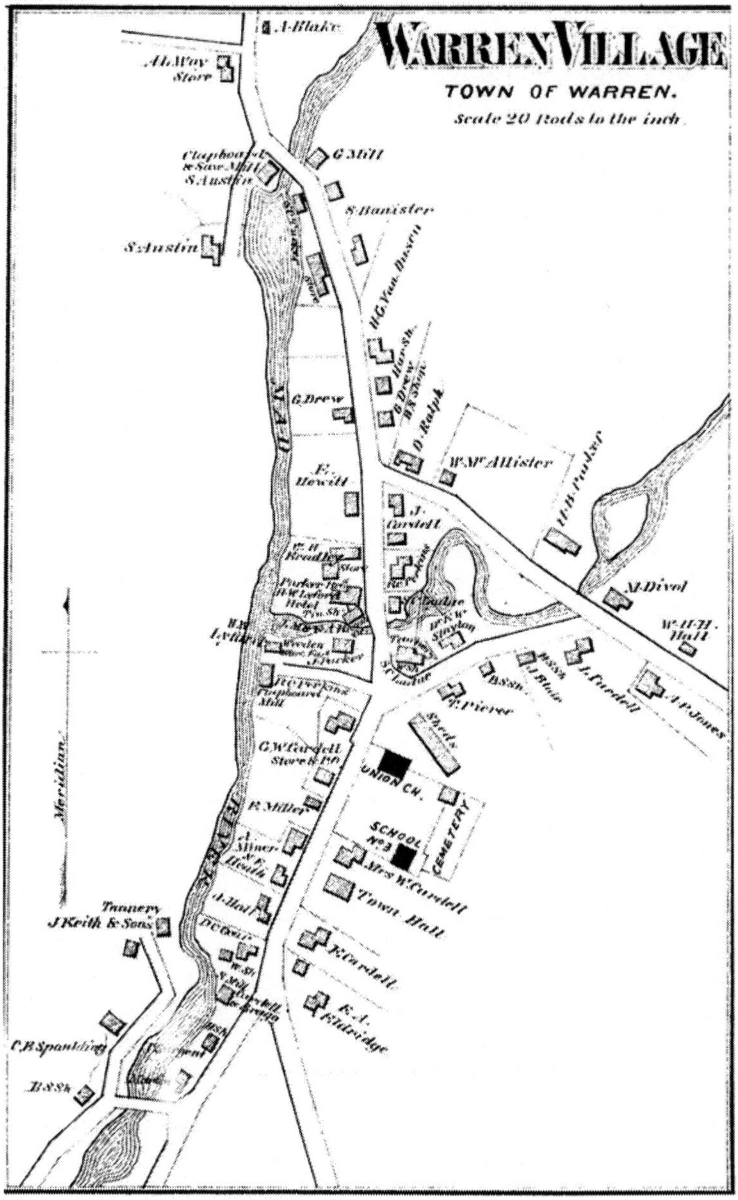

Beers, County Atlas of Washington, *supra* note 51, at 63.

dents such as the Lyfords and Cardells can be seen.[67] The 1880 United States Federal census established that John H. Senter, age thirty-one, was living in Warren, married with two children.[68] By 1884, Senter evidently had a separate law office in Warren, but whether that office was in his home or elsewhere remains unclear.[69]

Although small, Warren was far from completely isolated, and its small size required businessmen like Senter to travel frequently throughout the county.[70] In addition to traveling by wagon, which was fraught with perils of its own,[71] by 1881 Senter could avail him-

> Men employees will be given an evening off each week for courting purposes, or two evenings a week if they go regularly to Church. After an employee goes home from the office, he should spend his leisure time reading the Bible and other good books while contemplating the Glories and building up of the Kingdom. . . . Any employee who has performed his labor faithfully and without fault for a period of five (5) years in my service, who has been thrifty and attentive to his fellowmen as a law-abiding citizen, will be given an increase of five cents (5¢) per day in his pay, providing a just return in profits from the business permits it. Signed, James C. Moffett[.]

Cynthia L. Cooper, *Adapt or Follow: A Firm's Choice*, N.Y.L.J., May 23, 1988, at S13.

67. *Map of Warren Village*, in BEERS, *supra* note 51, at 64. Senter appears to have had a home or office in Warren Village. *See* Letter from John Henry Senter to H. Moore (Nov. 27, 1879), *in* Senter Letter Book, *supra* note 1, at 86 (asking a debtor to see him about a collection matter "the first time your up to the village"). A search of the Warren, Vermont registry of deeds covering the period 1860 to 1890 was conducted on October 13, 2005 by Warren Town Clerk Reta Goss. There is no record that Senter purchased any property in Warren during that time. However, Ms. Goss noted that the town often provided housing to schoolteachers, or perhaps Senter rented his home or apartment during that time. Interview with Reta Goss, Town Clerk, Warren, Vt. (Oct. 13, 2005).

68. UNITED STATES FEDERAL CENSUS (1880), *available at* http://www.ancestry.com (access link to 1880 census) (last visited Apr. 15, 2007).

69. Letter from John Henry Senter to Charles Pike (May 8, 1884), *in* Senter Letter Book, *supra* note 1, at 250 ("There are two cases set for trial at my office May 13th . . . .").

70. *See infra* pages 70-71 (discussing Senter's arduous travel schedule).

71. *See infra* pages 67-70 (discussing injuries Senter sustained due to poor road conditions).

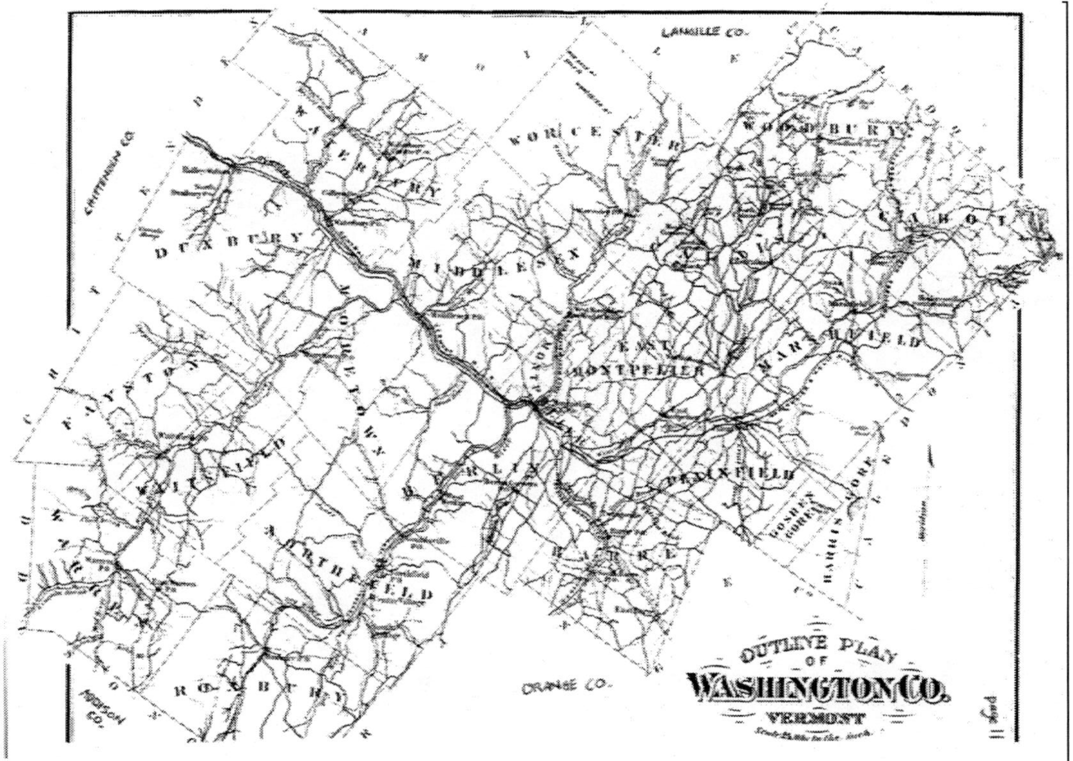

Figure 6. Map of Washington County, Vermont. Warren is at the lower left, Cabot is at the upper right, and Montpelier is in the middle. BEERS, COUNTY ATLAS OF WASHINGTON, *supra* note 51, at 11.

self of a daily stage to travel the seven miles from Warren to Roxbury, home of the nearest railroad station.[72]

Much of Senter's legal work during 1879 to 1884, the years covered in his copying book, centered in Warren and surrounding towns in Washington county, particularly Montpelier, the state capital. Warren is located in the southwest corner of Washington County, outlined faintly in Figure 3 and shown in detail in Figure 6, a map of Washington County. Washington County also includes the town of Cabot, where Senter was born. Warren is 34 miles from Cabot, at polar opposite ends of the county, and 17.3 miles from Montpelier as the crow flies.[73]

When Senter traveled to Montpelier, he conducted much of his business in various downtown hotels and the Washington County Court House. The latter was located in downtown Montpelier near the corner of State and Elm Streets. It was built in 1844, enlarged in 1879, and finished in 1880.[74]As described in 1889, it was "commodious, and warmed by steam, [and contained] pleasant, spacious rooms for the use of the county clerk and judge of the Probate Court; also convenient jury rooms."[75]

John Senter was listed as a lawyer in the Vermont Business Directory during all the years he practiced law in Warren. Prior to 1879, his name did not appear in the Directory. Between 1879 and 1885, Senter was among the one to three lawyers listed in Warren. Oddly, Senter's father-in-law, Carlos Martin, appeared sporadically during these years in the annual business directories as a lawyer in Warren, but Senter never mentioned him in his correspondence.[76] Senter made his final appearance in Warren in the 1885-86 edition of the Direc-

---

72. 4 Pt. 2 HEMENWAY, *supra* note 7, at 807. For a clever way that Senter paid his stage fare, *see infra* note 135 and accompanying text.

73. CHILD, *supra* note 13, at 2 (Table of Air Line Distances for Washington County, Vermont).

74. CHILD, *supra* note 5, at 346.

75. *Id.*

76. THE VERMONT BUSINESS DIRECTORY, FOR 1878-79, at 115 (Boston, Briggs & Co. 1878); THE VERMONT BUSINESS DIRECTORY, FOR 1883-84, at 126 (Boston, Briggs &

Figure 7. Washington County Court House, Montpelier, Vermont

WASHINGTON COUNTY COURT-HOUSE.

CHILD, PART FIRST: GAZETTEER OF WASHINGTON COUNTY, VT. 1783-1889 *supra* note 5, at 346.

tory.[77] That year marked a transition for Senter, who also listed himself in the Montpelier section of the Directory in his new partnership with Harlan W. Kemp,[78] where theirs was one of twenty-one lawyers or law partnerships listed for the town.

In comparison to the twenty-two lawyers practicing in Warren and Montpelier, the 1883-84 Vermont Business Directory listed eleven blacksmiths working in these two towns,[79] sixteen carpenters and builders,[80] nineteen grocers and country stores,[81] nine hairdressers,[82] one circulating library,[83] two photographers,[84] twelve physicians,[85] three plumbers,[86] nine saloons,[87] seven stables,[88] one telephone company exchange[89] and two undertakers.[90]

Co. 1883); THE VERMONT BUSINESS DIRECTORY, FOR 1884-85, at 137 (Boston, Briggs & Co. 1884). The versatile Carlos Martin was also listed as a carpenter in the 1880 *Walton's Vermont Register.* WALTON'S VERMONT REGISTER FOR 1880, *supra* note 10, at 169.

77. THE VERMONT BUSINESS DIRECTORY, FOR 1885-86, at 137. (Boston, Briggs & Co. 1885).

78. *Id.* at 135.

79. THE VERMONT BUSINESS DIRECTORY, FOR 1883-84, *supra* note 76, at 30, 32.

80. *Id.* at 50, 52.

81. *Id.* at 76, 102.

82. *Id.* at 105, 106.

83. *Id.* at 127.

84. *Id.* at 161.

85. *Id.* at 164, 166.

86. *Id.* at 168.

87. *Id.* at 175.

88. *Id.* at 191-2.

89. *Id.* at 200.

90. *Id.* at 204.

Warren in the 1890's. Memorial Day speech by John Senter, famous lawyer and talker from Montpelier, in front of the Warren Inn (now Warren Store).

Figure 8. Postcard of Senter giving a speech in Warren, Vermont. Undated postcard courtesy of the Vermont Historical Society Library. The original of this photograph can be found at the end of Volume 4 of the Warren Public Library's photo album collection. This handwritten note is included with the photo: "Memorial Day - 1890. John Senter, born in Warren (*sic*) and self-educated, became a lawyer and a state leader in Montpelier. Here in front of Lyford's Hotel he addressed a group that includes Henry Hartshorn, Warner Moore and Ivan Greenslit." E-mail from Deborah Kahn, Director, Warren Public Library (Nov. 2, 2005). Lyford's Hotel is now the Warren Store, and the photo actually shows the side of the building rather than the front. The benches might still be present in the Warren Town Hall. *Id.*

Figure 9. Closed view of John Senter's letterpress copying book

Figure 10. Inside front cover and flyleaf

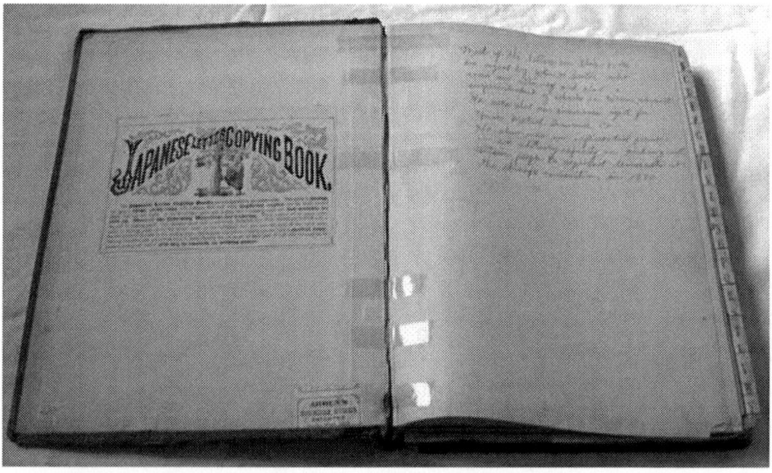

Photographs by Paul Baskett

CHAPTER 2

John Senter's Copying Book

John Senter's copying book is a rather modest-looking volume, measuring approximately nine inches wide by eleven inches tall by one inch thick and bound in dull brownish cloth. The word "LETTERS" is stamped in gold on the spine in courier type.[91] Over the years the book has been crudely mended by strips of clear adhesive tape which attach the front and back covers to the spine, and which hold the insides of the covers to the flyleaves. Apart from this, the book is in remarkably good condition. (See Figure 9.)

On the front flyleaf of Senter's copying book, someone has written in ballpoint pen (See Figure 10):

> Most of the letters in this book are signed by John H. Senter who was an attorney and also a superintendent of schools in Warren, Vermont. He was also an insurance agent for Union Mutual Insurance Co. He also was an influential person in an advisory capacity in picking out certain people to represent democrats at the Chicago convention in 1884.

On the inside front cover is pasted a label titled "JAPANESE LETTER COPYING BOOK." This label boasts of the copying book's advantages and also explains its use. (See Figure 11.)

---

91. As we shall see, Senter's copying book is quite typical of its kind. By the late 1870s, copying books were often bound in full cloth, like Senter's, and its dull brown canvas binding was typical. BARBARA RHODES & WILLIAM WELLS STREETER, BEFORE PHOTOCOPYING: THE ART AND HISTORY OF MECHANICAL COPYING, 1780-1938: A BOOK IN TWO PARTS 69 (1999). Rhodes is the author of Part I: Materials and Methods [hereinafter RHODES]; Streeter is the author of Part II: History of the Letter Copying Press [hereinafter STREETER]. In a typical copying book of the period, the

Figure 11. "Japanese Letter Copying Book" label

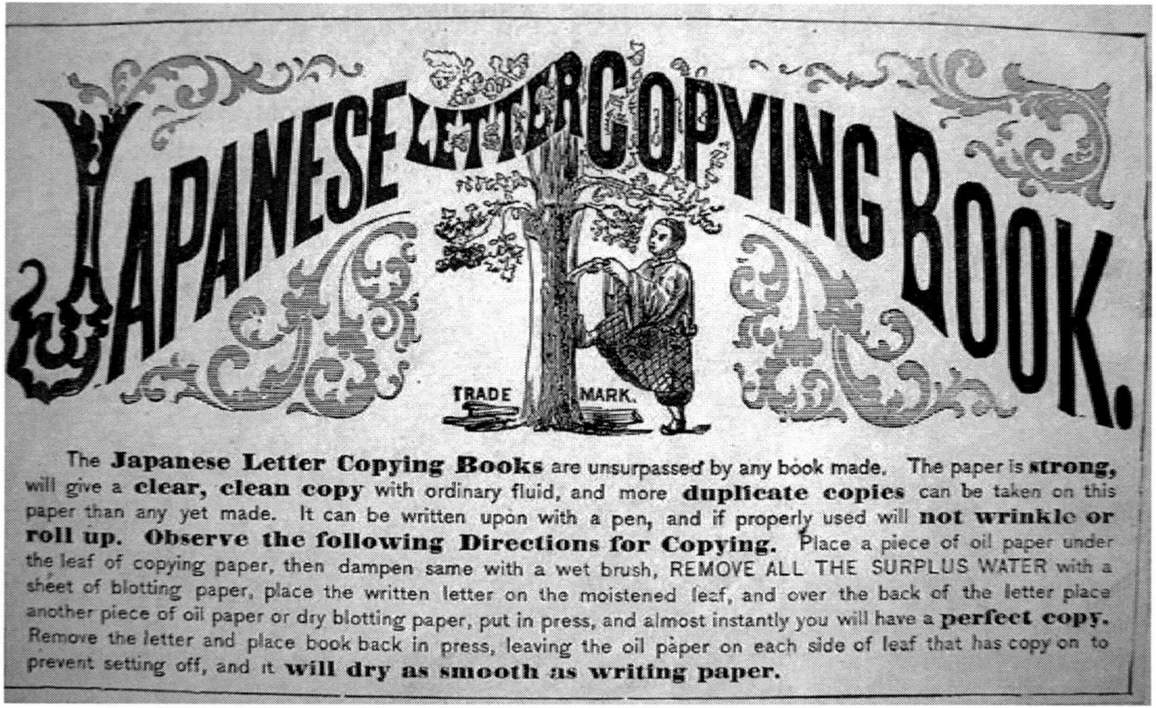

Photograph by Paul Baskett

The copying process required two pieces of equipment: the copying book and a copying press. Copying presses were first patented in England in 1780 by James Watt, who sold them by subscription for six pounds apiece with great success.[92] Copying presses had crossed the Atlantic to America by 1782 and were in wide use by the early part of the nineteenth century.[93] By the middle of the

---

title "Letters" was usually stamped in black on the spine, whereas Senter's was stamped in gold. RHODES, *supra* at 69. Although finely bound copying books were available, most were simple, utilitarian and inexpensive, as was Senter's.

92. RHODES, *supra* note 91, at 10. The equivalent cost in 2007 dollars is approximately $920. Current values are calculated using ERIC NYE, POUNDS TO DOLLARS HISTORICAL CONVERSION OF CURRENCY, http://uwacadweb.uwyo.edu/numimage/Currency.htm (last visited June 20, 2008).

93. RHODES, *supra* note 91, at 10; STREETER, *supra* note 91, at 207. In the grand tradition of legal scholarship, I am compelled to tuck some of the juiciest nuggets of research into the footnotes because they do not advance the main point of the story. My favorite tidbit is a nineteenth-century broadside advertisement for Frank G. Johnson's Portable Letter Copying Press, *available at* the LIBRARY OF CONGRESS, AMERICAN MEMORY, http://hdl.loc.gov/loc.rbc/rbpe.13400500 (last visited Apr, 15, 2007). This wonderful advertisement is part of the collection "An American Time Capsule: Three Centuries of Broadsides and Other Printed Ephemera." Fans of hyperbole in early advertising will enjoy the following excerpts from the ad, which also illustrates the many uses to which copying presses could be put.

GREAT MEN ATTENTION!

ATTENTION, LITTLE MEN!! ALL MEN ATTENTION!!!

Those who expect to be Great, —Men, Women and Children, — Attention, All!!!

THERE IS A NEW THING UNDER THE SUN.

It is a Useful thing. It is an Ornamental thing. It is fit for the Office: It is fit for the Parlor: It is fit for the Library: It is fit for the Study: It is fit for the School-room: It is fit for the Camp: It is fit for Field: It is fit for the Trunk: It is fit for Males and Females—

HERE IS A PICTURE OF IT, LOOK AT IT. . . .

century, letterpress copies were widely accepted in government and private businesses, particularly banks, railroads, and steamship lines in England and America. They were accepted by British and American courts as authentic copies of the originals, and thus could be used as legal evidence in courts of law.[94]

Various types of copying presses existed. The earliest presses copied only single sheets of paper; only later were they able to copy letters into blank copying books created for that purpose.[95] Other variations included portable models that doubled as writing desks and, later, extremely portable roller copying models that fit inside a suitcase. Copying presses were quite common pieces of office equipment; in fact, office desks sometimes were constructed to accommodate them.[96] Although inventors created many different variations on the theme, by the middle of the nineteenth century many presses looked similar to the one shown in Figure 12.

{illustration}

FRANK G. JOHNSON'S PORTABLE LETTER COPYING PRESS. . . .

. . . No person who hopes to rise to fame and distinction (and who does not?) should neglect to preserve such copies when it can be done so cheaply, and with so little time and trouble as at present. . . .

What person of eminence is there now living, who would not give the half his fortune for a full collection of his or her writings. With such a process of preserving copies as is now offered, there can be no excuse for not having such a collection. The constant use of such a press constitutes one his own Auto-Biographer. Its low price brings it WITHIN THE MEANS OF ALL. . . .

94. "About 1848, the late Lord Campbell, then Lord Chief Justice of England, decided that as a press copy must in every case be a perfect one, which many certified copies were not, they should be received as evidence in the English courts, and since then nearly all law courts have acknowledge them as such." RHODES, *supra* note 91, at 8; quoting John Underwood, Writing Inks, 6 AM. STATIONER 7 (1878). However, the exact date that letterpress copies were admitted as evidence in American courts has not been determined. RHODES, *supra* note 91, at 8.
95. STREETER, *supra* note 91, at 207.
96. RHODES, *supra* note 91, at 10.

Figure 12. Letterpress in the Conservation Lab of the John J. Burns Library, Boston College, Chestnut Hill, Mass. Senter's copying book is resting between the plates.

I am grateful to Mark Esser, Book Conservator at the John J. Burns Library, Boston College, Chestnut Hill, Mass., for permission to take this photograph, and for providing much useful information about letterpress copying. Photograph by the author.

This typical design featured a base plate upon which the copying book would be placed, and a second plate that would be pressed down by means of a hand-turned screw onto the copying book. The mechanism permitted the operator to press and release the upper plate quickly.

Senter, or his office clerk if he had one, would have followed these procedures every time he wished to copy a letter:

1. Place a piece of oiled, moisture-resistant paper underneath the leaf of thin copying paper in the copying book. This prevented moisture from transferring to surrounding leaves.

2. Dampen the sheet of copying paper with a dampening cloth or a brush dipped in water. This was the trickiest part of the operation. "Moisture evenly distributed, and neither scant nor excessive, is the secret of success."[97] Too little water and the copy of the letter was too faint to read; too much water and the copy was blurred and illegible.

3. Remove excess moisture from the copying paper with a sheet of blotting paper. Again, this was something of an art. The copying paper had to be evenly saturated and damp, but not wet enough to be shiny.[98]

4. Place the letter to be copied so the writing side is in contact with the dampened leaf of copying paper.

5. Place another sheet of oiled paper or blotting paper behind the original letter. Again, this step prevented moisture from transferring to surrounding leaves.

---

97. RHODES, *supra* note 91, at 84 (quoting *Writing Ink*, 21 AM. STATIONER 170 (1887)).

98. RHODES, *supra* note 91, at 84.

6. Close the book, place it in the copying press, and make the impression.

7. Open the press, remove the original letter, and return the (closed) copying book to the press with the two sheets of oiled paper still surrounding the copy. This step allowed the page to dry flat and prevented moisture from transferring to other leaves of the copying book.[99]

If the copying paper had been dampened correctly, there should have been little evidence on the original letter to show that it had been copied. However, smudges, blurs, and various telltale marks made by ink or water must have been quite common. Interestingly, some people who received letters that had obviously been copied in a letterpress appreciated the evidence that they were receiving a personal piece of correspondence.[100]

John Senter's copying book consists of two main parts: an index in the front, followed by five hundred numbered sheets of very thin, lightweight copying paper. Senter's last letter appears on page 280; the remainder of the pages are blank except for the page numbers in the upper right corners.

A small label pasted into the inside front cover of the copying book alerts us to the presence of "ARDEN'S DOUBLE INDEX" within, as shown in Figure 13.

---

99. This process, and much more about the history and use of copying books and copying presses, is explained generally in RHODES & STREETER, *supra* note 91. For those who would appreciate a more visual description of the process, Streeter describes the process with illustrations of the many layers of pages involved. STREETER, *supra* note 91, at 191.

100. RHODES, *supra* note 91, at 91. Advertisers quickly caught onto this. In an early example of the fake blue signatures emblazoned on the junk mail we receive today, or the notorious yellow sticky notes from "J" that most law librarians have received from time to time, nineteenth-century advertisers actually tried to make their mass-distributed letters look more personalized by running them through dampening mechanisms! *Id.*

Figure 13. Arden's Double Index label

Photograph by Paul Baskett

Figure 14. Pages from the index to Senter's copying book

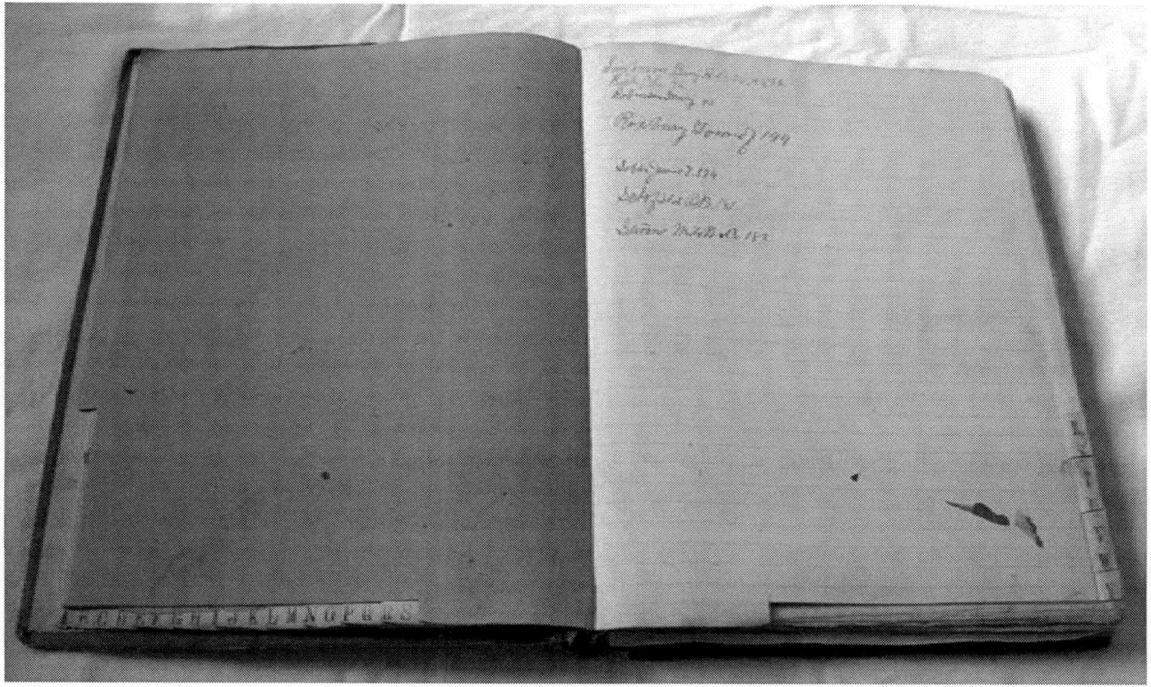

Photograph by Paul Baskett

Patented July 25, 1871, the index consists of regular blue-lined notepaper divided into twelve alphabetical tabs: AB / CD / ... / VW / Y. Between each lined sheet is an unlined sheet of purplish paper, probably used as a blotting sheet. The index is called a double index because the alphabetical tabs run along the outer edge of the page and also along the bottom, enabling the copying book's owner to quickly locate the appropriate letter, as shown in Figure 14.

Indexing was a standard feature of letterpress copying books. Like Senter's, most indexes were bound into the front of the book.[101] Writers typically wrote the name of the person to whom the letter was addressed under the appropriate alphabetical index heading, followed by the page number where the copied letter could be found. In Figure 14, the index is opened to the "RS" page. The fourth line shows that Senter's letter to the Town of Roxbury, Vermont appears on page 144 of the copying book.

If well indexed, copying books were a useful way to store and retrieve copies. Since the pages were thin, many copies could be stored in a relatively small space, and there was no danger of leaves getting lost; assuming you did not lose the book, you would not lose an individual copy of a letter.[102] However, if poorly indexed, or if the copies were poorly made, the books were less useful, and this is true in Senter's case. Occasionally his indexing appears to be slipshod, incomplete or illegible. Moreover, a significant minority of the letters were poorly copied – either due to too much water (resulting in a blurred impression), insufficient water (resulting in a faint impression), or a mistake in making the impression, such as erroneously copying one letter on top of another, as seen in Figure 15.

The example in Figure 15 shows all three of these problems: very minor blurring of the word "Boston," a very faint impression of Senter's signatures at the ends of the two letters, and multiple letters copied on top of each other. However, Senter wrote in a fairly clear hand, so as long as the impression was a good one, as it was most of the time, the letters are easy to read.

101. *Id.* at 66.
102. *Id.*

Figure 15. Example of problems with letterpress copies: blurring, faintness, and double impressions

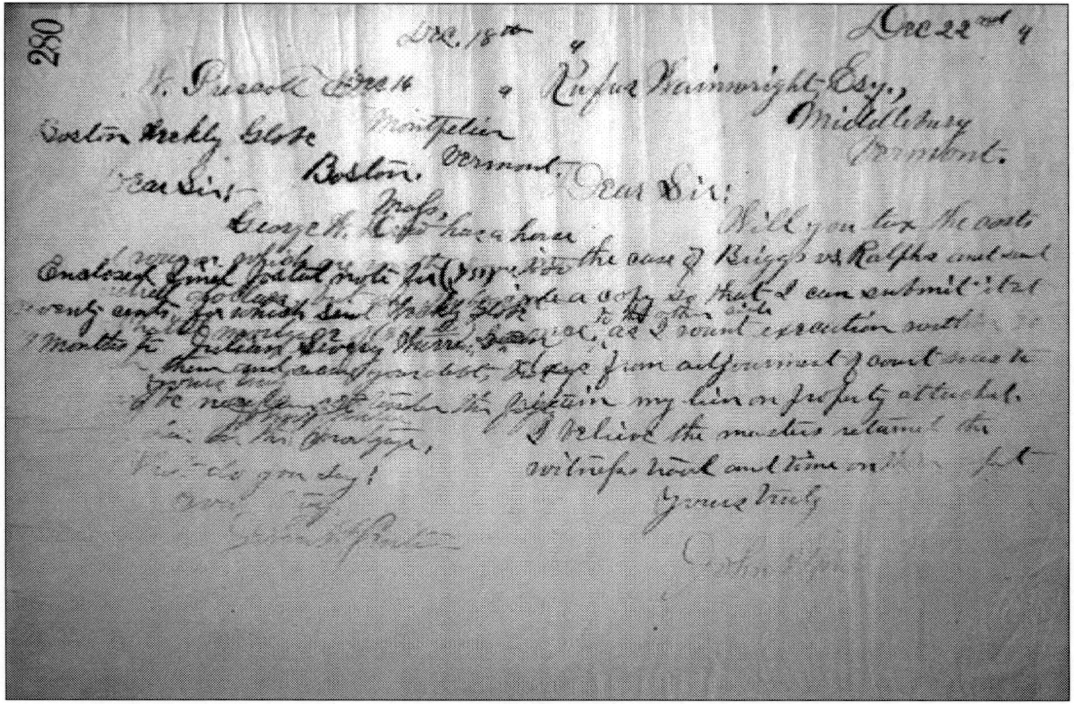

Photograph by Paul Baskett

One final shortcoming of copying books is painfully evident to scholars and researchers eager to unlock the past. Generally, the "other side" of the correspondence, i.e. the letters received by the copyist, were not placed inside the copying book but were filed elsewhere in the office, requiring the writer to look in at least two places to find both sides of any exchange of correspondence.[103] Unfortunately, this is true in Senter's case, and because we do not have the letters he received, we must piece together the events of his life from only one side of the story.

Notwithstanding these drawbacks, it is evident that Senter used his copying book as its creators intended. In his letters, he mentioned on more than one occasion that he had referred back to his copying book to refresh his memory about previous correspondence with clients and associates.[104] Imperfect as it may have been, the copying book served its purpose.

Following the index, the five hundred leaves of copying paper begin. The number of each leaf appears in the upper right corner, stamped in blue ink. Again, Senter's book appears to be a typical example of its kind; five hundred pages seems to have been a standard size.[105]

As expected, most of Senter's letters appear chronologically in the copying book, generally one or two to a page, although he quite often squeezed in copies of brief letters wherever there was room, without regard to the date of the letter. The copying paper sheets are thin, so one cannot read the copied letters without inserting a

---

103. *Id.* at 67.

104. In one such letter, Senter wrote to a debtor, "I find on referrence to my letter book, that I wrote you a letter on the 30th [illegible], and I have no answer from you as yet. . . ." Letter from John Henry Senter to Charles Newcomb (Sept. 14, 1881), *in* Senter Letter Book, *supra* note 1, at 171.

105. RHODES, *supra* note 91, at 63. Around 1850, copying books began to be sold pre-numbered, paginated by machine. Women operated the paginating machines, which must have been mind-numbing work; every leaf had to be turned by hand, and a chain carrying the numerals passed over the upper right corners of each leaf. The women worked a treadle to make each impression. *Id.* at 63-65.

Figure 16. Photograph demonstrating thin sheets of copying paper, pagination, and slight dampening and wrinkling of the pages

Photograph by Paul Baskett

blank white sheet behind each leaf. Figure 16 illustrates the machine-made pagination, the thinness of the individual sheets, and the slight wrinkling of the pages caused by the dampness of the copying mechanism.

Before moving on to the contents of John Senter's copying book, it is worth pausing to reflect on this useful piece of technology from the past. Although it is a stretch for us to recall the days of carbon paper and mimeograph machines in this age of computing, the copying press remained viable for a long time. Letterpress copiers were owned by Benjamin Franklin, George Washington, James Madison, and Thomas Jefferson.[106] Many other presidents used the copying press; the last to do so was Calvin Coolidge.[107] The Smith Charities of Northampton, Massachusetts used the letter-copying press process until 1954, and Frank W. Symonds, the former treasurer of Smith and Wesson in Springfield, Massachusetts, observed "the use of a nineteenth-century transfer copying press until approximately the year 1960."[108] William Streeter asserts that the copying press was the most significant piece of office equipment in the nineteenth century.[109] Its demise was gradual, and it was only completely put out of business by the photocopier.[110]

Streeter believes that "perhaps over sixty percent of government, military, medical, religious, business, labor, and industrial correspondence has been kept in letter copying books."[111] Imagine what these rich sources could tell us about the daily working lives of lawyers and other professionals in centuries past.

---

106. *Id.* at 10.
107. *Id.*
108. STREETER, *supra* note 91, at 224.
109. *Id.*
110. RHODES, *supra* note 91, at 113.
111. STREETER, *supra* note 91, at 223.

CHAPTER 3

The Letters

Copied into the first 280 pages of John Senter's letterpress copying book are approximately 326 of his letters (the number is approximate because a few of the letters are copied on top of each other and hence are illegible; a couple of other letters in the book are written not by him but by his clients) and a few miscellaneous items such as notes, receipts, drafts of math problems for a textbook, and, most interestingly, copies of Senter's legal bills to his clients. The latter will be discussed later, but first, a summary of the letters.

The 326 letters can be divided into the broad categories of law, education, politics, and miscellaneous. Because some letters can be classified into more than one category, the total number of "hash marks" used to tally up the letters actually amounts to 333. Table 1 illustrates some odd gaps in Senter's copying book. Why did he write so many letters in 1879 and 1884, and so few in 1880 and 1883? His correspondence provides no clue; there is no mention of illness, extended travel, or personal matters that might explain such a dearth of correspondence in certain years. Perhaps he simply got out of the habit of making copies for some periods of time; this explanation seems rather out of character, however, since in other respects he seems to have been a most attentive record keeper, as will be shown.

Table 1 also illustrates Senter's gradual transition from educator to lawyer. In 1879, 86 of his 136 letters pertained to education, and only 35 pertained to law. Senter wrote his last education-related letter in 1882. In this same year he began to write about politics, and the proportion of law-related letters increased each year.

Table 1
Summary of Senter's Letters

Year	Law	Education	Politics	Miscellaneous	Total
1879	35	86	0	15	136
1880	6	0	0	0	6
1881	38	7	0	5	50
1882	39	1	1	3	44
1883	4	0	0	1	5
1884	79	0	4	9	92
Total	201	94	5	33	333

Senter as Educator

While studying to become a lawyer, Senter taught forty-three terms of school.[112] During this time he remained entrenched – more so than he would have liked, it appears – in the world of education. "I have been for several years while studying for my profession in the habit of teaching two or three terms of school each year, (although now I am happy to say, I have broken of that habit) . . . ."[113]

Senter first referred to himself as an attorney in his copying book on May 10, 1879, when he noted that he was the attorney for G.B. Newcomb, treasurer of the Methodist Church.[114] Even as Senter commenced his new career, he remained firmly entrenched in his work as superintendent of schools for the town of Warren, and the task that occupied most of his time in 1879 was his work on the Washington County Textbook Selection Committee.

---

112. *See supra* text accompanying note 6.

113. Letter from John Henry Senter to Benjamin Sanborn (Apr. 14, 1879), *in* Senter Letter Book, *supra* note 1, at 21. In his copying book, Senter mentioned nothing about his former teaching duties, but interested readers may wish to consult Martha B. Currie, *A Teacher and Her Students: My Mother, Ellen Peck, and Her One-Room Schoolhouse in East Montpelier*, 39 VERMONT HIST. 55 (1971), to get an idea of what a difficult occupation it must have been.

114. Receipt (May 10, 1879), *in* Senter Letter Book, *supra* note 1, at 53.

The Textbook Selection Committee

In 1879, Senter was appointed to a committee charged with selecting and purchasing the textbooks for Washington County. His fellow committee members were Professor Charles Dole of Norwich University in Northfield, Vermont, and W.W. Ainsworth, Principal of Calais High School, also in Vermont.[115] From April 1879 through the end of the year, Senter wrote eighty-six education-related letters, most of which had to do with selecting textbooks for the county. In this capacity he read and evaluated textbooks, solicited the recommendations of others, and corresponded with book agents – sometimes heatedly – about securing the most favorable terms of sale. During this time he met with book agents almost daily, [116] sometimes for hours at a stretch.[117]

Senter took his responsibilities as a textbook evaluator quite seriously, as we can see from this excerpt of a letter to G.B. Damon, a Boston book agent: ". . . I believe I have a copy of twenty one different arithmetics and have compared them page by page . . . ."[118] Many other letters reveal a similar sense of thoroughness and dedication to his appointed task (mixed in with a bit of acerbic wit), which is quite impressive when we consider that he was struggling to get his legal career off the ground at the same time.

> To day I have had a lawsuit to attend to, but have found time to look over the picture book a little, and will now give you the result. First on page 5 first column, 6 ¶, the definition of Archipelago,

---

115. Letter from John Henry Senter to Messrs. Clark and Maynard (Apr. 8, 1879), *in* Senter Letter Book, *supra* note 1, at 2.

116. "A book agent comes to see me every day almost." Letter from John Henry Senter to Benjamin Sanborn (Apr. 21, 1879), *in* Senter Letter Book, *supra* note 1, at 36.

117. "Appletons man was here yesterday and stayed nearly all day . . . ." Letter from John Henry Senter to Hiram Huse (Apr. 17, 1879), *in* Senter Letter Book, *supra* note 1, at 32-35.

118. Letter from John Henry Senter to G.B. Damon (Apr. 15, 1879), *in* Senter Letter Book, *supra* note 1, at 26-29.

> strikes me as "original," it goes back on Webster somewhat. . . . Third compare the west coast line of the U.S. as given on 25 & 28, 30 & 58 pages. I have compared them by sketching on tissue paper, and think the result would convince any one, that whoever drafted those maps, had no idea of the "Eternal fitness of things." In the same book one would, naturally suppose, they would have some similarity to say the least. . . . Fifth . . . notice the Sierra Nevada Mtn's on page 30 (in California) at the south end near Mt. Whitney, they make an almost square turn to the left, then on page 58 the same mountains have gone on a "tour" and now turn to the right, also observe the same mountains on page 28 then on page 30, which of the four different directions and twists does the author (if the book ever had one, which I doubt) swear by? . . .[119]
>
> Well I have spent just one hour on this book to day and the foregoing is the result. What would be the result of a man well [footed] in geography should spend a week on the book, don't you think such a man could make some "splendid illustrations." . . . Well if you are not bored, I shall be glad.[120]

During this time Senter had at least one run-in with some temperance advocates while selecting textbooks for the town of Warren. In a letter to the editor of the *Argus and Patriot* newspaper, based in nearby Montpelier, Senter wrote in part:

> I notice also that Appleton's Readers are held by some gentleman, through the medium of the Argus as detrimental to the temperance interest . . . . Notice the tenth ¶ [of the textbook] which is the last in regard to wine drinking, "According to the old time code of good manners, now happily falling into disuse, it was considered extremely uncivil to decline taking wine when invited, although politeness demanded no more than a sip, and it was

119. Altogether, Senter identified ten errors in the book.

120. Letter from John Henry Senter to Hiram Huse (Apr. 17, 1879), *in* Senter Letter Book, *supra* note 1, at 32-35. In addition to his textbook work, Hiram Huse was a justice of the peace in Montpelier. THE VERMONT BUSINESS DIRECTORY, FOR 1884-85, *supra* note 76, at 258.

> regarded as ill-bred to empty one's glass on such occasions, yet this custom has often proved the first step toward ruin."
>
> Now I in my ignorance, am of the oppinion that the sentiments quoted are strong arguments for temperence, and I can see nothing in that article . . . which they could object to have taught to their children. I ask each man and woman in the county to read this article, which will be found on the 387 page of Appleton's fifth reader, and judge for themselves. . . .[121]

Senter's work as a textbook selector reached its fever pitch in early June 1879, when interested parties gathered at a convention to select the county's textbooks. Shortly after the convention, Senter proudly recounted his triumph to his friend G.B. Damon, the book agent.

> We had a big fight at the convention. I handled the Arithmetic and Geography question. I know that when the convention was called in the afternoon Greenleafs book had more friends than Fisk [Damon's book], but I went in to win, and I won. I talked two hours on that question. I took your book and Greenleaf, and went through them from begining to end. . . . [S]ome one moved to adopt Greenleaf and it was voted down flat, then I moved to adopt Fisk and it was adopted almost unanimously. . . . Friday morning the air was full of rumors that I was bought for Fisk's Arithmetic. I got the book agents to gather and . . . I spoke my piece. The agents all exonerated Dole and myself, and took back all they had said about us. . . . These things are not very pleasant for one who has tried to do his duty [conscientiously.] Well I came out of the fight all right . . . . When you can find time to recreate a little

121. Letter from John Henry Senter to Hiram Atkins, Editor of the Argus and Patriot newspaper (June 2, 1879), *in* Senter Letter Book, *supra* note 1, at 70-73. Senter's approval of the temperate life, as expressed in the letter above and also in a character reference in 1882, *see infra* note 137 and accompanying text, did not stop him from defending a fellow accused of drunkenness in 1881. *See* Letter from John Henry Senter to Henry Kew (Dec. 12, 1881), *in* Senter Letter Book, *supra* note 1, at 180.

> I should be happy to see you, and give you a vivid description of the fight. I am all tired out now but hope now the fight is over to take some peace. . . .
>
> One thing I want you to remember. If I am alive five years from this time I shant be a text book committee man.[122]

It appears that young Senter's skills as an orator and a fighter were already in evidence. However, he did soften his tone a bit when corresponding with female teachers about textbooks. At the close of a long letter thanking Miss Ellen F. Van Deusen, a teacher in Waitsfield, Vermont, for her previous opinions on several textbooks, he wrote, "I hope you will come to Warren, I want to talk with you about Text books very much, I have so many books to look, that I dream of them nightly. . . ."[123]

Senter's Duties as Superintendent of Schools

In his capacity as superintendent of schools for the town of Warren, a position to which he was appointed in 1879 and held

---

122. Letter from John Henry Senter to G.B. Damon (June 8, 1879), *in* Senter Letter Book, *supra* note 1, at 81-83. Senter drove the point home again in another letter: "Well the County fight is over and I am out of it, and I shall never again be fool enough to act on a text book committee." Letter from John Henry Senter to F.B. Winnie (June [9], 1879), *in* Senter Letter Book, *supra* note 1, at 85-87. And yet again: "[O]ne thing you may remember if you and I are alive when the next book fight comes five years from this time I shall not be on a text book committee." Letter from John Henry Senter to Benjamin H. Sanborn (June 9, 1879), *in* Senter Letter Book, *supra* note 1, at 88-89.

123. Letter from John Henry Senter to Ellen Van Deusen (Apr. 21, 1879), *in* Senter Letter Book, *supra* note 1, at 38. Occasionally his devotion to the textbook cause seems to have gotten the better of him. In a letter to a book agent, Senter wrote that he liked the look of the arithmetics: "[t]hey look neat and tasty . . . ." Letter from John Henry Senter to G.B. Damon (Aug. 17, 1879), *in* Senter Letter Book, *supra* note 1, at 134.

through 1882, Senter administered examinations to prospective teachers, supplied letters of recommendation, and attempted to fill vacant teaching positions. Six of the letters he wrote in 1879 fall into this category. One of these letters, which again reveals a rare softer side of Senter, must have been quite difficult to write.

> With reluctance I have to inform you of your failure to pass the required per ct on your examination, but I must do my duty although it is disagreeable. Your average is only 44-1/2 and I have marked it very high, you have not reached fifty on any one subject, so you can readily see that it is not possible for me to grant a certificate on these answers.
>
> I think you capable of passing a much better examination, think you were frightened, hurried, and cold, and I am willing to give you another chance, will give you a private examination, free any day this week, give you all the time you want and if you can pass an average of 65 without going below fifty on any one subject, I shall be happy to grant you a certificate.
>
> I suppose Katie you will feel badly to hear that I deny this certificate, but you certainly will not feel any worse about it than I do, if I could do it, Katie, honorably I would willingly sacrifice more than your whole wages for the term.
>
> I think you had better try a private examination, because I think you are capable of doing better.
>
> If you wish to try again let me know at once.
>
> Although perhaps you may not think so I am your friend
> John H. Senter
> P.S. Let me know by return mail when you will come, if you conclude to come again.
> Yours, J.H.S.[124]

Evidently Senter's exhortations had no effect. In a letter to a Miss Nichols dated April 29, 1879, he mentioned that he "did not

---

124. Letter from John Henry Senter to Katie Prentice (Apr. 28, 1879), *in* Senter Letter Book, *supra* note 1, at 39-40.

give Miss Prentice a certificate," and offered the vacant position to Nichols at a salary of $2.25 per week.[125]

Senter took his duties as Warren's superintendent of schools quite seriously, as this brief, and unintentionally funny, excerpt of a letter to Professor Edward Conant reveals: "I am glad you are to adress the people of my town [and] I will try and have a good audience present. I am trying to get my teachers interested in education more than they are at present, and shall endeavor to have them all present . . . ."[126] Perhaps the lack of interest in education on the part of Warren's teachers prompted Senter's comment in another letter that he was willing to discuss methods of teaching in Warren's common schools, but he did not want "any fine spun theories shot over the heads of the teachers."[127]

Senter's Diverse Law Practice

Like many small-town sole practitioners, the bulk of Senter's law business involved debt collection, especially in the earliest years of his practice. Also like many lawyers just beginning to build a practice, he probably was eager to take nearly any case that walked in the door, no matter the nature of the dispute. Table 2 illustrates the wide-ranging nature of Senter's law practice. Of the 204 law-related letters in Table 2,[128] the majority (seventy-one letters) pertained to collections issues, including collecting on notes and accounts, taxes, securing property to settle debt, and collecting on

---

125. Letter from John Henry Senter to Miss [F.L.] Nichols (Apr. 29, 1879), *in* Senter Letter Book, *supra* note 1, at 42.

126. Letter from John Henry Senter to Edward Conant, (n.d., probably May 10 or 12, 1879), *in* Senter Letter Book, *supra* note 1, at 52.

127. Letter from John Henry Senter to Zed Stanton (Sept. 2 or 3, 1881), *in* Senter Letter Book, *supra* note 1, at 165.

128. Senter wrote 201 law-related letters. *See supra* Table 1. A few of these letters dealt with more than one legal subject, resulting in the slightly higher total of 204 letters shown in Table 2.

judgments. Numbering fifty-eight letters, procedural matters such as filing papers and setting dates for depositions and trials ranked second. A most interesting category, which is labeled "Practice of Law" in Table 2 but which really refers to the business of practicing law, ranks third with thirteen letters. These letters show us what Senter actually did for his clients, how much he charged them for doing it, and how he tried (often unsuccessfully) to collect his fees. These will be discussed in detail below.

Table 2
Subject Matter of Senter's Law-Related Letters

Subject Matter	Number	Percentage
Collections	71	34.8
Procedure	58	28.4
Practice of Law	13	6.4
Insurance	10	4.9
Personal Property	10	4.9
Opinion Letters	9	4.4
Real Property	5	2.5
Wills, Trusts & Estates	5	2.5
Insanity	4	2.0
Municipal Law	4	2.0
Other & Miscellaneous	15	7.4
Total	204	100.2

Collection Work

An early account of the bench and bar of Vermont notes that many nineteenth-century lawyers earned the bulk of their fees from collection suits that arose from the "general custom" of people who bought goods and services on credit and paid only when sued.[129]

Looking at Senter's correspondence, this account seems to have been an accurate reflection of his law practice in Warren. The very first law-related letter in Senter's copying book, which is also excerpted at the beginning of this discussion, is typical of many of his letters in form and content. "I have in my hands for collection a note against you in favor of G.W. Cardell[130] amounting today to $6.50. An early settlement will save you costs. Yours with respect, John H. Senter."[131]

Straightforward collection-related letters such as these comprise the single largest category of letters in the copying book: forty-four letters in all. Also part of the "collections" category are letters in which he attempted to collect back taxes (four letters), to secure property to settle debt[132] (thirteen letters) and to execute judgments (four). Amounts at issue ranged from a few dollars to $1,250 – the amount Miss Louisa Allen claimed was owed to her for her interest in a house.[133]

Senter's correspondence reveals that there was an art to securing property. In several letters with sheriffs or attorneys in nearby towns, he often discussed whether the debtors had any property worth securing, and how best to secure it. Timing could be tricky; often

---

129. CHILD, *supra* note 5, at 51.

130. George Cardell was a merchant who ran a lumber mill, manufactured eave spouts, served as postmaster, and represented Warren in the stage legislature. *Id.*, at 481.

131. Letter from John Henry Senter to A.F. Martin (Apr. 14, 1879), *in* Senter Letter Book, *supra* note 1, at 7. Interestingly, Senter's wife Addie's maiden name was Martin. One hopes her husband did not embark upon his legal career by dunning a member of his wife's own family.

132. *See, e.g.*, Letter from John Henry Senter to R.H. Mardin, Bristol, Vt. (Sept. 9, 1881), *in* Senter Letter Book, *supra* note 1, at 170 ("Dear Sir, Can you secure a bill of fifteen dollars against Wesley E. Dana of your place? If you can let me know at once and I will send you a writ. I don't care to dun him, I have done that enough, what I want is to secure it. If you will inform me I will be much obliged and if you secure it I will pay you for all your trouble.").

133. Letter from John Henry Senter to F.J. Green (Nov. 1, 1881), *in* Senter Letter Book, *supra* note 1, at 175. Louisa Allen is listed in *Walton's Vermont Register* as a milliner. WALTON'S VERMONT REGISTER FOR 1880, *supra* note 10, at 169.

Senter – or the sheriffs or attorneys he engaged to secure property and serve papers – had to be stealthy.

> I find your name in the list of attornies of the Wilber Mercantile Agency, and so send you the enclosed note for collection. The signor Williams is at work in your town for a farmer by the name of Parks, I believe.
>
> Do not let Williams know that you have the claim untill you can secure it. He does not mean to pay and would be on his guard if he knew that you had the claim.[134]

In attempting to settle debts, Senter was nothing if not ingenious. The best example occurred in 1884, when Senter and a debtor agreed to work out a debt by allowing Senter to ride the stage for free until the debts were paid off.

> I return uncollected assessment receipts, except that I retain D.H. Stut's receipts for the sum of $16.95 which I am in the way of working up by [fare] on the stage, he agreed to let me [ride] out part of it, by making a discount and as that is the only way to get it I accepted the proposition. When I have rode all I can on that account I will divide with the company.[135]

In addition to the bread-and-butter practice of securing property and collecting debt, Senter engaged in a wide variety of other legal work. Some of his more interesting activities are discussed below.

---

134. Letter from John Henry Senter to Giles Whitney, Winchendon, Mass. (probably June 1882), *in* Senter Letter Book, *supra* note 1, at 189. In an excerpt from another example, Senter advised creditors that he had investigated the debtor, a Mr. White, and found that White had no attachable property but that he earned good wages. Based on this, Senter advised the creditors to "get judgment against him, and that will bring the amount above ten dollars and then when he leaves the bars down muster his wages." Letter from John Henry Senter to Richardson and Fullerton (Aug. 6, 1884), *in* Senter Letter Book, *supra* note 1, at 267.

135. Letter from John Henry Senter to H.N. Taplin, Montpelier, Vt. (June 30, 1884), *in* Senter Letter Book, *supra* note 1, at 263.

Character References

A small town is like a family of sorts, and its residents become intimately acquainted with fellow townspeople whether they like it or not. Perhaps a town attorney such as Senter had even more opportunity to get to know his neighbors. Senter occasionally was called upon, or took it upon himself, to issue character references for people in his town. Five of these appear in his copying book, including this one, a letter to an editor of an unidentified newspaper.

> Your correspondent, who reported the particulars of the burglary committed in this town on the 6th inst, and the arest of Edgar H. Van Deusen, must, most assuredly, have been but little acquainted with the truth of the matter. . . . [O]ne of his statements is entirely untrue, and does injustice to an honest well deserving young man, Eugene Van Deusen the brother of Edgar. Your correspondent says that "suspicion at once rested upon Edgar and his brother." It is true that suspicion at once rested upon Edgar but [illegible] the least suspicion of Eugene . . . . [much of the remainder of the letter is illegible].[136]

This is interesting not only for Senter's eagerness to distinguish Eugene from Edgar, obviously the rogue of the family, but also because the Van Deusen brothers must have been related to Miss Ellen Van Deusen, the schoolteacher with whom Senter so perfervidly corresponded about textbooks.

In several sentence fragments in his copying book, Senter jotted the following observations about O.D. Greene, M.D. of Warren, Vermont: "A very good country Practice. Excelent. Temperate."[137]

---

136. Letter from John Henry Senter to an unidentified newspaper editor (Aug. 1879), *in* Senter Letter Book, *supra* note 1, at 135.

137. Undated notes probably written around mid-June 1882, *in* Senter Letter Book, *supra* note 1, at 188. Greene appears several times in Senter's correspondence; Senter did some collection work for him, acted as a newspaper agent on his behalf, and referred to him in a letter to an insurance agent. *See infra* text accompanying note 146.

In 1882, Senter wrote Daniel Barnard of Franklin, New Hampshire, asking him to collect on a note for $22 against Wells Blake, formerly of Warren and now residing in Franklin. Senter had a rather poor opinion of Blake, as can be seen in this excerpt:

> Unless [Blake] has changed very much from what he was when he left here, it will be better not to let him know that you have the note untill you can secure it.
>
> If you can find any chance to secure this debt I will send this note at once, as the owner is very anxious to secure and cares very much more to make Blake pay it than he does for the money.[138]

Evidently Senter was not the only resident of Warren with a low opinion of Blake.

Town Agent

As attorney for the town of Warren during the years covered in this copying book, 1879 to 1884, Senter occasionally took part in townwide enterprises extending beyond strict legal representation. He appears to have acted as a newspaper agent for his fellow townspeople, buying subscriptions to the *Argus and Patriot*, the *Boston Globe*, and other newspapers for himself and other members of the town.[139] Seven letters capture his activities in this area.[140] Beyond serving as a newspaper agent and insurance agent (discussed below), Senter occasionally functioned in the capacity of a general town agent, acting

---

138. Letter from John Henry Senter to Daniel Barnard, Franklin, N.H. (probably early July 1882), *in* Senter Letter Book, *supra* note 1, at 194.
139. While in Warren, Senter subscribed to the *Argus and Patriot* newspaper, published by his friend and mentor Hiram Atkins, a frequent correspondent in Senter's copying book. All told, there were two daily newspapers, the *Evening Argus* and the *Daily Journal*, and two weekly newspapers, the *Vermont Watchman* and the *Argus and Patriot*. All were based in Montpelier. *The City of Montpelier*, *supra* note 6, at 148.
140. E.g. Letter from John Henry Senter to *Boston Globe* (Oct. 23, 1884), *in* Senter Letter Book, *supra* note 1, at 271.

on the town's behalf in a variety of matters, as in the following letter written to a Boston physician.

> I write you for information as regards the expense at your Infirmary of opperating on eyes. A young lady of this town has a cataract over each of her eyes, her parents are poor, and as she is [an] estimable young lady several of the people here are willing to help pay the expenses of the opperation and her traveling expenses.
>
> You will oblige me very much by giving what information in regard to the matter you can conveniently.[141]

This is an interesting example of the members of a small community banding together to help one of their own; one wonders what the community would have done if the young lady had not been "estimable." Senter, at least, may have been less inclined to pitch in. Here is another letter that Senter wrote in a similar capacity as agent for a number of townspeople. In two letters sent to the same correspondent on the same day, Senter took pains to distance himself from the people on whose behalf he was writing.

> We, here in Warren, are trying to raise money to pay Beeman H. Campbell's bail, you will reccollect he was one of the men convicted of arson, from Warren. We think that he is inocent, and we know well enough that he is, now we want to get all the evidence there was in the case against him as cheap as possible, and I write to ask you how much it will cost, together with his own testimony.

And then,

> In looking over my copy book I notice I forgot to add that I wrote the first letter to you by request. I was acting merely as an amanuensis. I am not a part of the <u>We</u>.[142]

---

141. Letter from John Henry Senter to B. Joy Jeffries, Boston, Mass. (Aug. 21, 1879), *in* Senter Letter Book, *supra* note 1, at 136.
142. Letters from John Henry Senter to Henry Oviatt (Apr. 12, 1879), *in* Senter Letter Book, *supra* note 1, at 13.

Senter also acted as a real estate agent at least once, attempting to broker a deal between a mill owner and a prospective buyer.[143] All of these diverse roles he played – newspaper agent, insurance agent, real estate agent and general town agent – may have been part of the regular job duties of a small-town lawyer trying to make ends meet, or they may have been examples of Senter's efforts to obtain work wherever he could get it.

Insurance

Senter's ten letters pertaining to insurance matters are split nearly evenly between routine correspondence in his capacity as agent – securing and canceling policies and the like[144] – and strongly worded letters to insurance agencies on behalf of his policy-holding clients. Mr. J. Francisco, Secretary of the Vermont Accident Association, came in for some harsh words from Senter on more than one occasion. In August 1882, Senter scolded Francisco for failing to communicate with several policyholders whom he represented: "What is the matter? Do you receive the communications? And if you do receive them, why do you not answer? Or have they been miscarried?"[145]

Some months later, Senter wrote Francisco again regarding his client Hiram Wood, who had been severely injured in an accident. It is worth quoting this long letter in full, for it weaves together and reveals several themes that recur in the letters: Senter's fair and forthright nature, his tenacity, his refusal to recoil from a fight, and his

143. Letter from John Henry Senter to D.D. Hemenway (Dec. 3, 1879), *in* Senter Letter Book, *supra* note 1, at 139.

144. Senter's first letter to his future employer, Union Mutual Fire Insurance Company, involved a routine policy cancellation on behalf of one of his clients. Letter from John Henry Senter to Union Mutual (Sept. 3, 1881), *in* Senter Letter Book, *supra* note 1, at 165.

145. Letter from John Henry Senter to J. Francisco (Aug. 17, 1882), *in* Senter Letter Book, *supra* note 1, at 202.

willingness to go to bat for fellow citizens whom he deemed to be of deserving character.

> Hiram Wood of E. Warren, Vermont, on the 15th day of August, A.D. [1882] took out an insurance certificate, No. 2640, in the Vermont Accident Association of Rutland Vermont. About the middle of November 1882, while engaged at his work as a wood chopper, he was thrown backwards over a [log], and was injured in his spine just below his shoulder blade on his right side. The place injured became very much discolored and swollen, but he is an ambitious hard working man, and he thought he would not stop work, although very lame and stiff, after two or three days he was obliged to, and did stop work, on the 22nd of Nov. a medical examiner here, Dr. O.D. Greene [was] called, as Mr. Wood continued to grow worse. Soon after this Dr. Halett of Moretown was called, both of these M.D.s examined Mr. Wood and both were satisfied that his disability was occasioned by the fall and injury above mentioned.
>
> He had neglected notifying you untill after this examination, as I understand because he was in hopes to be able to work, and did not wish to make any call on the [association] if he could avoid it.
>
> He has not done an hours work since he tried those two days, after his injury, and has been ever since, and is now entirely helpless. All of these statements can be proven to your satisfaction. He has written to you or had others several times about the matter, but for some, to him, unknown reason, you seem to entirely ignore him. What he wants is that you should thouroughly examine this matter and satisfy yourself [about it] and if you find it an honest claim to settle honestly with him, if not an honest claim, or if you are not satisfied that it is, he wants nothing, but you will either fairly hear and investigate this claim [or] the <u>courts</u> will. I don't intend this as a threat, as I have always found you square [and] upright, I expect to now.
>
> This man is an honest, hard working man and I do not think the Vermont Accident Association, cares to [several words illegible] settling an honest claim with such a man for a technical quibble, if they do it shall be made known.
>
> I request you to lay this matter before the directors, and to at

> least treat [him] with consideration enough to answer [this] letter, and not remain as you [have] with Mr. Wood entirely dumb.[146]

Unfortunately, nothing in Senter's copying book reveals the outcome of Mr. Wood's plight.

Opinion Letters

Sprinkled throughout the copying book are letters that could best be described as legal opinion letters. In some of these, particularly in the early years of the correspondence, Senter sought legal advice from his mentor, Clarence Pitkin of Montpelier, with whom he studied law before embarking on his own practice. A typical example follows:

> Friend Pitkin
>
> A. sells B. a house, in the house is a sink the frame of which is fastened to the house, the iron sink set in the frame is not fastened to the frame & cannot be a discharge pipe fastened to the sink [passes] out through the house, no reservation was made of the sink. [Qare.] Does the sink pass as part of the realty, and a fixture, or is it a chattel?
>
> Please to answer and oblige,
> Yours truly John H. Senter [147]

In the latter part of the copying book, Senter posed fewer questions to his mentor and offered more of his own opinions. In these later letters, he occasionally cited to various legal authorities – primarily Vermont cases and statutes. The most recent of these was written May 17, 1884, and its content and tone shows how Senter's

146. Letter from John Henry Senter to J. Francisco (June 4, 1883), *in* Senter Letter Book, *supra* note 1, at 206-07.
147. Letter from John Henry Senter to Clarence Pitkin (Aug. 18, 1879), *in* Senter Letter Book, *supra* note 1, at 136.

confidence and expertise had increased over the five-year time span of the copying book.

> I have investigated the matter of your claim for a horse, which you sold to Ashly Wolcott during his life, and which horse by the terms of the sale was to be and remain your property until paid for, although no record was made of the lien in the town Clerks office, and although the said Ashly Wolcott has since deceased and the horse has come into the possession of the administrator of his, Wolcott's, estate.
>
> The law of conditional sale is well settled in this State, the purchase money having become due and being unpaid, you are the absolute owner of the horse in question, and entitled to possession on demand which right of possession can only be defeated by the payment of the purchase money.
>
> See West vs. Bolton 4 Vt. 558.
> Buckmaster vs. Smith 22 Vt. 203
> Burnell vs Marvin 44 Vt. 277 & cases therein cited
>
> . . . .
>
> Your course then Mr. Allen is to demand of the Administrator the horse in question and if he neglects to either pay the sum due upon the horse or to deliver him to you, he is liable in trover for the value of the horse.[148]

At some point in his future, after the years encompassed by his copying book, Senter was said to have amassed one of the largest and most complete private law libraries in New England, numbering more than ten thousand volumes.[149] One cannot help but wonder whether he delved into his private stash of Vermont reporters to find the answers for his client Mr. Allen. In all likelihood, he did. In an 1884 letter to George Wing, Senter wrote:

---

148. Letter from John Henry Senter to S.D. Allen (May 17, 1884), *in* Senter Letter Book, *supra* note 1, at 264-65. S.D. Allen was a clapboard manufacturer and a merchant. WALTON'S VERMONT REGISTER FOR 1880, *supra* note 10, at 169.
149. *The City of Montpelier*, *supra* note 6, at 155.

> Since my return from County Court I have been mousing around my library hunting for law to fit my views and wishes in divers and sundry cases in which I am anxious to thrash the other party, and as one of the results of my labor I have found the case of Pinnock vs Clough reported in the 16th Vt 500, and if that case is not a clinker in the case of which you have heard . . . then I am at sea. . . .[150]

The Difficult Life of a Small-Town Lawyer

Unsafe Roads

Even though bad roads are still an unfortunate fact of life, it is easy for us to forget that in Senter's day, roads were made of dirt; travel was by horse and buggy or by stage; and, with no alternate routes available, a bad road meant that travel ground to a halt. Senter wrote several letters about the hazardous condition of local roads, and these letters serve as sharp reminders to twenty-first century readers about the everyday difficulties of middle-class life in a small nineteenth-century New England town. In 1879, Senter warned the selectmen of the town of Granville, Vermont, about the unsafe condition of its road.

> You are hereby notified that the highway leading from the town of Warren to the town of Granville known as the Main or River road . . . is badly out of repair and unsafe for travel. The said road being full of holes, stones and roots and standing and running water. . . .[151]

Less than a month later, Senter was injured due to bad road conditions in his own town:

---

150. Letter from John Henry Senter to George Wing (Apr. 25, 1884), *in* Senter Letter Book, *supra* note 1, at 236.
151. Letter from John Henry Senter & H.W. Lyford to the Select Men of Granville (May 12, 1879), *in* Senter Letter Book, *supra* note 1, at 54.

> I hereby notify you, that on Tuesday June 3rd 1879, I was riding in my wagon, drawn by two horses, over and upon the highway, leading from the main or river road in said town of Warren . . . . I turned my team from [illegible] in order to pass another team, and [illegible] wagon wheels striking a stone which was only three feet from the travel of said road, it being within the highway, and also in consequence of the . . . traveled part of said highway, it being but 10 feet wide at this place, and in consequence of the said highway being [gullied] at this abovedescribed place, and of the general insufficiency and want of repair of said highway, I was violently thrown from my wagon to the ground, and I was severely injured in my shoulders, and back, and left side, and in consequence of which I am now confined to my bed, for which injuries I claim dammage of the Town of Warren.[152]

These letters remind us that in Senter's time, routine events such as commuting could be dangerous as well as inconvenient and time-consuming. Before becoming too sympathetic to his injuries, though, it is worth noting that a week later, Senter wrote to his mentor Clarence Pitkin that "[b]usiness is very brisk with me, for the last two weeks I have worked night and day, hope it will continue[,]"[153] leading one to wonder just how incapacitating his wagon accident really was.

Only six letters appeared in Senter's copying book in 1880. Sadly, in one of these he described another wagon accident in which he was injured, this time more seriously than before. Note how this letter is larded with much more "legalese" than the letter he had written as a fledgling lawyer just one year before.

> To the Select Men of the Town of Roxbury in County of Washington and State of Vermont,
> Gentlemen,

---

152. Letter from John Henry Senter to unspecified "Gentlemen" (probably June 17, 1879), *in* Senter Letter Book, *supra* note 1, at 97-98.
153. Letter from John Henry Senter to Clarence Pitkin (June 24, 1879), *in* Senter Letter Book, *supra* note 1, at 98.

> I hereby notify you, that on the 29th day of September A.D. 1880 I was riding in my wagon drawn by my horse, over and upon the highway in the Town of Roxbury in the County of Washington, an open public highway in said Town of Roxbury . . . my horse and wagon were thrown off the bank on the easterly side of said highway; said highway being insufficient and out of repair at that point, in that there was a steep bank on the easterly side of said highway at that point, and the said highway at that point was not protected by any railing or other guard to prevent teams from going over the said bank, and by said accident solely caused by the said insufficiency of said highway my wagon was broken and injured, ... and the spokes were broken out of both off wheels of said wagon, and the wagon was otherwise scratched and marred, and I was thrown from my wagon, and severely injured in my spine near my shoulder so that I have had no use of my arms since that time, but have been and am now confined to my bed, entirely helpless, and I was otherwise injured in and about my back and spine, and internally, and I was so severely injured that the clothes had to be cut from my back. All of said injuries to my person and wagon were solely caused by the said insufficiency of said highway in said Town of Roxbury, and I shall and do claim damage of said Town of Roxbury for each and all of said injuries to my person and wagon . . . .[154]

Senter also did battle with town managers on behalf of clients injured by unsafe roads. The next letter, quoted in full, is another example of Senter's trademark brew of tenacity and plain-spokenness, coupled with his sense of fair play and kindness toward his fellow townspeople and clients.

> Selectmen of Hancock,
> Gentlemen;-
>
> Mr Charles Stone informs me that [you] undertook to

---

154. Letter from John Henry Senter to Town of Roxbury (Oct. 18, 1880), *in* Senter Letter Book, *supra* note 1, at 144-46. In the excerpts presented here, Senter used the word "said" sixteen times – anathema to modern-day legal drafters.

play a sort of hocus-pocus settlement with him about his injury which happened to him by reason of the insufficiency of a bridge in your town.

Gentlemen perhaps you can make yourselves believe that you have accomplished a shrewd financial stroke in what you have done with this poor simple man, but you cannot make anybody else think so. The kind of settlement you [have tried] to force onto Charley will not stand as long in law as you were in making it. You must either make an honest settlement with him, paying what is just and square or I shall procede to bring suit against your town and give you a chance to explain your so called "Settlement" in court.

Yours truly
John H. Senter
P.S. Write me your determination what you will do, and I will give you untill June 16th to answer this letter, after that costs will be made if I do not hear from you.
John H. Senter[155]

Constant Travel

Reading through the letters, one is struck by how much travel was required of a small-town lawyer like Senter. Attorneys in the capital city of Montpelier probably would have had to travel less frequently, but for Senter frequent absences from home were a way of life. Not mentioned in the letters is the toll his absences must have taken on Addie Senter and their children. On July 5, 1879, Senter reported that he had to go to Hyde Park, Vermont, for at least a week.[156] In November 1881, he again reported in a letter that he was anticipating a week-long absence;[157] he alluded to a similar such ab-

155. Letter from John Henry Senter to the Selectmen of Hancock (June 4, 1883), *in* Senter Letter Book, *supra* note 1, at 208.
156. Letter from John Henry Senter to C.F. Clough (July 5, 1879), *in* Senter Letter Book, *supra* note 1, at 114.
157. Letter from John Henry Senter to Robert Long (Nov. [20], 1881), *in* Senter

sence in June 1882,[158] and another the following month.[159] In 1884, he reported a week-long stay at Montpelier House Hotel in early March,[160] followed by another stint in Montpelier in late March. He announced plans to travel to the capital yet again in early April,[161] and visited Granville, Vermont for three days in early May, where he engaged in the trial of seven cases.[162] In June 1884, he was at Middlebury.[163] During this time, Senter reported to his soon-to-be law partner Harlan Kemp that he had had "more business this spring than usual."[164]

Although there is no evidence in his copying book that Senter ever traveled out of state, he did have at least one client, and probably more, as far away as Iowa. Senter's copying book contains four letters written to clients and counsel in Iowa, mostly involving procedural matters relating to scheduling depositions. One other letter was addressed to a client in Kansas, pertaining to a matter being litigated in Washington County, Vermont.[165]

Letter Book, *supra* note 1, at 179.

158. Letter from John Henry Senter to Joseph Wing (June 12, 1882), *in* Senter Letter Book, *supra* note 1, at 187.

159. Letter from John Henry Senter to Silas B. Whitney (July 13, 1882), *in* Senter Letter Book, *supra* note 1, at 198.

160. Letter from John Henry Senter to C. Hubbard (March 9, 1884), *in* Senter Letter Book, *supra* note 1, at 217. Montpelier House Hotel was located at 100 State Street, very near the Washington County Courthouse. CHILD, *supra* note 13, at 248.

161. Letter from John Henry Senter to B.B. Smalley (March 30, 1884), *in* Senter Letter Book, *supra* note 1, at 220-25.

162. Letter from John Henry Senter to Clarence Pitkin and Hiram Huse (May 4, 1884), *in* Senter Letter Book, *supra* note 1, at 244.

163. Letter from John Henry Senter to Charles Wilds (May 10, 1884), *in* Senter Letter Book, *supra* note 1, at 251.

164. Letter from John Henry Senter to Harlan Kemp (May 10, 1884), *in* Senter Letter Book, *supra* note 1, at 252.

165. Letter from John Henry Senter to C.O. Graves (June 30, 1884), *in* Senter Letter Book, *supra* note 1, at 263.

The Business of Running a Law Practice

Perhaps the most interesting group of letters in John Senter's copying book reveals details about the daily work of a small-town lawyer embarking on his law practice in the late nineteenth century – what he did for his clients, how much he charged them, and how much he ultimately was able to collect from them. Senter's copying book contains thirteen such letters, plus copies of fourteen legal bills he submitted to his clients.

Senter often had the unpleasant task of collecting his fees from recalcitrant clients. The first of Senter's so-called "dunning" letters appears in 1881. Writing to Henry Kew, he states: "My acct against you for defending Robert [in] his liquor prosecution is long over due. I sent you a statement long ago, and I now desire it to be paid soon."[166]

By 1884, Senter had become wiser in the ways of running his law practice. For one thing, he began to record copies of bills for legal services in his copying book. This section of the book is especially interesting because it shows firsthand the types of legal work he did, how much he charged, and how he ran the business side of his law practice. Since the earlier sections of his copying book contained no such correspondence, it is reasonable to assume that he developed his procedures for assessing and collecting legal fees as he went along, taking more of a "get tough" stance as the years went by and his confidence and client list grew.

The first such letter/bill combination went to H.B. Cady of Waitsfield, Vermont. Senter had done some legal work for Cady in 1879 and 1880, and by 1884 had at long last grown tired of waiting for his fees.

> Enclosed I send you bill of services [for] Parker's case, and I will say right here [that] this bill must now be paid or fixed up [some] way or I shall bring suit against you. The services were rendered for you and at your request and are very reasonable, and must [be] paid. I do

---

166. Letter from John Henry Senter to Henry Kew, Waitsfield, Vt. (Dec. 12, 1881), *in* Senter Letter Book, *supra* note 1, at 180.

> not desire to hurry anyone [but] it is time this matter was closed up and unless I hear from you by May 1st I shall send an officer.

H.B. Cady on account with John H. Senter.							
1879							[Dr.]
June 18	To 1 day defending Parker Cady						5.00
Sept Term	" Term & Atty fees. State vs. Cady (two cases)						10.00
1880							
March Term		"	"	"	"	"	10.00
Sept	"	"	"	"	"	"	10.00
		" Int on above					8.00
							$43.00

> I suspose you [have] a charge against me for pictures, and I have not figured the interest very fine on you, but if you wish to settle now, and I make this offer only for the purpose of settling with out costs or trouble, send me $30.00 and I will square accts with you, otherwise I shall seek to recover for the last cent my due.[167]

Having waited for four years to collect, Senter could be forgiven his rather brusque tone.

It is worth reproducing a few more of Senter's bills to give an idea of the costs of legal services and the fees he charged.

C.H. Clay in account with			
John H. Senter			
1882			Dr.
June 17	To writ you vs Wheeler		1.00
"	"	" Cash Pd Officer	1.50
"	"	" Intr	.30
			2.80[168]

167. Letter and bill from John Henry Senter to H.B. Cady, Waitsfield, Vt. (Apr. 21, 1884), *in* Senter Letter Book, *supra* note 1, at 227.
168. Bill from John Henry Senter to C.H. Clay (Apr. 21, 1884), *in* Senter Letter Book, *supra* note 1, at 228.

Ellen Mahuron
in account with
John H. Senter

1881		Dr.
November 26	To writ You vs. Joseph P. Tucker	$1.00
December 19	"One Day Trial of Your Case vs. Tucker	3.00
" "	" Execution	.25
" "	" Interest on Same	.75
		5.00[169]

Perhaps the difficulties of collecting legal fees that were past due by several years, as were the two examples above, prompted Senter to begin sending regular statements to his clients. The first of these was dated April 22, 1884:

Warren Vermont April 22nd 1884
Fred Parker
In account with
John H. Senter

1883		Dr.
Sept. Term Wash. Co. Ct.	To Term and Atty fees Grundy vs. You	7.00
" " "	" Cash Paid Clerk's bills	1.48
March " "	" Term and Atty fees Grundy vs. You	7.00
		$15.48

> Fred I do not send this to dun you or any thing of the kind but I have adopted a rule to send a statement of acct. to each of my clients at the close of each term of court so that they may know just how big my bill is as they go along, and not think I am bleeding them.[170]

169. Bill from John Henry Senter to Ellen Mahuron (probably Apr. 21, 1884), *in* Senter Letter Book, *supra* note 1, at 229.
170. Bill from John Henry Senter to Fred Parker (Apr. 22, 1884), *in* Senter Letter Book, *supra* note 1, at 232.

Figure 17. Bill from John Henry Senter to Fred Parker (Apr. 22, 1884)

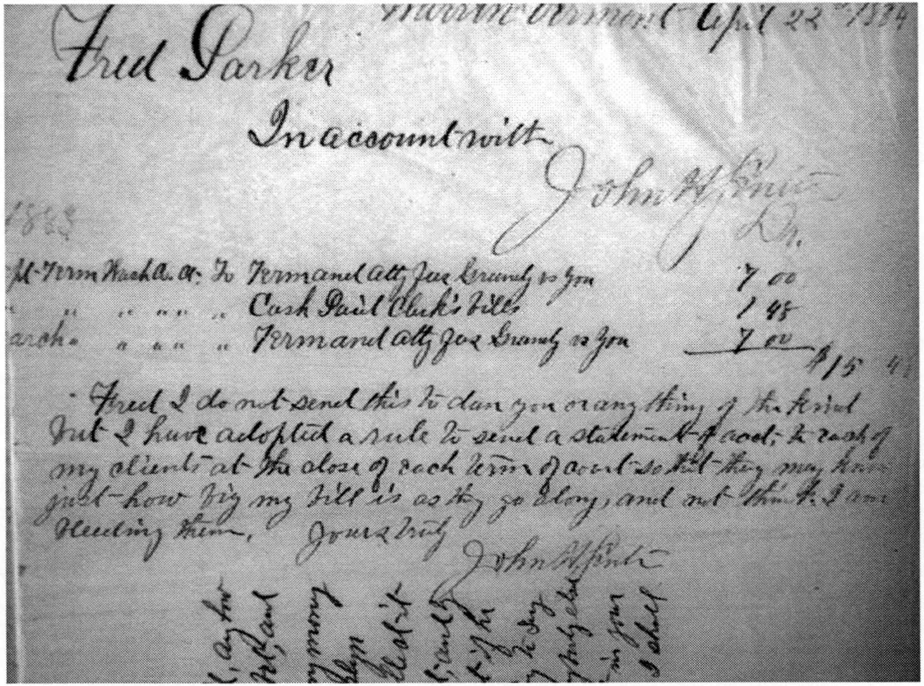

Fred Parker

In account with John H. Senter Dr.

Fred I do not send this to dun you or any thing of the kind but I have adopted a rule to send a statement of acct. to each of my clients at the close of each term of court so that they may know just how big my bill is as they go along, and not think I am bleeding them. Yours truly John H. Senter

Photograph by Paul Baskett

George A. Atkins
In account with
John H. Senter

Statement		Dr.
[illegible] 7th	Writ Robinson vs. Miller	1.00
[illegible] 3	To Letter to [Hartshorn]	.50
	" Retainer	5.00
	" Letter to Sherbino	.50
[illegible]	" Writ you to Sherbino	1.00
Feb 2	" 1 Day trial You vs Sherbino	5.00
March Term of Wash. Co. Ct.	To Term and Atty fees You vs Sherbino	7.00
		$20.00

> George this is not a dun, but I have made a rule to send a statement of account to every client at the close of each term of court so they may know just [how] their bill stands, and so they wont be disappointed when they come to settle at last, as under the new fee bill, no discount is made.[171]

Looking at these bills and several other similar ones, we can see that in 1884 Senter charged $5 per day to represent a client at trial,[172] $5 to retain a client,[173] 50 cents to write a letter,[174] and $1 to $3 (usu-

171. Bill from John Henry Senter to George Atkins (probably Apr. 22-25, 1884), *in* Senter Letter Book, *supra* note 1, at 235.
172. In 1881, Senter charged a day rate of $3. *See supra* text accompanying note 169, Bill from John Henry Senter to Ellen Mahuron.
173. Senter explained his retainer policy in an 1884 letter to George Berry:

> On my return from Montpelier I received a letter from you, in which you say you expect some trouble with Godfrey Sumner about a cow and that you shall want my services, if you do. I shall be happy to assist you, but perhaps you do not understand my terms. If a client wishes to retain me against a prospective lawsuit, I charge five dollars retainer. If you want me on those terms, I will charge you five dollars whether I do any thing or not. If you do not wish me to do that, I shall feel at liberty to act for Mr. Sumner should he desire. Let me hear from you at once.

ally $1) to prepare a writ. He charged his court and officer's fees back to his clients;[175] these costs ranged from .48 to $1.48 for clerk's fees to $7 each term for "term and attorney fees." Senter also charged back fees for obtaining copies of documents (generally $1 per document) and postage as well – usually a matter of a few cents.[176]

One hopes that Senter's policy of twice-yearly statements made it easier for him to collect his fees in 1884 and thereafter. However, in October of 1884, Senter prepared another round of bills and, as of that time, neither George Atkins nor Fred Parker had yet paid their April 1884 bills, whose amounts Senter appended to their October bills. In fact, of the five bills recorded in Senter's copying book in October 1884, only one of these did not include a balance carried forward from April 1884. Rather plaintively, Senter added a single sentence to the end of Fred Parker's October bill: "Fred this will come very handy to me at this time if you can pay it."[177]

Letter from John Henry Senter to George Berry (Apr. 21, 1884), *in* Senter Letter Book, *supra* note 1, at 226.

174. Senter made that charge plain to his clients in several letters, such as this one: "Your favor enclosing twelve dollars came promptly to hand, and I [return] your note, which amounts to $11.52, writing letter 50. = $12.00." Letter from John Henry Senter to Lervis Story (Feb. 26, 1884), *in* Senter Letter Book, *supra* note 1, at 213.

175. In one letter, Senter asked E.W. Howe to serve a writ on behalf of Senter's client Kelsey. Senter directed Howe to use his "own discretion about serving this writ. If Kelly has wronged the old man [Kelsey], serve the writ, and if he has not, put the old man off. If you serve it, charge your fees to Kelsey. I do not have officers fees charged to me." Letter from John Henry Senter to E.W. Howe, Northfield, Vt. (Sept. 12, 1881), *in* Senter Letter Book, *supra* note 1, at 170.

176. As a matter of comparison, it is interesting to note the costs of other items written in Senter's copying book. A three-month subscription to the *Boston Daily Globe* newspaper cost $1.50, as mentioned in a letter to the *Globe* (Oct. 23, 1884), *in* Senter Letter Book, *supra* note 1, at 271. An account that was copied into Senter's book for some reason lists costs of $3.25 for five bushels of oats and $1.88 for a sack of flour. Account between L.L. Durant & S. Banister (probably late Nov. 1884), *in* Senter Letter Book, *supra* note 1, at 276.

177. Bill from John Henry Senter to Fred Parker (Oct. 23, 1884), *in* Senter Letter Book, *supra* note 1, at 269.

Figure 18. Bill from John Henry Senter to Fred Parker (Oct. 23, 1884)

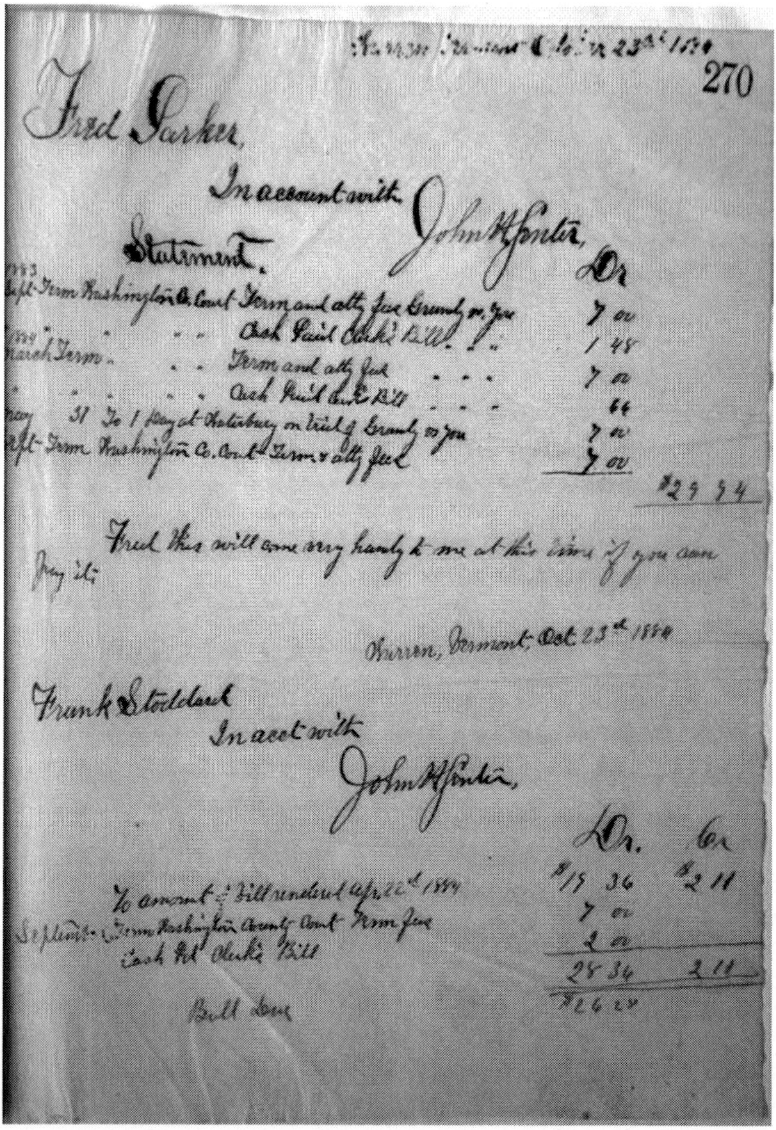

270

Fred Parker,

In account with John H. Senter,

Statement. Dr

1883 Sept Term Washington Co. Court	Term and atty fees Grand ...	7 00
1884 " "	Cash Paid Clerk's Bill	1 48
March Term " "	Term and atty fees	7 00
" " "	Cash Paid Court Bill	66
May 31	To 1 day at Waterbury on trial of Grand ...	7 00
Sept Term Washington Co. Court	Term & atty fees	7 00
		$29 14

Fred this will come very handy to me at this time if you can pay it.

Warren, Vermont, Oct. 23rd 1884

Frank Stoddard

In acct with John H. Senter,

	Dr.	Cr
To amount of bill rendered Apr. 22nd 1884	$19 36	$2 11
September Term Washington County Court Term fees	7 00	
Cash Pd Clerk's Bill	2 00	
	28 36	2 11
Bill due	$26 25	

Photograph by Paul Baskett

In the event lawyers cannot collect their fees through the usual channels, they must resort to more drastic measures, and Senter occasionally was forced to do likewise. In one letter, Senter referred to an attorney's lien for over $100 he had secured against a judgment. Remembering that $100 in 1884 equaled about $2,128 in 2007,[178] it is no wonder Senter sounded as adamant as he did when discussing his lien.

> I have a lien on the judgment which is a prior lien by force of my being the attorney of record for my fees and disbursements which amounts to over one hundred dollars. I shall insist on that and according to all the decisions, I think it clear my attorneys lien will hold. If you think otherwise, we shall have to fight for I do not propose to let up a hare on my lien. I have filed notice of my lien in clerks office on the docket and shall strive to maintain the same.[179]

Senter also streamlined his law practice by enclosing reply cards in his business correspondence. He would send letters to clients or counsel and ask them to reply to him using the enclosed card, which probably helped speed the pace of his affairs.[180] In May 1884, he placed an order for two-hundred-fifty such cards with his old friend the newspaper publisher Hiram Atkins of Montpelier.[181]

One other means of communication was the telephone. Senter mentioned a telephone only once, in a letter dated August 5, 1884, so it is rather difficult to determine how much the lawyers of Warren and Montpelier relied upon it as a commonplace means of communication.[182]

---

178. Current values are calculated using ROBERT SAHR, INFLATION CONVERSION FACTORS FOR DOLLARS 1774 TO ESTIMATED 2017, http://oregonstate.edu/cla/polisci/faculty-research/sahr/sahr.htm (last visited June 20, 2008).

179. Letter from John Henry Senter to F.N. Holman, Randolph, Vt. (June 23, 1884), *in* Senter Letter Book, *supra* note 1, at 260-61.

180. *See, e.g.*, letter from John Henry Senter to Charles Porter (May 5, 1884), *in* Senter Letter Book, *supra* note 1, at 243.

181. Letter from John Henry Senter to Hiram Atkins (probably May 4-7, 1884), *in* Senter Letter Book, *supra* note 1, at 244.

182. In early 1881, the first telephone exchange opened in Montpelier for thirty-

I tellephoned you the other day, but have received no answer, and to-day I cannot find you. Harlan is here and is growing impatient about this case and that to with good reason. Can you not see Judge Rudfield and get some order so that progress can be made in his case.

He has a right to be impatient and if any thing can be done, Do it [183]

Senter's Relations with His Clients

Lawyers have always had to contend with disgruntled clients, and have occasionally become disgruntled with them in turn. While Senter generally communicated with his clients in a polite, direct and businesslike way, in one instance he changed his tone when a client dared to cross him. In a letter that unfortunately is illegible in part, he set the client straight.

> Your favor of the 4th inst is at hand and its contents duly noted. In reply I will say that I do not exactly understand what you mean, or how you expect I or any one else can get your papers served until we find out where your husband is I have writen several letters [to] find out where he is and so far have been unable to find him, if you want to be to the [expense of] advertizing the bill by publication [in] some newspaper, all right – but it will [cost] you some twenty dollars extra, or if you [line is illegible] satisfy you, you had better employ [some other] lawyer, as I do not care to be found [failing] when I am doing all that is possible.

three subscribers; by 1889, the exchange served about two-hundred fifty, and some four hundred miles of lines extended into twenty-seven towns in five counties. CHILD, *supra* note 5, at 337.

183. Letter from John Henry Senter to George Wing, Montpelier, Vt. (Aug. 5, 1884), *in* Senter Letter Book, *supra* note 1, at 266. Perhaps due to letters like these, George Wing eventually left the practice of law to become Vermont state librarian. However, as of 1884-85, Wing was serving as a justice of the peace in Montpelier. THE VERMONT BUSINESS DIRECTORY, FOR 1884-85, *supra* note 76, at 258.

> I have explained this matter to you when I have seen you the best I could. I do not understand what you [blame me] for, and as I have done my duty by you [in] the matter I do not care.[184]

Even someone with the highest standards of professional conduct in dealing with clients could be pushed too far. In this rather amusing letter to the Honorable Frank Plumley, Senter had this to say about his client Mr. Cardell:

> Cardell is raving [around] me about that ten dollars in the matter of Bishop vs Cardell, recognisance, and I said you would pay it and stop his howling.
>
> I have got heartily sick of it and you would if you had it for breakfast, dinner, supper and for lunch.
>
> Please to close it out. . . .[185]

And then later, after he had Cardell's $10 in hand, he wrote again:

> Friend Frank: Your favor of yesterday enclosing check for ten dollars in payment of costs in the matter of Bishop et ux vs Cardell is duly received. Frank don't think I should have hurried you about this matter if it had been my business, but it was not, and I was punched until I got sore. As for interest you may put that in your eye. Yours fraternally, John H. Senter.[186]

Beyond this rare episode of frustration with his clients, however, Senter nearly always adopted a straightforward, civil and businesslike tone. In fact, in a letter to H.H. Van Deusen,[187] a current or

184. Letter from John Henry Senter to Lizzie Griffith, Waitsfield, Vt. (March 8, 1884), *in* Senter Letter Book, *supra* note 1, at 216.
185. Letter from John Henry Senter to Frank Plumley (Apr. 23, 1884), *in* Senter Letter Book, *supra* note 1, at 237.
186. Letter from John Henry Senter to Frank Plumley (May 7, 1884), *in* Senter Letter Book, *supra* note 1, at 247.
187. Van Deusen, of East Warren, Vermont, is probably related to Ellen Van

potential client battling with a neighbor over a shared water conduit, Senter truly appeared to have placed Van Deusen's best interests ahead of any opportunity for his own financial gain.

> Mr. Goodspeed has been to see me today in relation to his rights about the water conduit which heretofore has supplied your house and his. He presents some different phases of the matter than you did. It seems there is a deed from Childs to him [for] the surplus water, also a reservation of the same rights for Goodspeed, in Childs' deed to Powers he also claims that he has always been ready and willing to do, and always has done his equitable share of repairs on the aquaduct. This makes a different [object] than the one you presented to me, and under the circumstances I advise you as I do him [several words illegible] you have neither of you any idea [one line illegible] litigate it in the courts, and when you get through very likely you will neither of you be any better for your experience.
>
> If you and Goodspeed cannot agree and most likely you cannot, I would suggest that you refer the whole matter to som disinterested man whom you both can agree upon and let him decide, and then abide by his decission. This will be by far the least expensive and I presume more satisfactory in its results to both of you, than a chancery lawsuit costing from two to five hundred dollars.
>
> Of course I do not pretend to dictate to either [of you] but you have neither of you any money [to pay] fighting about those water rights. I [have sent] this letter to Goodspeed and sent it by [illegible] hope it will accomplish its [last lines and signature illegible][188]

Deusen, the schoolteacher who advised Senter on textbook selection, and to Edgar and Eugene Van Deusen, the brothers who got mixed up in the burglary. *See supra* text accompanying notes 123, 136.

188. Letter from John Henry Senter to H.H. Van Deusen, East Warren, Vt. (May 17, 1884), *in* Senter Letter Book, *supra* note 1, at 256.

Senter's Final Days in Warren

In April 1884, Senter wrote to H.H. Hall in Chelsea, Vermont, that he was looking for a place to build a house.[189] Perhaps Senter was beginning to find life in Warren a little too stifling or inconvenient. Shortly thereafter, he found a place in Montpelier and appeared very eager to make the move.

> Nathaniel Stockwell is dead and buried, and of course I cannot make any purchase of the premises now until after the action of the Probate Court. Now I should like the place but I cannot hang up on a [pinhook] until doomsday waiting for it, and as I cannot buy now, can I rent it? I will pay forty dollars rent for it this year if I can have it at once, and will buy it just as soon as it can be sold. What do you say? Let me know at once what can be done as I am about to do something.[190]

The very last letter in Senter's copying book is noteworthy only for that reason. Rather fittingly, as the very first law-related letter pertained to collections, the most common type of letter, the very last letter pertained to procedural matters, the next most common category.

> Will you tax the costs in the case of Briggs vs Ralphs and send me a copy so that I can submit it at once to the other side, as I want execution within 30 days from adjournment of court [three words illegible] my lien on property attached. I believe the masters retained the witnesses travel and time on their report.[191]

---

189. Letter from John Henry Senter to H.H. Hall, Chelsea, Vt. (Apr. 28, 1884), *in* Senter Letter Book, *supra* note 1, at 241.
190. Letter from John Henry Senter to Homer Heaton, Montpelier, Vt. (May 6, 1884), *in* Senter Letter Book, *supra* note 1, at 246. Homer Heaton was a justice of the peace in Montpelier. THE VERMONT BUSINESS DIRECTORY, FOR 1884-85, *supra* note 76, at 258.
191. Letter from John Henry Senter to Rufus Wainwright (Dec. 22, 1884), *in* Senter Letter Book, *supra* note 1, at 280.

CHAPTER 4

Senter's Character

> John Henry Senter was a lawyer of striking and original personality. In the rough and tumble of debate, whether at the bar or in the legislative or political field he had few equals. His mind worked with remarkable rapidity and his fund of information on a great variety of subjects equipped him for the duties of the disputant. He was, moreover, a well-read lawyer and in the department of evidence especially skilled. He was frank, open and honest with the court and took pleasure in assisting in the right decision of questions, as well as in the progress of the trial.[192]

This snippet from a biography of Senter was published in 1923, seven years after his death, which gave the biographer the luxury of looking back on Senter's entire life and summing it up in a few well-crafted sentences. In the copying book, prepared by Senter himself some forty years earlier, we can comb through his letters and find bits and pieces of evidence that indeed support the biographer's lofty assessment of Senter. Recall that in 1879 Senter proved himself a worthy disputant in the "rough and tumble" atmosphere of the textbook selection meeting, where he lobbied for two solid hours on behalf of his favored textbook.[193] While we do not see him addressing a court of law in his correspondence, we do find evidence of his "frank, open and honest" manner when dispensing advice to Mr. Van Deusen and his neighbor about their dispute over water rights.[194]

---

192. CROCKETT, *supra* note 3, at 410.
193. *See supra* note 122 and accompanying text.
194. *See supra* notes 187-88 and accompanying text.

Telling It Like It Is

The letters also reveal additional facets of Senter's character that never made it into published accounts of his life. Even a casual reader of Senter's copying book will quickly notice that Senter was intelligent, plain-spoken, blunt to the point of being caustic, wry and acerbic, fair-minded, thoughtful, and a tenacious fighter. These qualities were already much in evidence in 1879, in the letters written in his capacity as an educator and textbook selector. For instance, this one-sentence letter written in May 1879: "Is not my town entitled to as good terms on exchange of books as any other town in this County or State?, and if not why?"[195]

Modern-day collection development and acquisitions librarians may see a bit of their own situation in the one Senter recounts in this excerpt of a letter to Mr. Hazen, a book dealer.

> . . . I do not like to have a gentleman offer me terms with a caution to keep it confidential, and say [to me] that my town is especially favored, on my account when those same terms are common to all, and not as good as some. I had never asked for any special consideration because I favored your Readers, and should not have complained, if you had not, endeavored to pour a large stream of gush over me, but that part I do not relish very much. Now Mr. Hazen I am using plain language but it is my nature to be blunt, and when I think one is trying to humbug, I am very apt to say so. . . .[196]

In a subsequent letter, Senter dispatched Mr. Hazen once and for all. He first expressed surprise that Hazen seemed to be reneging on his promise to extend special introductory terms for the entire five-year period that Senter would be buying his texts.

---

195. Letter from John Henry Senter to G.B. Damon (May 15, 1879), *in* Senter Letter Book, *supra* note 1, at 31.
196. Letter from John Henry Senter to M.W. Hazen (date illegible but probably late May 1879), *in* Senter Letter Book, *supra* note 1, at 66-68.

Senter continued,

> . . . I am sory Mr. Hazen to find out that you are not a man that I can depend on but on the contrary to find you to be a quibbler. I say this because I know that you understood what terms I wanted for my town, and now I find when the time comes for your signing an agreement to the town, you write me a decidedly thin excuse.
>
> However I am glad to find right where you are before I have adopted any of your books. I do not want any connection with any man whose word is not as good as his bond, and I shall not have Yours John H. Senter[197]

In a letter dated April 21, 1879, to book agent Benjamin Sanborn of Boston, Senter stated that he would be happy to meet Sanborn at Montpelier's Bishop Hotel on May 2, but he insisted on paying his own expenses.[198] Evidently Sanborn took offense at this, prompting Senter to explain himself in a second letter:

> . . . I wrote you that if I met you [at Montpelier] I should prefer to pay my own expences, which was true, and for which perhaps I have good reasons, but it may have appeared rather crusty to you. I did not mean it to be [however], as I do not myself think but what it would be perfectly proper, but I know that you know that sometimes committeemen are just a little indiscreet. Now I am poor enough, and have got only one thing belonging to me which would be of consequence to loose and that is my reputation, . . . now when I know more of this book business, I am very glad I did not accept your offer, (and you know why).
>
> I should be very happy to see you Mr. Sanborn and talk over this book question, as long as you wished. I will try to use you as a gentleman should but untill you know where I stand, and what I know about some things, you will probably get a wrong impression. . . .[199]

---

197. Letter from John Henry Senter to M.W. Hazen (July [23], 1879), *in* Senter Letter Book, *supra* note 1, at 118-19.
198. Letter from John Henry Senter to Benjamin Sanborn (Apr. 21, 1879) *in* Senter Letter Book, *supra* note 1, at 36.
199. Letter from John Henry Senter to Benjamin Sanborn, Boston, Mass. (n.d.,

It should not surprise us that Senter retained his same forthright and "crusty" manner in his law-related correspondence. A few snippets from the letters will serve the point: "Dear Sir, You will find enclosed your accts, which were placed in my hands for collection. I have done nothing with them. They are not worth the paper they are written on and never were[.] My charges are nothing."[200] And:

> [My client] . . . desires me to say to you that while he denies all legal liability to Mr. Merill, he was missinformed about the [chair] and is willing to make that right, he has left with me five dollars which I will send you if you desire it, in full settlement, and if this does not satisfy you we will pay nothing, but fight.[201]

One of the most interesting letters in the copying book is a very long letter from Senter to the Honorable B.B. Smalley of Burlington, Vermont. The letter is noteworthy because, in addition to containing a characteristic mix Senter's of bluntness, honesty, and good sense, it shows his increasing involvement in Democratic politics [202] and his awareness of being in the political minority in a heavily Republican state. It also provides an interesting glimpse into the inner workings of party politics. Perhaps most striking of all, it shows Senter rather uncharacteristically backing down from a fight.

> You say, that of course you will see me at our State convention, that is not at all probable as you will observe from what follows....
>
> As to the personnel of the delegation [to the National convention], I quite agree with you, that they should be "cool level-headed men," and I would add one or two other to me quite as essential

---

probably May 8, 1879), *in* Senter Letter Book, *supra* note 1, at 45-49.

200. Letter from John Henry Senter to E.P. Barnham (Dec. 12, 1881), *in* Senter Letter Book, *supra* note 1, at 180.

201. Letter from John Henry Senter to Hon. Charles Heath (July 6, 1882), *in* Senter Letter Book, *supra* note 1, at 195.

202. Although Senter wrote only five letters in which he discussed politics, they

qualifications, i.e. they should also be clean and respectable men, with brains, men who will honor the office, and not be a reproach and disgrace to the party. If we can't do anything else here in Vermont, let us so conduct our party, that it shall be entitled to the respect even of our opponents. I for one do not wish the democracy of Vermont represented at Chicago with any such timber as our Republican friends used four years ago when the[y] sent L. Bart Cross, perhaps they can afford to be sneered at but we can't. Undoubtedly Bart contributed liberally to their campaign fund, the same as no doubt Bascom has to ours, but if that is to be the criterion of fitness, why not set the office up at auction and knock it down to the highest bidder and not go through the formula of a convention?

John C. Burke, Esq., of Albany is the right man for the place, I think, he is cool level-headed clean, able, and respectable. . . .

Then so far you and I agree, but now there comes a trifling difference of opinion, which [I] must express though with great hesitancy and diffidence. In the first place I will state my position in regard to, and my relations with the chairman of our State Committee.

Of Hiram Atkins[203] I have the greatest respect and esteem. He has always been very friendly to me both personally and politically, and I fully appreciate his kindness to me, he has conferred many favors upon me which have been far beyond my power to reciprocate, but I have in return done the best I could. I have stood by him through thick and thin, but there is a Rubicon over which my regard and respect for him will not ferry me, and so if I do cross it I must wade.

---

reveal that he was deeply involved at the state and local level. *E.g.* Letter from John Henry Senter to Hiram Atkins, Editor, *Argus and Patriot* newspaper (Montpelier, Vt.) (July 13, 1882), *in* Senter Letter Book, *supra* note 1, at 198.

203. Hiram Atkins was editor of the *Argus and Patriot* newspaper in Montpelier. As a youth he worked for three years as a dry goods clerk before apprenticing with printer in a newspaper office. He rose in the newspaper world despite the fact that "[h]is only capital was good habits, energy, and industry[.]" Sixteen years Senter's senior, Atkins was active in state Democratic politics for decades. CHILD, *supra* note 5, at 395.

I have always worked with him in our state politics, and while I remain in the party [I] shall never go into any fight against him, although in this matter of delegates, I cannot work with him. So much for my relations with him. Now Mr. Atkins has mentioned the name of Frank Haven Bascom to me as his choice for a delegate from this County and I have very frankly expressed my opinion to him about the matter, he has expostulated with me but to no avail, he has tried to convince me, but I have, as he well knows, remained unconvinced. Now I am struck with the to me wonderful coincidence of your solicitude for Bascom, and it has occurred to me, however strange and chimerical it may seem to you, that Hiram has been the moving [cause] of your favor to me in regard to Bascom. I am well aware with what [pertenasity] he sticks to those whom [he] thinks to be his friends, which is very commendable in him, so long as personal friendship does not produce party dishonor. I may be and probably am wrong in this surmise, but I answer your letter on that hypothesis.

Personally I am on good terms with Mr. Bascom and wish well, but that has nothing to do with his fitness as a delegate. In my opinion (since you flatter me by asking it) his selection as a delegate would be a very unwise move. I hardly think Mr. Atkins appreciates the position he will place the party of this County in by such a course, if he were to canvass even Montpelier with a purpose of finding how the matter was he would be astonished to find that the better class of democrats were disgusted with the idea, and throughout the county he would find that no other man than himself could pull Bascom through. I think Mr. Atkins has asked several leading democrats this question, "Which do you prefer Bascom or G.B. Evans of Moretown, and of course they have said Bascom, but that is not exactly fair, as one man of considerable influence said to me, "Who in hell wants either of them"? They do not think and I do not think we are driven to that alternative yet, if we are God help the party!

The selection of such men for delegates [and] the nomination of such men generally is one great reason why our party remains so weak in this state. Many young men of liberal ideas are deterred from voting with us by such a course, and such a course [persisted] in will drive others out of the party. . . .

> Are we so d—d hard up that it must be either Bascom or Evans, if so good bye for me, I will step down and out.
>
> However I do not wish to make any disturbance in the party, if I could, nor to try to force my opinions against the wishes or the policy of either you or Mr. Atkins, and I shall not, for two reasons, the first, because I am not, so egotistical as to think it would amount to any thing, if I should, and secondly, because I will not under any circumstances go in to any fight with a man who has placed me under as many obligations to him as has Mr. Atkins, and as I am convinced from your letter that he is bound to push Bascom at all hazards and I can't prevent it by peacfull means, I will take a back seat.
>
> Therefore I think that I will not attend the State convention, as under the circumstances [I] think it would not be best, for I certainly [should] kick if Bascom's name was proposed, [as] I never will be an abettor of my party's dishonor, so I will as gracefully as possible retire from the battle and the party and [let] those wiser than I run the machine [illegible] themselves, I do not mean that I shall ever be anything else but a democrat, but simply that I will take my foolish head out of politics as far as any active service is concerned. . . .[204]

Despite Senter's intimations that the Vermont Democratic Party would not have him to kick around any longer, he in fact went on to hold numerous local, state, and national offices and appointments, as noted earlier.[205]

---

204. Letter from John Henry Senter to B.B. Smalley, Burlington, Vt. (March 30, 1884), *in* Senter Letter Book, *supra* note 1, at 220-25.

205. *See supra* notes 21-27 and accompanying text. In fact, newspaper columnist Dorman B.E. Kent wrote in 1933: "When I was a boy, Harland (sic) Kemp, John Senter . . . and half a dozen other war horses like them could be counted on as being present at every town meeting in the old Capital hall on State street and later at the armory. They were without exception men of high ability, not one of them was in the slightest afraid of any opponent on the floor of a town meeting in those olden days . . . ." DORMAN B.E. KENT, EVENTS OF THIS DAY: FACTS OF INTEREST TO MONTPELIER FOLKS BRIEFLY TOLD 107 (Michael R. Doyle ed., 2005).

Senter's Way With a Dollar

Because the vast majority of the letters in Senter's copying book were strictly business-related, the few glimpses of his personality and character that shine through become all the more tantalizing. One of these facets is his way with a dollar, which we first glimpse in a letter dated April 10, 1879 that he wrote to his friend and mentor Hiram Atkins, the newspaper publisher. "I received to night from your office a bill for [illegible] notice of R. Shattuck. You will recollect I think that I paid you that dollar when I gave you the notice for publication. I paid to you personally, hope you will rember."[206]

Evidently this was not the end of the dispute. While we unfortunately do not have a copy of Atkins' reply, we do have the following response from Senter:

> No I do not think that I am mistaken, I think I can give you the date by the Hotel register, when I am at Montpelier, it was not far from the 20th of February. I gave the order to you and at the same time told you that Shattuck was intending to send it to the Journal office, but that I had told him that your paper was the better one for him, and so I had brought it to you. You thanked me for that, and then asked me whose law office I was going into at Montpelier, and I told that I was going into C.H. Pitkin's office. You then said that I had made a good selection, and that was glad that I did not go to Heath's. Now do you not remember this? . . .[207]

The final piece of the dollar debate correspondence occurred on April 18: "I am very positive about the dollar am sure I paid you, and think I can convince you when I see you. I shall be at Montpelier

206. Letter from John Henry Senter to Hiram Atkins, Editor, *Argus and Patriot* newspaper (Montpelier, Vt.) (Apr. 10, 1879), *in* Senter Letter Book, *supra* note 1, at 15.
207. Letter from John Henry Senter to Hiram Atkins, Editor, *Argus and Patriot* newspaper (Montpelier, Vt.) (Apr. 14, 1879), *in* Senter Letter Book, *supra* note 1, at 14-15.

the 3rd of May, and will see you then and we will [avenge] this matter someway."[208]

Not to snicker too much at Senter's parsimony, the money seems to have been less important to him than the principle of the matter, as is evident in this example from five years later. In 1884 Senter engaged in an uncharacteristically foolhardy enterprise when he bet a Mr. Joslyn[209] five dollars[210] that Senter's cow could give eleven quarts of milk per day. Given that by this time he charged clients five dollars per day to represent them,[211] this bet of a full day's pay seems rather astonishing, particularly when he and his wife Addie had several mouths to feed. Senter must have been doing fairly well in his law practice, or else he felt very confident in the capabilities of his cow. At any rate, the entire milk dispute turned sour when a disagreement arose over exactly what the bet was. In these two heated letters to William Strong, who was charged with holding Senter's and Joslyn's five dollars until the bet was concluded, we again see evidence of Senter's stubbornness, sense of justice and fair play, and cutting humor.

> Sometime last winter as you will remember, I and one Mr. Joslyn made a bet of five dollars which was deposited in your hands. The bet was as follows. I said I had a cow that would come in in April that was giving eleven quarts of milk per day. Mr. Joslyn turned up

---

208. Letter from John Henry Senter to Hiram Atkins, Editor, *Argus and Patriot* newspaper (Montpelier, Vt.) (Apr. [18], 1879), *in* Senter Letter Book, *supra* note 1, at 29.

209. The only other reference to a Joslyn in Senter's correspondence is a single mention of an L.R. Joslyn, whom Senter represented in a collection action against Robert Riley of Granville, Vermont. Senter attempted to collect on Joslyn's behalf on an account against Riley for $4.74. Letter from John Henry Senter to Robert Riley (June 18, 1884), *in* Senter Letter Book, *supra* note 1, at 258. HAMILTON CHILD'S BUSINESS DIRECTORY OF 1889 lists Oramel S. Joslin and Louis R. Joslyn, both of Waitsfield, as livestock breeders and dealers. CHILD, *supra* note 13, at 252.

210. Five dollars in 1884 was worth about $106 in 2007. Current values are calculated using SAHR, *supra* note 178.

211. *See supra* text accompanying note 171.

> his nose at the statement of 11 qts per day for any cow, and I said that I had a five dollar bill in my pocket that said my cow would give 11 qts that day or the next day he immediately put up the money and I did the same. Well sir I did not bet that my cow would calve in April, or any thing of that kind, I bet she would give 11 qts of milk that day or the next. I measured her milk carefully for a week and she gave 82 qts that next week, and I can prove it, she gave 12 ½ qts. the next day which was the day I bet on but I took her average for week so Joslyn would not say there was any hocus pocus about one day. I now understand that he claims the money on the ground that she will not calve this April, and has sent a man to see her, to find out, well I don't myself think she will calve this April, but I do claim that when she would calve is no part of my bet, but if he insists that it was, one thing is sure no particular April was named and I will endeavor to accomodate the gentleman and have her go to bull in [summer] so that she will calve next April, any how.
>
> But joking aside I claim that bet, and I hereby notify you not to pay my money to any one but myself. If Mr. Joslyn claims his of course I cannot collect it but I claim I have fairly won it; and by all the wager rules it is mine, but if he demands his money I have nothing to say but you must not pay him or anybody else my money, the five dollars I put in your hands to any one but me. If you do I shall hold you responsible.[212]

Senter must have received an unsatisfactory reply from Mr. Strong, the contents of which we regrettably can only infer from Senter's caustic riposte.

> I have the honor to acknowledge your very effusive favor of the 23rd inst. And in reply I will say that for a disinterested party who has very little to say, it is quite an interesting document.
>
> In reply to query why I had not called for the Stakes, I must say that perhaps I am less ravenous than you thought, but my main reason has been that I have had no opportunity without putting myself out, and I thought the money quite safe in your hands, and

212. Letter from John Henry Senter to William Strong, Waitsfield, Vt. (Apr. 21, 1884), *in* Senter Letter Book, *supra* note 1, at 231-32.

> I should not have written you when I did, but that I was informed that Mr. Joslyn and the [one line illegible] ground of the April [clause].
>
> [Well] sir, I should have been a little astonished at your fervor in the matter had I not heard some talking you had done about the matter before I received your favor signed with the additional title of stake holder, which I concluded was done so I should not infer that an interested party was the author.
>
> I made the bet that my cow would give 11 qts. of milk that day or the next. I did not bet she would calve in April.
>
> I did make the statement that she would calve in April, and she shall if she lives another year.
>
> Now as to your very plainly expressed determination to pay Messrs. Joslyn and Reed ten dollars, I have this to say, you can pay [illegible] or anybody else, whatsoever you see fit and as for me I want no revenge out of you or the old cow either, but I have already notified you that I claim my money, and now I demand it, and I mean exactly what I say. I have no quarrell with you and want none, or with anyone else. But if you choose to have one why that is all right have one. Now if you pay the money you do so with full notice, and assume your own responsibility. . . .
>
> Don't for a moment my dear sir think I care very much for five dollars, for [while] I am poor enough, I can manage [to] [one line illegible].
>
> [If] Mr. Joslyn and Reed will [agree to it] you may pay that money (I mean the $10) to the most needy family in your village and you may be the judge who it is. So please don't howl about that.
>
> Hoping you are serene and contented in the office of stake holder.[213]

Not surprisingly, given the furor surrounding this silly bet, there is no further mention of any other bets in Senter's copying book. One suspects that after this debacle, Senter's betting days were over. Perhaps Addie Senter had a hand in this decision as well.

---

213. Letter from John Henry Senter to W.M. Strong, Waitsfield, Vt. (Apr. 25, 1884), *in* Senter Letter Book, *supra* note 1, at 238-40.

Senter's Sense of Humor

Occasional gems of wit appear in the letters, as in this one to Mary Robinson, whom Senter considered hiring as a teacher.

> I could have recomended you as far as your education is conserned very highly, because I know that you are well grounded in our elementary branches, which to me are of great importance either for a teacher, or for an accomplished young lady. I am afraid that many young ladies of today are neglecting plain english for bad French, and poor latin. I have more respect for our mother tongue, and think it should be learned first, and then others will be an advantage. . . .[214]

More often, though, Senter's humor was of the wry, pugilistic, even abusive, kind. In quite a few letters to attorneys who also were his friends, Senter let his competitive nature shine through: "In accordance with your request . . . the case . . . will be continued untill June 29th 9 a.m. same place, at which time and place I am desirous of cleaning you out."[215]

Senter wrote the ultimate "with friends like these, who needs enemies" letter to his (supposed) friend Zed Stanton, also a lawyer.[216] In between bits of legal business involving a case with which they were involved, Senter fired off a stream of colorful prose that would have made Shakespeare proud.

> Thou art violently carried away from grace; there is a devil haunts thee in the likeness of a fat, lazy man; a tun of man is thy

---

214. Letter from John Henry Senter to Mary Robinson (n.d., probably May 8, 9, or 10, 1879), *in* Senter Letter Book, *supra* note 1, at 50.

215. Letter from John Henry Senter to Charles Heath (June 12, 1883), *in* Senter Letter Book, *supra* note 1, at 209.

216. In addition to his legal work, Stanton represented the town of Roxbury in the Vermont state legislature, and was an assistant judge of Washington County Court from 1884 to 1888. CHILD, *supra* note 5, at 117.

companion; thou [bolting-hutch] of beastliness; thou swolen parcel of dropsies; thou huge bombard of beer; thou stuffed [cloak] bag of guts; thou, my sweet creature of bombast, how long ago is't since thou sawest thine own knee? Thou has more flesh than another man, therefore more frailty.

Out upon thee for a sordid wretch t'would beat his doctor of his physic. Away, you starveling, you bull's pizzle, you vile [paunch] of sin. O, for breath to utter what is like thee! I am accursed to rob in such a thief's company, ye fat-kidneyed rascal, you [illegible-presser], you horse back-breaker; you huge hill of flesh.

Thou art so fat-witted, with drinking Gotham's beer, and unbuttoning thee after supper and [one line illegible] to demand that truly which thou wouldst truly know.

Has not my worthy client who handles the [mortar] and pestle called thine to a reckoning many [illegible] and oft, without avail? . . . But by the Lord [if ye] are glad ye have the money and out of that great store I will demand only sixty silver buzzards, besides which you shall fully recompense that faithfull minion of the law, i.e. Orcutt for his well done labor in behalf of [rest of line illegible].

> I'll have my debt, speak not against my debt;
> I have sworn an oath that I will have my debt;
> Thou callest me pelican; before thou had'st a cause;
> But since I am a pelican beware my beak;
> For the justice with his fat round belly shall grant me my most righteous cause.
> I'll not be a soft [and] dull eyed fool;
> To shake the head, relent and sigh and yield
> I'll have my debt.[217]

Have I not interceded by letter with your stony hearted client all to no purpose? And now because I have him in my power by the strong arm of the law shall I relent? Shall I throw away my

217. Senter was indebted to Shakespeare for these lines. In *The Merchant of Venice*, Shylock says:

physic on such a craven dog as he, because thou [threw the better] fight. Why if fight is what you want "[Pile] on McDuff and damned is he who first cries hold enough." Hads't thou cried for mercy you would have had it, but that mercy would have been tempered with justice.

Well Zed, Julia's acct. amounts to	$18.83
Marshalls acct. amounts to	37.00
Two writs amount to	2.00
Orcutt's officer fees amount to	5.70
Total	$63.53

Sixty three and 53/100 dollars will be [required to liquidate].
Verily I say unto thee thou parody on justice it must be [63.50] or fight, fight, fight.
Thine fraternally
John H. Senter[218]

> I'll have my bond; speak not against my bond:
> I have sworn an oath that I will have my bond.
> Thou call'dst me dog before thou hadst a cause;
> But, since I am a dog, beware my fangs:
> The duke shall grant me justice. . . .
> I'll have my bond; I will not hear thee speak:
> I'll have my bond; and therefore speak no more.
> I'll not be made a soft and dull-eyed fool,
> To shake the head, relent, and sigh, and yield
> To Christian intercessors. Follow not;
> I'll have no speaking: I will have my bond.

William Shakespeare, The Merchant of Venice, act 3, sc. 3. Senter's ability to paraphrase Shakespeare is quite impressive, and shows that the words in one of his biographies were more than mere flattery: "[D]uring the years of his greatest activity, [he] has never ceased to be a student, both in his profession, in literature, and in municipal and educational problems." *The City of Montpelier, supra* note 6, at 155.

218. Letter from John Henry Senter to Zed Stanton (May 11, 1884), *in* Senter Letter Book, *supra* note 1, at 253-54.

Figure 19. Partial view of letter from John Henry Senter to Zed Stanton (May 11, 1884)

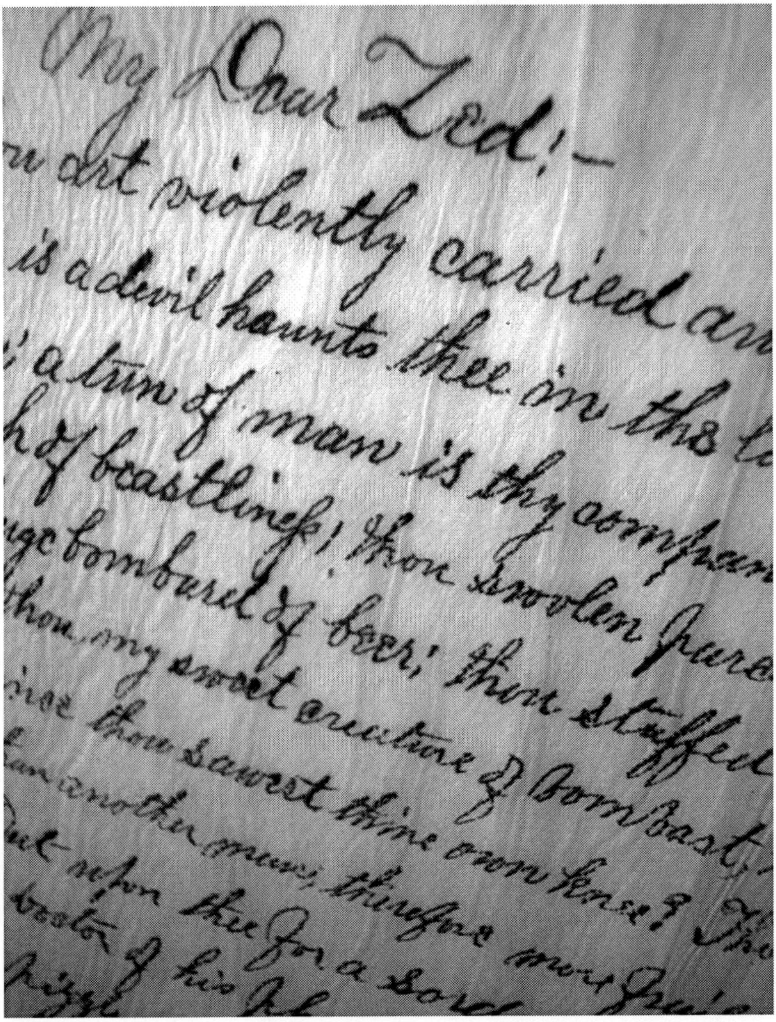
My Dear Zed:—
...u art violently carried aw...
...is a devil haunts thee in the l...
...a tun of man is thy compan...
...h of beastliness; thou swollen parc...
...ge bombard of beer; thou stuffed...
...thou, my sweet creature of bombast...
...since thou sawest thine own knee?...

Photograph by Paul Baskett

Pushing The Envelope

In his law office correspondence, Senter showed himself to be an upstanding man and, except for the ill-fated cow bet, a cautious one as well. Nevertheless, two Vermont Supreme Court cases in which he was a party showed that he was not averse to pushing the envelope a bit. Both of these cases arose after the period covered in his copying book; one in 1885, the other in 1900.

In 1885, when Senter still had close ties to Warren, he was a party in *D.H. Downing v. Lyford & Senter.*[219] Lyford was a sheriff in Warren and in that capacity sold butter-tub machinery on an execution issued against Downing. Evidently Lyford and Senter had an agreement whereby Senter bid on the property with the "tacit understanding" that Lyford would later take it off his hands for $125 or less. The court held that the sale was invalid on the grounds that a sheriff's sale to his agent is void.[220]

Fifteen years later, Senter was a party in *City of Montpelier v. Senter.*[221] Senter had been elected mayor in March 1898. At the time of his election, compensation for the mayor was prohibited. However, a statute effective November 30, 1898 granted the mayor a salary of $300. Senter immediately grabbed the full $300 and the city sued him to get it back. Rather unsurprisingly, the court held that the city was entitled to recover the portion of the $300 covering the period from March through November 1898, with interest, on the grounds that a statute should not be given retrospective effect.[222]

Senter also engaged in rather zealous advocacy on at least one occasion, which should not surprise readers of his letters one bit. In *Foss v. Smith,*[223] he represented defendant Smith in a case involving a new trial. In his argument to the jury, Senter said, "Mr. Redmond

219. 57 Vt. 507 (1885).
220. *Id.* at 508.
221. 47 A. 392 (Vt. 1900).
222. *Id.* at 393.
223. 65 A. 553 (Vt. 1907).

said to you, gentlemen of the jury, 'granted that he, Foss, is a knave,' and I guess it is generally granted." Immediately after the plaintiff lodged an objection, Senter continued, "And I repeat, gentlemen, Mr. Redmond says, 'Granted Ernest Foss is a knave,' and I don't dispute it."[224] Chief Judge Rowell mildly chastised Senter for his remark:

> Mr. Senter's argument was not provoked by Mr. Redmond's and he incorrectly stated what Mr. Redmond said; but the jury knew that, and would not be misled by it. Mr. Senter stated nothing as a fact, but only as a guess, and as an assent to what he represented Mr. Redmond as saying. While this was not a style of advocacy to be commended, it was not so vicious as to require reversal.[225]

---

224. *Id.* at 556.
225. *Id.*

Figure 20. Signature of John Henry Senter

Photograph by Paul Baskett

CHAPTER 5

Conclusion

> John Senter is a self-made man. He has obtained his education almost wholly by himself; studied law and been admitted to the bar, and makes a success of his business.[226]

After John Henry Senter had gotten his legal career off the ground and left Warren for Montpelier, he went on to a distinguished and multifaceted career as a lawyer, politician, and civil servant, and the many accomplishments of his later years were recorded in brief biographical sketches published near the end of his life and after his death.

How fortunate we are to have this copying book from the earliest days of his career, which bears witness to his daily struggles and successes and reveals firsthand evidence of the intellect, temperament, and hard work that would eventually take him so far from his humble beginnings in Warren. More than that, the copying book reveals glimpses of the man behind the published accounts – his integrity, bluntness, and acerbity on full display. The copying book also takes us into the world of one small-town lawyer in the late nineteenth century, introducing us to his clients, revealing the types of legal matters he worked on, showing us how he ran his business, and giving us a firsthand look at the daily difficulties he encountered: frequent travel over dangerous roads, long stays away from home, and constant struggles to get his clients to pay their bills.

This single volume of letters has revealed so much. How many other unique manuscripts lie waiting in our rare book rooms for their secrets to be unlocked?

---

226. 4 Pt. 2 HEMENWAY, *supra* note 7, at 812.

Part II

Letters

A note about the transcription: The transcription is literal; misspellings and omitted words are transcribed as they appeared in the letters. Words that are either completely illegible or illegible enough that I have had to guess at their meaning are indicated in [brackets]. For the most part, punctuation marks have been transcribed as they appeared in the original letters. However, since Senter's periods and commas are often indistinguishable, I have chosen the mark that makes the most sense to our modern eyes. Occasional explanatory notes have been inserted in the transcription in [bracketed italics].

[*Page 1 of the copying book*]
Warren April 21st 1879
[*The rest of the page appears to be a test of the copying system – illegible writing in both forward and backward directions appears on the page.*]

[*Page 2*]
April 8th 79
Messrs. Clark & Maynard
New York
Gentlemen,

I received your sample coppies of Reed & Kellogg's grammars, for which please except thanks. I have not as yet had time to give them a thorough examination but am well pleased with so far as I have examined them.

At the annual meeting of the Superintendent of this County, Charles Dole of Northfield, W.W. Ainsworth of Calais and myself were appointed to select a list of textbooks for the County under the new law. We shall probably recomend an entire new list of books, and I will give your grammars a fair chance.

Yours truly,
John H. Senter

[Page 3]
April 8th 79
E.C. McClintock Esq.
I have received the readers & spellers you sent me, for which please accept thanks. I have not had time as yet to examine them, but will before [we decide.]

At the annual meeting of the Superintendents for this County, Prof. Charles Dole of Northfield, W.W. Ainsworth of Calais and myself were appointed a committee to select a list of books for the County. We have not as yet decided on any books, but we shall probably report a nearly entire change. If you wish to enter the field on any other books, we will give your books a fair trial.
Yours truly,
John H. Senter

[*Pages 4-5*]
April 8th 79
G.B. Damon Esq.
Boston
Dear Sir,

Your favor of the 27 [inst.], is at hand and in reply I have a few suggestions to make in regard to the Arith question. At the annual meeting of the Superintendents of this County Prof. Charles Dole of Northfield, W.W. Ainsworth of Calais, and your humble servant were appointed a committee to select a list of books for the County. Northfield has a great many of [Harpers] Geog's & Greenleaf's Arith's in use, and Dole [hangs] that way a little, now I would suggest that you write to every Superintendent in the County, about the changes you purpose to make in the Arith, especially the work on the Vt method of interest & <u>taxes</u>, also if possible I would like to have you see this committee. We meet at Bishops Hotel Montpelier on Saturday May 3rd, and I should be happy to meet you there, [and] I should be very happy to see you at Warren also. We shall probably reccomend an entire new list of books, especially Readers, Spellers, Arith's, Grammar's, Histories & Geog's.

Hoping your Arith. will be successfull I remain yours &c,
John H. Senter

[*Page 5*]
April 8th 79

A.C. Stockin Esq
Boston
Dear Sir

At the annual meeting of the Superintendents of this County, Prof. Chas. Dole of Northfield, W.W. Ainsworth of Calais and myself were appointed a committee to select a list of books for this County under a new law. I shall be happy to hear your terms, on Readers, Spellers, Grammars, Histories, & Arithmetics. Your Geographies are now in use in part of the County and will stand a good chance, I think.

Yours truly,
John H. Senter

[*Page 6*]
April 8th 79
M.W. Hazen Esq
Boston
Dear Sir

At the annual meeting of the Superintendents of this County held at Montpelier April 1st, Prof. Chas. Dole of Northfield, W.W. Ainsworth of Calais and myself were appointed to select a list of school texts for this County. We shall probably select an entire new list of books.

I should like samples of your publications and prices.

Yours truly
John H. Senter

April 14th 79
A.F. Martin Esq.
Dear Sir

I have in my hands for collection a note against you in favor of G.W. Cardell amounting to day to $6.50. An early settlement will save you costs.

Yours with respect
John H. Senter

[*Page 7*]
April 8th 79
J.H. Butler & Co.
Philadelphia
Gentlemen

At the annual meeting of the Superintendents of this April 1st, Prof. Chas. Dole of Northfield, W.W. Ainsworth of Calais and myself were appointed a committee to select a list of school text books for this County. We shall change Arithmetics, Grammars, Histories, Geographies, & Spellers. Samples & prices of your publications will [be] thankfully received if you whish to introduce any of your books.

Yours truly
John H. Senter

[*Page 8*]
April 8th 79
W.T. Whittemore Esq.
Boston
Dear Sir

Since I saw you at Northfield, the Superintendents of this County have held their annual meeting, and for the sake of uniformity throughout the County, they appointed a committee to select a list of books for the County, and Prof. Charles Dole of Norwich University, Northfield, W.W. Ainsworth, Principal of High School, Calais; and your humble servant were appointed such committee. I would sugest that you send samples of your publications to each member of this committee and that you see them personally if possible. We hold our first committee meeting at Bishop Hotel Montpelier on the 3rd day of May. Should be very much pleased to meet you there or here at any time.

Yours truly
John H. Senter

[*Page 9*]
April 9th
James N. Johnson Esq
Northfield V^{t}
Dear Sir

I find on the Town books, three chattel mortgages on Ashley Duttons property, the first one in favor of his Son Charles H. Dutton given to secure the payment of a promissory note dated July 5th 1876, with an endorsement May 1st, 77 of two dollars, and one Oct 1st 78 of ten dollars, the notes is on demand and given for $112.79.

The second mortgage to James Cardell for $95.73 the third one to Edwin Cardell for $[5]3.50. Will send you coppies if you wish, and will watch the old [case] the best I can.
Yours truly John H. Senter

April 9th 79
[Marshal] Hanks Esq.
Dear Sir
I have in my hands for collection, an order on your district, ammounting to about $25.00, in favor of Homer W. Heaton, it must be paid immediately to save cost.
Yours truly John H. Senter

[*Page 10*]
April 9th
Levi Wakefield Esq.
Dear Sir
I have in my hands for collection, an order on your district, ammounting to about $25.00 in favor of Homer W. Heaton, it must be paid immediately to save cost.
Yours truly
John H. Senter

April 9th 79
F.A. Trask Esq.
Roxbury Vt
Dear Sir
I have in my hands for collection a note against you ammounting today to ($4.03) owned by L.M. & E.A. Heath, an early settlement will save you cost.
Yours truly
John H. Senter

[*Page 11*]
April 10th 79
[*one or two words illegible*] Curtis Esq.
Lincoln Vt
Dear Sir

I have in my hands for collection an account against you amounting $3.75 owned by Dr. E.G. Hooker of Northfield, it being for his services. An early settlement is desirable.
Yours John H. Senter

Warren Vermont April 10th 1879
Hiram Atkins
Montpelier Vt
Dear Sir

I received to night from your office a bill for [*one word illegible*] notice of R. Shattuck. You will recollect I think that I paid you that dollar when I gave you the notice for publication. I paid to you personally, hope you will rember.
Yours truly
John H. Senter

[*Page 12*]
April 10th 79
Friend Huse

I have not a set of the readers, nor have I yet received the Geography from Mr Whittemore, neither has Mr. Ainsworth of Calais I believe.
Yours truly
John H. Senter

April 29th 79
E.A. Heath Esq.
Moretown Vt
Dear Sir

[*one word illegible*] can I secure a demand of $40.00 on John Kew Junior of Fayston, and if I can, on what, please inform me on this at once.

How did your examination turn out. I raised hell I guess, but not a d-d one got a certificate that did come to the standard, [it] cut pretty close on some of them.

Folks are well I shall come down as soon as the going is good.

By the way I should like your oppinions on the school books write and inform me of your choices.
Yours
[*Signature cut off at bottom of page.*]

[*Page 13*]
April 12th 79
Henry Oviat Esq
Dear Sir

We, here in Warren, are trying to raise money to pay Beeman H. Campbell's bail, you will reccollect he was one of the men convicted of arson, from Warren. We think that he is inocent, and we know well enough that he is, now we want to get all the evidence there was in the case against him as cheap as possible, and I write to ask you how much it will cost, together with his own testimony.
Yours truly
John H. Senter

April 12th 79
Henry Oviatt Esq.
Dear Sir

In looking over my copy book I notice I forgot to add that I wrote the first letter to you by request. I was acting merely as an amanuensis. I am not a part of the <u>We</u>.
Yours truly
John H. Senter

[*Pages 14-15*]
Warren Vt Monday April 14th 1879
Hiram Atkins
Montpelier
Dear Sir,

No I do not think that I am mistaken, I think I can give you the date by the Hotel register, when I am at Montpelier, it was not far from the 20th of February. I gave the order to you and at the same time told you that Shattuck was intending to send it to the Journal office, but that I had told him that your paper was the better one for him, and so I had brought it to you. You thanked me for that, and then asked me whose law office I was going into at Montpelier, and I told that I was going into C.H. Pitkin's office. You then said that I had made a good selection, and that was glad that I did not go to <u>Heath's</u>. Now do you not remember this?

And now I think I can explain what your brother and Mr. Sullivan are

thinking about, about the 7th or 8th of March I was at your office to get a town order book printed. I talked with your brother about it and he called your foreman Mr. Blair, (I think) his name is, and I bought the book of them, at the same time I gave Mr. Will. Sullivan a list of town officers elected in this Town for publication. Now is not that what those gentlemen are thinking about? I am quite sure you took this [*one word illegible*] notice from me yourself, and that we had this conversation which perhaps you will recollect.
Yours truly
John H. Senter

[*Page 16*]
[*The following letter appears to be in someone else's handwriting.*]
April 19th 79
Friend Heaton [*one word illegible*] Dear Sir

I wish to ask your opinion upon a leagal question that is liable to come up in a Town meeting to be held in this town two weeks from [*one word illegible*] to day the article in the [*one word illegible*] is this to see if the town will [*one word illegible*] to instruct [this] Select-men to indemnify E.H. Spalding for becoming [*one word illegible*] for B.H. Campbells [aperance] to the [*one word illegible*] Court to [bee held] at Montpelier on the 2nd Tuesday in August next.

The question is has the the Town the leagal right so to do & will it bind the Town if the Town do vote to instruct this Select men so to do. You will [*remainder of letter is illegible*]

[*Pages 17-19*]
April 14th 79
Friend Huse

Your favor of the 12th is at hand, also the Geog. for which accept thanks. Am sory to learn of your discouragement in regard to [Gugot]. When you next venture forth to encounter a [Sub] Prof's I wish you would have him explain one or two things which I find in Harper's. I will [commence] at home for my geographical knowledge, "may be limited," first our county. Will he look on the map of Vt in Harpers and explain the position of Fayston & Waitsfield in regard to Warren then he may look in the description just under the head of "Political Organization" and tell if he [can] what about two hundred and forty three members in the House

of Representatives, "one from each organized Town or city". Then he may glance at "Arizona Territory" and tell when Prescott was made the capital, then to South America and be sure to have the "[Sub] Prof" explain the northern and eastern boundaries of Bolivia & Paraguay also where on the map the Galapagos Islands are situated. [*several words illegible*] Point Aguja is. Then take this encyclopedia of geographical knowledge and turn to the [*one or more words illegible*] [map] of Vermont again, look over here to Warren, and ask Moore to give more explanations, first how long since Mad River and White River have had their source in Warren, and have him tell you how the Roxbury branch managed to climb the mountain. But my head grows dizzy and my heart grows sick, if he wants any more [*one word illegible*] I will [perish] on short notice but till these very slight mistakes are rectified or explained I shall be obliged to withhold my approval of the "picture book."
Yours
John H. Senter

[*Page 18*]
April 14th 79
H.B. Ward Esq.
Duxbury Vt
Dear Sir

I write you by request James Tillotson of this Town, his daughter expects to teach the school at North Duxbury this summer, and it will be very inconvenient for her to attend the public examination at your place. I write to ask if she can be examined here, and have me send her answers to you. Please answer & oblige.
Yours truly
John H. Senter

[*Page 19*]
April 21st 79
John McGreggor Esq.
Dear Sir

In looking over the problem I sent you I find a mistake in the statement, the [Tower] that is marked 90 ft on the diagrams should be 60 feet and the one marked 60 feet should be 90, they were misplaced by me on the plans.

The triangle of course is supposed to be a horisontal. Please excuse my blunder & oblige yours truly
John H. Senter

[*Page 20*]
April 14th 79
[*A full-page letter about school matters; a very faint copy, nearly completely illegible.*]

[*Page 21-22*]
April 14th 79
Benjamin H. Sanborn Esq.
Boston
Dear Sir

Your favor of the 12th is at hand, in reply I will say your samples were duly received, for which please accept [thanks.] I have been for several years while studying for my profession in the habit of teaching two or three terms of school each year, (although now I am happy to say, I have broken of that habit), and during that time I have had to encounter in several schools Mr. French's [apology] for an arithmetic which was adopted by our late State Board of Education. I then did all I could to establish Greenleaf and [allways] with success. I am as well acquainted with the book as I ever can be, and know of its merits and demerits in practical opperation. The committee for the County have not as yet made any selections, and have not even held a meeting, our first meeting will be on Saturday May 3rd at Bishop Hotel Montpelier where I should be happy to meet you, what action will be taken is more than I know, but will say that your book stands more than an even chance.

As far as my own town is conserned I am instructed by the Town to buy all the text books for the town and sell them to the scholars at cost, and I want your bottom wholesale price, you will understand of course the town is to be responsible for the bills. I should like your lowest prices, and should be pleased to meet you at Montpelier or here at any time.
Yours truly
John H. Senter

April 14th 79
Walter Pike, Esq.
Dear Sir

John L. Tuttle of Montpelier has sent me a bill of taxes against you amounting to $11.20 which he says <u>must</u> be <u>paid immediately</u> or he will make you cost and trouble. You must govern yourself accordingly.
Yours truly
John H. Senter

April 22nd 79
Mrs [Julia] Curtis
[Lincoln] Vermont
Dear Madam

Your favor of the 19th enclosing check for $3.75 is at hand for which please accept thanks. Enclosed you will find receipt [for] bill.
Yours truly John H. Senter

[*Page 23*]
April 15th 79
Miss Ella Van Deusen
Waitsfield Vermont

Please excuse this liberty, but I wish to inquire of you relating to Reed & [Heloys] grammars which were in use in your school last winter.

Knowing as I do that the school room is the best place to judge of text books, and also knowing of your ability to test such books, I am anxious to have your opinion of these grammars. I was appointed at the annual meeting of the Superintendents of this County one of a committee of three to select a list of text books, for this County, which are to be the books used in all the schools for the next five years, which is the reason I am anxious to select as far as I can the best books.

I will be so kind, as to pardon this liberty I have taken in addressing you and write your oppinion of the books you will much oblige, yours very respectfully
John H. Senter

[*Page 24*]
April 15th 79
John McGregor Esq.
Winooski Vermont
Dear Sir,

Your favor of Feb. 25th came to hand in due time, and I should have answered before this had I not been very busy. I have examined your problem and solution, and think it excelent, in fact it is perfect.

I have this winter made up a problem which perhaps may interest you, and so I send it to you like your solution of it and will send you mine and we will we will see how well we agree, if you think it worthy of a trial you may have it published in some newspaper. I will diagram it as well as I can, and when you want my solution I will send. I should like your opinion of the problem very much.

Yours very respectfully J.H. Senter

[*Page 25*]
[*At the top of the page is a red mathematical drawing of various lines and triangles, with distances of "300 feet," "600 feet," and so on written along the lines.*]

This diagram is intended to represent a triangle with a 600, 300, & 400 foot side respectively, with a tower at each vertex, 60 feet high at the 400 & 600 vertex, 50 feet high at the 600 & 300 vertex, 90 feet high at the 300 & 400 vertex.

The question is the length of a rope that placed at some one point will exactly touch the top of each tower and also the distance of this point from the foot of each tower respectively.

Hoping this may meet aproval I remain yours truly
John H. Senter

[*Pages 26-29*]
April 15th 79
G.B. Damon Esq.
Boston
Dear Sir

Your favors of the 14th are at hand and contents noted. In reply I have to say that if you do not meet some opposition from Ainsworth & Dole, in regard to Harpers Geog I shall be happily disappointed.

In regard to the arithmetic, Greenleafs is a very good book, and is very extensively in use throughout the County, it has some very excelent features, and some which are not so good, among which are, the position of U. S. Money, before decimal fractions which to say the least is absurd, and taxes, what Vermont boy if he learns Greenleaf's method of assessment of taxes, could make a V^{t} tax bill, yet on the other hand its metric system is placed where it should be in the body of the book, his definition of annual interest is the best I have ever seen in any arithmetic, although it is not quite correct, until I saw your book, I thought Greenleaf's the best book extant, I gave it a very thorough trial last winter, and became satisfied that your book, if it had the changes you propose to make would be my choice. I have received this spring eight or ten different ariths and have not yet seen any that could compare with Greenleaf much less with yours, I have never seen Olney's Arith and do not of course know any thing about that one, but I believe I have a copy of twenty one different arithmetics and have compared them page by page, and had made up my mind that your book exceded every book except Greenleaf and that it was better than Greenleaf in every point except the V^{t} int rule, and now with the proposed changes I think it the best book I have ever seen, but it will require a great deal of argument to convince some of the old fogies that we had better change, and I not think that to day your book stands an even chance in the County. I write this to you so that you may know where you stand and what you have got to do. I know that Mr. Ainsworth is in favor of your arithmetic, and I also know that he and Dole both favor Harpers Geography, it is a pretty picture book, but I think I can find some inacuracies that will bother them to explain or get over, you say that I did not say anything about Geogs well my mind has not changed in regard to them. I should like it if it had as many of them do have in their V^{t} editions, a full page map of V^{t}, but as it is will (unless I see some book different then I have so far,) receive my hearty approval, your grammar I do not like and shall not approve of its selection.

I wish you would send your work on the annual interest rule to Hiram A. Huse, Esq. of Montpelier for critisism, as I think he is capable of making some good suggestions on that subject, and I shall be pleased to do any thing I can for you in that line.

I received to night from you a copy of Herls Grammar Swetts Questions & Swinton History for which please accept thanks. I notice you never say anything about readers, we shall change readers without doubt.

You did well to avoid Mad River this trip, but by the third of May I think Turtles will sweetly sing from one end of the valley to the other, and that book agents will be as plenty as tadpoles. I dont get this from old "Prof." but venture this oppinion from observations taken from my [observatory].

Yours not very briefly John H. Senter

P.S.

Perhaps you may think a postscript to this already lengthy letter unnecessary, but I forgot about the Big Dic. perhaps I could show you several such letters, but you have no cause to order a Dic. for me, I am <u>not in the</u> habit of sharing <u>confidential communications</u>. As for the terms of your books when I see you I think I can explain what I want for terms in such a manner that it will not appear so <u>horrible</u> to you as it does now, if I cannot then, well we will wait till <u>then</u>.

Yours loquaciously
J.H.S.

[*Page 29*]
Warren V[t] April [18th] 79
Hiram Atkins
Dear Sir

I am very positive about the dollar am sure I paid you, and think I can convince you when I see you. I shall be at Montpelier the 3rd of May, and will see you then and we will [avenge] this matter someway.

Yours truly
John H. Senter

[*Pages 30-31*]
April 16th 79
H.F. Whittemore Esq.
Dear Sir

Your favor of yesterday is at hand also the books for which please accept thanks. I will give them a careful examination and will try and get rid of my *[several words illegible]* the Geogs, I have had quite [*several words illegible*] on the Geography question [*several words illegible*] some of my views of Harper's ["<u>Dictionary</u>."]

Today I have been visited by [Appleton's man] and he has tried hard to make me believe that Harpers Geog was not so good as any other. I believe there must be a <u>conspiracy</u> among you bookmen against Harper's book. I like Appleton's Readers & History very much, but do not intend to decide untill I have given them all a fair chance. I will say a word now about the terms I [expect] and <u>shall have</u>. The books must be put at the [*two words illegible*] wholesale price. Then I will pay for all books [*several words illegible*] 90 days, and all books not sold must be [*several words illegible*] end of my official [career] or turned over to my [*two words illegible*] the same terms, the Town to be responsible for all losses by fire and so forth, and for the payment for the books and the return of unsold books, also all books now in the hands of our merchants, and they are but a small number, must be replaced by the new ones, free from expence to the merchants.

What do you say to this, and what will be your bottom price for five years

I await your reply

Truly yours

John H. Senter

[*Page 31*]

April [15th] 79

Friend [E.L.H.]

By request of Joseph P. Tucker I write you for him, he wants you to make him a petition for insolvency of his creditors, their names, are E. Cardell, [Chaney] Murry, Mary Ann Tucker, James Hewitt & Albert Murry & E.W. Tucker & James Priner. He wants it made immediately.

John H. Senter by request of J.P. Tucker

May 15th 79

G.B. Damon Esq.

Boston

Dear Sir

Is not my town entitled to as good terms on exchange of books as any other town in this County or State?, and if not why?

Yours,

John H. Senter

[*Pages 32-35*]

April 17th 79

Friend Huse,

Your favor of the 16th came to hand last night, I also recv'd a sett of books and a leter from Mr. Whittemore. I am down on Prescott question, but shall lay the mistake to the Government because I got my information from the official P.O. register. To day I have had a lawsuit to attend to, but have found time to look over the picture book a little, and will now give you the result. First on page 5 first column, 6 ¶, the definition of

Archipelago, strikes me as "original," it goes back on Webster somewhat. Second on Page 6, second column ¶ 10. The natural divisions of water are oceans, rivers, lakes, all other divisions of course then must be artificial. Third compare the west coast line of the U. S. as given on 25, & 28, 30 & 58 pages. I have compared them by sketching on tissue paper, and think the result would convince any one, that whoever drafted those maps, had no idea of the "Eternal fitness of things." In the same book one would, naturally suppose, they would have some similarity to say the least. Fourth look on the same maps cited and see the various directions they have given to the Columbia river, if any one should try to find Bryant's "vast [canals] where rolls the Oregon and hears no sound save his own dashings," he would conclude that they, the dead were still there, and that no one had ever lived who had once seen it. Fifth (I give my [heads] as the parson does his text) notice the Sierra Nevada Mtn's on page 30 (in California) at the south end near Mt. Whitney, they make an almost square turn to the left, then on page 58 the same mountains have gone on a "tour" and now turn to the right, also observe the same mountains on page 28 then on page 30, which of the four different directions and twists does the author (if the book ever had one, which I doubt) swear by? Sixthly notice the mountains on the south west boundary of California, on page 30, then look on page 58 for the same, most assuredly the engraver of those maps forgot something. Seventhly, observe the small lakes in the southern part of Oregon, on page 30 & 58, "how artistic," what "splendid illustrations" although they have nary an outlet, how much care has been taken with the two maps to have them alike. Eighthly, notice Lake St. Francis (they forgot to give the name in this book) as the boundary between Missouri and Arkansas, N.E. of Arkansas, on page 30, then look on page 57 and see there is no lake there, nothing but a river, then on page [75] another change, and also see that chain of lakes and rivers reach uninterruptedly from the Mississippi to the Mississippi, then on page 55 see now it is entirely different, don't you think the illustrations are just splendid, only just a little overdrawn in these areas. Ninthly look at the Cumberland Mountains on page 30, then on page 45, how well they compare. Lastly I notice on page 106 that Pekin is the largest city in China, and on page 120 the population is given at 1,648,000, well what about [*one word illegible*] or [*one word illegible*] on the Yang-tse River with its two million?

Well I have spent just one hour on this book to day and the foregoing is the result. What would be the result if a man well [footed] in geography should spend a week on the book, don't you think such a man could make

some "splendid illustrations." I am going to look up your [*one word illegible*] on Swinton tomorrow, and then I will look over [Gazette] and give you the result. I should like very much to have a talk with you about these books don't think I should be bored very much, think I can stand it if you can. Yes there will be a change in readers certainly, and the more I hear about arithmetics I think will be changed to, I have no idea that our County committee will agree on the Geographies. I have pretty straight that, Dole & Ainsworth, are both hot for Harper and I presume that you have heard that the member from Warren don't lean that way. Appletons man was here yesterday and stayed nearly all day, he thinks his books are the best of course. I like their History & readers very well. Well if you are not bored, I shall be glad.
Very truly yours
John H. Senter

[*Page 33*]
May 12th
Charles Sawyer agt,
Moretown Vt

Will you please forward that title bill at your earliest convenience, I need it much.
Yours truly John H. Senter

[*Page 34*]
W.W. Ainsworth Esq.
Dear Sir

Our next meeting will be at Northfield on May 14th if it will be satisfactory to you
Yours truly
John H. Senter

Rev. J.P. Demeritt
Dear Sir

Our next meeting will be at Northfield Wednesday May 14th shall be very happy to meet you there.
Yours truly
John H. Senter

[*Page 35*]
April 21st 79
Bro. Durant
Dear Sir

I received your favor, and in reply would say that the morning I before I left Montpelier I received a remmittance from Mr. Stevens enclosing $7.00. I went to your office and it was not open, and as I was in a hurry, I left the $7.00 with the County Clerk for you, where you will find it all right. I supposed you had long before this or I should have written.

Yours truly
John H. Senter

Warren May 12th 1879
C.L. Rich Esq.
Dear Sir

Our next committee meeting will be at Northfield Wednesday May 14th

Yours
John H. Senter

[*First line is too faint to read.*]
I want your wholesale prices & lowest discount to Towns. I am to buy all books for my Town and am interested in those prices more than I am in [introduction] [I was]
Yours
John H. Senter
To Clark and Maynard
New York

[*Pages 36-37*]
April 21st 79
Benjamin H. Sanborn Esq.
Boston .
Dear Sir

Your favor of the 18th is at hand, and contents noted.

There is a lively competition going on here in regard to arithmetics. A book agent comes to see me every day almost. I notice you do not give but 5% off and that you say, that your list price is lower than houses which give larger discounts. I have received terms from several houses and 16-2/3% is the smallest yet before yours, as for list prices you may look at

Appleton's list and you will see their list is 63 cts for their practical. How is this, then look at Van [Century Brigg] & Co's list of White's book, wholesale 65 cts list, then at Clark & [Maynard's], wholesale price list of Thomson's book list 70 also recollect that Thomson's book is cloth bound. Then look at The New American list price 50, not one of these but what are willing to give a disc of 1/6 of some one 1/5 off, and one will give ¼ off. Your prices are nearly as high as ever, the book we adopt is to be used for 5 years, and cannot be changed. School books are higher than any other class of books, and why is it? You cannot keep your book in our schools, when there are fully as good books in the market, at very much lower prices. You say, you prefer to give the schools the lowest price, and not make so large a [ass] to the truth. That reasoning fails, when you get at the facts and find nearly all the books lower on the list than yours.

The fact is my dear sir your prices must come down or your books go out. I should be happy to see you and talk the matter over, I shall be in Montpelier May 2nd & 3rd but I had rather pay my own expenses, should have plenty of time to see you on the afternoon of May 2nd at Bishop Hotel. May 3 the County text book committees meet there, and I think it would be for your interest to be there and see each member. I have a great deal of [preducice] in favor of Greenleaf's books, they are old friends of mine, but there is a Rubicon, over which I shall not cross.

I am glad to learn that you are a Vermonter, & a teacher. You will know something of what you talk about, wich I am sorry to say all book agents do not.

Very truly yours John H. Senter

[*Page 38*]

April 21st 79

Miss Ella F. Van Deusen

Waitsfield

Your kind favor came to hand last night, and I am much obliged for the trouble you have taken to answer my inquiry.

I have a copy of Reed & [Kelog's] grammar and I liked it very much, which was the reason I wanted your oppinion.

The agent for the Franklin Readers and Mac Vicar's Arithmetic's was here last and I told him I wanted a sett of readers for you, he left them with me, and I take the pleasure in presenting them you, he enclosed a primary Arithmetic and will send you the complete by mail.

I should like your oppinion of the readers very much also of the Arithmetic when you look it through. I hope you will come to Warren, I want to talk with you about Text books very much, I have so many books to look, that I dream of them nightly.

I have to copies of Swinton, I will present you with one also with [*one word illegible*]

Yours in haste J.H. Senter

[*Pages 39-40*]

April 28th 79

Miss Katie Prentice

With reluctance I have to inform you of your failure to pass the required per ct on your examination, but I must do my duty although it is disagreeable. Your average is only 44-1/2 and I have marked it very high, you have not reached fifty on any one subject, so you can readily see that it is not possible for me to grant a certificate on those answers.

I think you capable of passing a much better examination, think you were frightened, hurried, and cold, and I am willing to give you another chance, will give you a private examination, free any day this week, give you all the time you want and if you can pass an average of 65 without going below fifty on any one subject, I shall be happy to grant you a certificate.

I suppose Katie you will feel badly to hear that I deny this certificate, but you certainly will not feel any worse about it than I do, if I could do it, Katie, honorably I would willingly sacrifice more than your whole wages for the term.

I think you had better try a private examination, because I think you are capable of doing better.

If you wish to try again let me know at once.

Although perhaps you may not think so I am your friend

John H. Senter

P.S. Let me know by return mail when you will come, if you conclude to come again. Yours J.H.S.

[*Page 41*]

April 29 79

Charles T. Sabin Esq.

Montpelier V^{t}

Dear Sir

The treasurer of the Methodist Church Society of this town, Mr. G.B. Newcomb has placed in my hands for collection, a demand against the farm known here as the [New] Farm now owned by Mrs. James Thurston, it is for a ballance of interest due last year, of $2.00, overdue 13 months, and $12.00 overdue one month.

I am informed that you are her agt, if so will you attend to this at once & save costs

Yours truly
John H. Senter

May 7th 79
Friend [E.L.H.]

I am just home from Montpelier, and have just got your letter. I do not know what to tell you as Parker is now at your town, and perhaps you may see him, the court is sett for the 12th, I was anxious that he should employ you, and if he has I want you to go on if he has not, why of course, you will work for the other [side] but I hope he has, if he were here I should insist that he should retain you.

Yours fraternally
John H. Senter

[*Page 42*]
April 29th 79
Miss [Frank] L. Nichols

I did not give Miss Prentice a certificate she was to teach up the river, consequently the committee Mr Muray, is out of a teacher, I have recomended you. The term is to commence next Monday, to continue eight weeks, he will pay $2.25 per week. I think you will do well in that school if you wish to teach at all, this summer.

Please let me know by return mail if you will teach or not.

Yours truly
John H. Senter

May 7th 79
C.L. Rich Esq.
Dear Sir

Your favor of the 3rd was not handed me untill yesterday which is the reason I have not answered before.

Our report of Saturday's procedings is not public we shall meet again before long at Northfield. I am to call the meeting and will let you know when I know myself. McGregor sent me the correct solution of the town problem I knew he would in time, I will try that quadratic as soon as I have a little leisure. I want to see Sanborn very much.
Yours truly
John H. Senter

[*Page 43*]
April 20th 79
H. B. Ward Esq.
Duxbury Vt
Dear Sir

I herwith send you examination papers, I have marked them according to my [ideas] and have given the true answers in ink. I think her answers good, and she has passed as high as my teachers average. I mark the answers just as I think they should be, whether they are to keep school in my town or elsewhere. I gave her a certificate and I wrote you some time since, about sending her answers to you but presume I sent it to the wrong office.
Yours truly
John H. Senter
P.S. My ans to the 8th I see is [blotted] so I will give it over
Dominion of Canada, N. Foundland, B. [Guyana,] B. Honduras, [Jamaica] Trinidad, Tobago, Grenada, St. Lucia, St. Vincent, St. Christopher, [Dominican] Anguilla, Montserat, Bahamas, Barbados, Bermuda, Barbados [*one word illegible*] [answer] Falkland Islands, I called half of these as correct.

[*Page 44*]
May 8th 79
[*Nearly the entire letter is blurred from faulty copying – the letter pertains to textbook selection. The last few lines are mostly legible, and are as follows:*]
[. . .] report that if a change is to be made, that [we can] reccomend the books [and we] determine [one as] the best. I have many reasons for this course which I will give you, when I see you. Write at once and let me know how this idea strikes you, for come what will, you and I <u>must</u> act as one
Yours truly
John H. Senter

[*Pages 45-49*]
May 8th 79
Benjamin H. Sanborn Esq.
Morrisville Vt
Dear Sir

Your favor of yesterday is at hand, and I have carefully noted all you say. In regard to price your discount is now with the other competing Arithmetics, but to day just before your favor arrived, another book is brought squarely into the field, and claims consideration at the hands of committees. It is Olney's, published by Sheldon & Co., its list price is a little lower than yours, what the book is I do not know, I purpose to find out if I have time. However, perhaps Mr Sanborn you have got the wrong idea of me, the price of the books will not govern my choice, but all other things being equal, of course then cost is a valid consideration. I infer from your letter that you think that I am not a friend to your book, and perhaps you think that I have something [hid] carefully away against the firm of Robert S. Davis & Co. Now my dear sir if such is the case your are laboring under a wrong impression. I most assuredly know of the [many] tricks I will not call them arguments, because to me they are not, of some gentlemen, so called, engaged in this textbook competition. Because Benjamin H. Sanborn was [an accredited] third house member of the legislature that abolished our late board of Education, or that the firm of R.S.D. & Co. have done certain things in regard to that matter which were questionable, viewed from a stand point of strict morality & public policy, these are no conserns of mine. I am not to judge of the integrity of publishing houses, but of their books, and if I was to pass sentence on them I think I should consider it as a mitigating circumstance that we had got rid of that board of Education.

What reports you may have got regarding the member from Warren on this comm. I do not know, and I do not know as I care very much, if any one knows what the report of this committee will be they have got a long distance in advance of me. I have tried to the best of my ability to give all these books a carefull consideration and to make up my mind conscientiously as to what I thought to be for the best interests of my County, if I fail it will be through ignorance, but I hope not through prejudice. Now my dear sir I understand from your letter that your books are in use in one half of the towns in this County, and that as far as you can learn from teachers and officers are giving good satisfaction. Now did you in this statement give the whole truth as they say in court. Is it not a fact that in almost every town were your books were used French's are also used to some extent, and did you find your books giving good satisfaction when you interviewed Mr. Blair of the Montpelier town school, and his teachers.

Now Mr. Sanborn I do not mention these things to injure your book, or as an argument against your book, but that you may see that if the argument of no change is good that Frenches book stands as well as yours. I have not doubt but what some teachers like Frenche's book, and I have no doubt but that it is used more in this County than your book, but I should hate to have my name attached to a reccomendation of that book, and I should not think I was disgraced if it was attached to a reccomendation of yours, because I know your book is a good one, and no one ever heard me say that it was not. Now as I am in the explanation business I will mention one thing more, you wrote sometime since about meeting you at Montpelier or somewhere else, and that you would pay my expences, if I would. I wrote you that if I met you I should prefer to pay my own expences, which was true, and for which perhaps I have good reasons, but it may have appeared rather crusty to you. I did not mean it to be however, as I do not myself think but what it would be perfectly proper, but I know that you know that sometimes comitteemen are just a little indiscreet. Now I am poor enough, and have got only one thing belonging to me which would be of consequence to loose and that is my reputation, and if some men in this county don't know anything, I have got to [toe a crack] to offsett their [dull] foolishness, now when I know more of this book business, I am very glad I did not accept your offer, (and you know why).

I should be very happy to see you Mr. Sanborn and talk over this book question, as long as you wished. I will try to use you as a gentleman should but untill you know where I stand, and what I know about some things, you will probably get a wrong impression.

Our next committee meeting will be at Northfield Wednesday May 14th A.D. 1879. Hoping to meet before long, I remain yours truly
John H. Senter

[*Page 49*]
May 8th 79
Prof. Charles Dole
Northfield Vt
Dear Sir

I have fixed the day of our next meeting for Wednesday May 14th.

Since I saw you an idea has found its way into my cranium, (an unusual thing by the way) which is that we report to the convention that where any book is in universal use throughout the County no change had better be made, and then give our reasons, and then further that we are not advised of how extensively any one book is in use, and then report if any change is to be made what books think the best. I have many reasons for this which I will give you when I see you, write at once and let me know how this idea strikes you, for come what will <u>you</u> and <u>I</u> must act as <u>one</u>.
Yours truly
John H. Senter

[*Page 50*]
Miss Mary Robinson
Moretown Vt
Dear friend Mary

I have not answered your favor before, for the reason that I have been waiting to find out if the teacher which had been hired, was qualified. I examined her yesterday, and she passed the required per ct. If you had written me a few days before you did, I could have secured you the school, and would have been glad to do so. I could have reccomended you as far as your education is conserned very highly, because I know that you are well grounded in our elementary branches, which to me are of great importance either for a teacher, or for an accomplished young lady. I am afraid that many young ladies of today are neglecting plain english for bad French, and poor latin. I have more respect for our mother tongue, and think it should be learned first, and then others will be an advantage. If I can do anything for you hereafter I shall be happy to do so, am sory your were to late. Yours very truly
John H. Senter

[*Page 51*]
May 10th 79
Hiram Atkins
Montpelier Vt
Dear Sir

I never knew any one to get rich by mixing up in these things much, but as you have always been a friend to me I will do the best I can by you. The names you have sent me are owned by men, not in the habit of paying their bills, but I think most of them would not like to have their names in the black list.

These men are all my fellow townsmen, and I must insist that you keep what I have said on their credit strictly confidential.

Prof. Conant State Superintendent of Education will lecture at Warren Village Tuesday Eve, May 20th on education.

Please notice this in your paper.

Yours
John H. Senter

May 12th 79
Prof. Charles Dole
Northfield Vt
Dear Sir

Your favor of the 10th is at hand in reply would say, that I think we will let Ainsworth work out his own destruction. I will try and be at your place as early as I can get there.

Yours truly
John H. Senter

[*Page 52*]
B. Winnie Esq.
Burlington Vermont
Dear Sir

Your favor of the 9th is at hand, and I have also received a partial list of your books, although I did not receive your arithmetics, for these please accept my thanks. Our committee will meet again at Northfield on Wednesday May 14th, after that day I shall be happy to see you here any day this week except Saturday. I should be happy to meet you in Burlington, if I was not a member of this county committee, as it is I think I had better see you here. You had better send Ainsworth a sett of your books, as that sett which you gave Dole got lost or mislaid or stole at the Pavillion, is adress is W.W. Ainsworth, Calais Vt.

Hoping to meet you I [am] yours truly,
John H. Senter

May 12th 79
Prof. Edward Conant
Randolph Vt

Dear Sir

Your favor of the 10th is at hand and contents noted. I am glad you are to adress the people of my town [and] I will try and have a good audience present. I am trying to get my teacher interested in education more than are at present, and shall endeavor to have them all present, shall be happy to visit any school with you.

Yours John H. Senter

[*Page 53*]

May 10th 79

Received of George W. Curtis ($14.19) fourteen dollars and nineteen cents, it being interest due to Methodist Church association, of Warren from Mrs. James T. Thurston, on [*one word illegible*] held by said association on the farm know as the [Kew] Farm, said sums being for two dollars interest unpaid, due April first A.D. 1878, and $12.00, due April 1st 1879, with interest on each sum to date.

John H. Senter Attorney for

G.B. Newcomb, Treasurer of Methodist Church

May 13th 79

Thompson, Brown & Co.

23 Hawley Street Boston

Gents

I write you by request of Prof. Charles Dole of Northfield, a member of the county text book committee, for coppies of Eatons arithmetics & Bradbay's Algebras, he has spoken highly of them to me, and wants me to examine them before we decide on our list

Yours truly John H. Senter

[*Page 54*]

May 12 79

To the Select Men of the town of Granville

Gentlemen

You are hereby notified that the highway leading from the town of Warren to the town of Granville known as the Main or River road commencing at the northerly line of said Granville [to] the premises occupied by Mrs Austin in said Warren and recurring southerly up Mad River in said Granville to near the head of said river, thence over the hills to the premises occupied by R.H. Bostwick in said Granville is badly out

of repair and unsafe for travel. The said road being full of holes, stones and roots and standing and running water. Also that many of the bridges and [sluices] have holes through the plank and by the side of the abutments.
Yours truly
H.W. Lyford
John H. Senter

[*Page 55*]
May [14th] 79
E.C. McClintock Esq.
Boston
Dear Sir

I sent you a telegram last night at the sugestion of Mr. Ainsworth, we have been considering your book (Geog) which we have just received, and to day they stand a good chance with any other book

The great objection which I have to meet in my own town to any change, is the expense, we have changed so often that it is hard to introduce any new book, and of course I must make the best terms for my own Town I can. I want as good a chance on the exchange for my town, as Dole does for Northfield.

I am authorized by my town to buy all the books for my town on the credit of the town and I want your bottom wholesale price list for five years & discount to my town, and the best terms you will give this town on exchange
Yours John H. Senter
P.S.

By request of Mr. Ainsworth, who thinks well of them will you send me Berard's History & [Brodrick's] Child's History

Yours J.H. Senter

[*Page 56*]
May 15th 79
M.W. Hazen Esq.
Hawley Street Boston
Dear Sir

The Washington Co. Text book committee of which I am a member, are now considering the subject of readers, an objection which has been raised to your readers, was poor binding. I understand that you are

changing the method of binding, and that your first reader is being rewritten, are these reports true, and if so will you send me a specimen of the new binding, that I may have it to refer to in the convention which is to meet June 7th, also in regard to terms, In exchanging books Mr. Hazen I in my town have got to meet a great opposition, on account of cost. We have changed so often of late years, that it is hard for me to do so now, I want as good terms for my Town as Northfield or any other town, send me your best terms. I am to buy all the books for my own town as agt. for the town and I want wholesale prices & disc. and I want special exchange prices.
Yours John H. Senter

[*Page 57*]
May 16th 79
Hiram A. Huse Esq
Montpelier Vt
Friend Huse

Thinking you might like to know something about the situation, I write a few lines. We met at Northfield last Wednesday, and as I expected the fluctuating gentleman was with me for Swinton. I dont know what to make of him, he has heard some intimations that somebody has heard something, and that bothers him, by the way there is a new geography in the field Warrens, and Dole is favoring that now, of course this is strictly confidential. I dont know any more about what our report will be than I did when I saw you. I mentioned my plan to Dole and he favors it so I guess we will suprise them with that report. Sanborn saw me the other day, he seemed to think I was working hard to beat Greenleaf. Somebody has put a bug in his ear as big as a beetle, the thing is getting *[one word illegible]* mixed and I shall send for Tuttle, if you know any thing new let me know and oblige Yours John H. Senter

[*Page 58*]
May 16th 79
E.C. McClintock Esq.
Boston
Dear Sir

Your favor of the 15th is just at hand, also maps and proof sheets of special N.E. [Matter] for which please to accept thanks. In regard to criticism on readers Mr. W.W. Ainsworth informed me that you had criticisms on Appletons and Franklins readers, and as I am desirous of finding out, all I can in regard to these books I should like them both. I am sory that your geographies were not brought to my notice earlier, so far as I have examined them I like them, and I like one thing very much in regard to the way you work your books that is you have not hired superintendents and text book committees by the dozen, who don't know any thing about books, to canvass this county, but have let your books speak for themselves, legitimate canvassing is all right but I don't like the illegitimate. I rec'vd Berard's history last night, I wrote you in regard to terms last night, hoping to hear from you soon, I am yours truly John H. Senter

[*Page 59*]
May 28th 79
M.W. Hazen Esq.
Dear Sir

We have reported in favor of your readers, and as soon as it is made public, there will be war in this county. J.H. Butler & Co. [Tarnton] Brothers, & others, have laid a nice lot of plans to break the report, now very naturally I want it sustained, they will make a thorough [*one word illegible*] of this county, just as soon as our action is made public, [we] the county comm'r, want you to make as good a fight as they do. I [cant] write you all the the particulars in a week, but sett your agents at work in this county & Orange just as soon as you get this, then come and see me at once I will give you what information I can, and I think we can carry this county, Orange & Caledonia unanimously for Appleton's readers
Yours in haste
J.H. Senter

[*Pages 60-61*]
May 26th 79
M. W. Tewksbury Esq.
Boston.
Dear Sir

Your favor of the 22nd is at hand, and I have noted contents. I received from your house in N.Y. last Dec. a letter asking me to act as agent for the introduction of your books. I was suprised at the time, because I had had no dealings with your house or books, and I supposed that I was an entire stranger not only to the books but the house, but I answered the leter, gave them the list of books in use, probable changes, and sent them a copy of the new text book law, and informed them that I did not know any thing about their books, and that I could not act as agent for any books unless I believed them to be the best, and that if I liked their books I should like to act as agent. I never heard any thing more from your house, and I concluded, first, that your house did not believe their books to be the best, second that they had written me simply for information, which when I can, I am always happy to give. I did receive from you about a month since a partial list of the books you mention although I never saw your arithmetics or gram'. The intermediate geography you did send but no other, and that was so misbound that I could not tell much about it, as I have never heard from you, I did not suspose, you were pushing your books in this State. I was chosen Superintendent of our town schools this year, and at the County meeting I was appointed one of a committee of three to select a list of text books for this county, so that now I am in a position that I cannot act as agent for any house if I should wish to. I have heard your books well spoken of by several times recently, but am not acquainted with them myself, because I have had no opportunity of examining them, or rather most of them. I notice on your list sent me, one book which is required to be used in our schools, by law, which no other house that I know of publishes that is, "Gow's Good Morals and Gentle Manners." I wish you would send that to me, and also "Andrews Manual of the Constitution." Hoping to hear from you again

I am very respectfully yours
John H. Senter

[*Page 61*]
June 4th 79
Frank A. Trask Esq.
Dear Sir

I have in my hands for collection, a note and claim against you, which amounts to day to $[19.34], owned by Myron R. Goodspeed. It must be paid immediately or I shall make you cost.
Yours truly
John H. Senter

[*Pages 62-63*]
May 28th 79
E.C. McClintock Esq.

Boston
Dear Sir,

Our county comm. were in session last week, as you already know, we telegraphed you to meet us but you could not meet us, unaccount of the Boston fight which was reason enough. I hope you will beat them to night, because I know that book, I mean Harpers. I think it would have been recommended in this County if I could have been brought over, but I did not start an inch, and never should. However we have now unanimously recommended, Swinton's Elementary and Warrens Common School, also Goodriche's Child History, and what we wanted to see you for, was about canvassing this County. Your <u>friends</u> the Harpers will do every thing to break down our reccomendations, that they can, their agent has threatened it and done every thing he could to get a report in his favor, he has failed, and now he will make a hot fight, and of course I am quite as anxious to sustain it, as he is to break it, for that reason I sugested to Dole and Ainsworth that we telegraph you to meet us, which they agreed to, and we did, when Dole received your letter he showed it to me, and wanted I should state how matters stood to you. I want you to send immediately to every text book committee man, in this county and Orange County, your new map of Vermont & Special Geography of V^{t}, we want you to submit that special work to us and many more for criticism, and to make as near perfect as possible, we want you to put an agent into this County, and one into Orange to canvass these Counties immediately, because these books are late in the field, and very few know any thing of them.

Perhaps I ought to tell you, Rev. J.P. Demeritt of Williamstown the Secretary of the Superintendents of Orange has been with us in all our meetings, agrees with us on all the books. Orange County naturally wants to go with our County, our conventions meet the same day, and what one does will help the other. You will see readily that your agents are needed here <u>now</u>. As soon as you can I want to see you personally. I think I can give some hints that will help you, & I want to arrange terms for my town.
Yours truly
John H. Senter

[*Page 64*]
May 28th 79
Miss Ella F. Van Dusen

I have requested many agents to send you text books, from time to time, because I wanted your oppinion and also wanted you to have the

books, among others I had Fisk's arithmetics sent to you, now I want your opinion of them, both of the primary & complete, you will confer a favor by giving it to me. I have worked hard on this book business, trying the best I could to select the best books and hope I shall succeed. Please give me your oppinion at once, as my time is getting short. Yours in haste
John H. Senter

May 27th 79
M.W. Hazen Esq
Dear Sir

I am unfortunate in not making myself understood by you. I want to know your prices & discount after introduction for five years and I must know before this town votes in convention
Yours
J.H. Senter

[*Page 65*]
May 27th 79
H.A. Huse Esq.
Dear Sir

I want you to know that this County committee, did not make any such report as I saw in the papers you sent me. I never heard of that dispatch untill I read it in your leter. Our report was, that when a book was in uniform use through out our County and giving good satisfaction, we would reccomend no change and that if any book of the following list was to be changed, we would reccomend as the best the following. Appletons readers, Fisk's Arith, Swinton's Elementary & Warrens Common School Geogs, Payson Dunton's & Scribners Penmanship, Nordhoffs Politics, Townsend Civil Gov, & Olney's Arithmetics [*two words illegible*]. You may publish this list if you wish, if you will publish all of it not garble, it makes a d—d difference, whether a man is a d—d fool or a knave, more tomorrow.
John H. Senter

[*Pages 66-68*]
[*Letter to M.W. Hazen about book matters; page 66 was copied too faintly to read. Beginning at the top of page 67:*]
[influence] what little I have, for Appleton's Readers [*one word illegible*]. I have thought them so for the best series I have seen, but I do not like to

have a gentleman offer me terms with a caution to keep it confidential, and say to me that my town is especially favored, on my account when those same terms are common to all, and not as good as some. I had never asked for any special consideration because I favored your Readers, and should not have complained, if you had not, endeavored to pour a large stream of gush over me, but that part I do not relish very much. Now Mr. Hazen I am using plain language but it is my nature to be blunt, and when I think one is trying to humbug, I am very apt to say so. I want to see you personally and talk over this matter of terms with you, and I think if you knew how decidedly interesting the situation was getting in this county, you would appear on the scene immediately. I enclose in this, an article cut from the [last] Argus. I have replied to the article, which will appear next week, a half sheet of the Argus, with that article marked with a blue pencil, has been sent to each text book committee, in the County, so I conclude some opposing book agent has taken this way to beat your books. You will see by this article that there is a large sized battle looming up in near future, if you can possibly make it convenient, I wish you would come and see me, the first of this week
Yours John H. Senter

[*Page 67*]
November 21st 79
Charles [Porter] Esq
Dear Sir,
I have in my hands, an account against you in favor of E.G. Hooker. [*several words illegible*] about it as soon as you can [*several words illegible*].
John H. Senter

[*Page 68*]
June 2nd 79
E.C McClintock Esq.
Dear Sir

I wish you would send your geography the common school, to the several text book committees in this County. I find many have not seen your book and I don't think they will be very liable to adopt a book they have never seen, if you want your book adopted, you must make something of a canvass and that directly. Harpers, J.H. Butler & Co., Scribner Brothers, & [*one word illegible*], [Blakeman & Taylors], agents are already in the field, and you will find your books out in the cold the first

you know, and for the reason that your book has not been shown up, give me your best terms, so that I can anounce them in convention
Yours truly
J.H. Senter

[*Page 69*]
June 1st 79
G.B. Damon Esq.
Dear sir, I have seen your man Smith and think him a good one. I think you will have to offer a free exchange on Greenleaf in order to get your book adopted. I hear nothing but, the expence a change howled in favor of Greenleaf, if you will authorize me to state in convention next Saturday that Fisk's book will be exchanged for Greenleaf's free, it will take the wind all out of Sanborn's sail & will you do it? All kind of rumors are afloat here in regard to Ainsworth but think they won't amount to much. I should like to see you very much, answer the exchange question as soon as you can. Yours in haste,
J.H. Senter

June 25th 79
William Blake Esq.
Northfield
Dear Sir

You spoke to me sometime since about securing an account against A.F. [Kingsbury].

I think I can do it, if it is not to large I found some property belonging to him the other day

If you want I should secure the account send it immediately.
Yours John H. Senter

[*Pages 70-73*]
June 2nd 79
Mr. Editor,

I notice in the Argus of May 28th, some comments, on the report of the Washington County text book committee, which, had you received the full report, as our secretary was directed to make it, I think you would admit were unjust. The report, as Prof. Dole and I understand it, was as follows. Where any book is in uniform use throughout the County, and giving good satisfaction we recomend no change, but if the convention desire to change in any of the following books, we recomend this list as the best we have examined, all things considered for our common schools. Appleton's Readers, Swinton's Elementary and Warren's Common School Geographies, Paysen, Dunton & Scribner's Pennmanship, Nordhoff's Politics, Townsend's Civil Government, Anderson's Popular History of the U.S., Vt. Ed., Goodriche's Child history of the U.S. Bartholemews drawing series, Fisk's Arithmetics, Reed & Kellogg's Grammars.

Now instead of the sweeping changes spoken of in the article in the Argus, we recomended no change only such as were necessary for uniformity and good satisfaction, and as we had but a limited knowledge regarding those matters, we left the subject of change entirely with the convention, where every part of the county would be represented, we were strongly in favor of county uniformity, and when a change was necessary to bring that about, I think it should be made as a matter of economy. Judging from the report as published in the Argus, Burlington Free Press and others, I conclude our secretary forgot to make the first part of our report public in those papers.

Had you received our report, as Prof. Dole and I authorized it, I think you would not have made those comments, regarding "sweeping" changes.

I notice also that Appleton's Readers are held by some gentleman, through the medium of the Argus as detrimental to the temperance interest, now if the gentleman had published this article which he refers to, "Table Manners," I think he would have been answered. Notice the tenth ¶ which is the last in regard to wine drinking, "According to the old time code of good manners, now happily falling into disuse, it was considered extremely uncivil to decline taking wine when invited, although politeness demanded no more than a sip, and it was regarded as ill-bred to empty one's glass on such occasions, yet this custom has often proved the first step toward ruin."

Now I in my ignorance, am of the oppinion that the sentiments quoted are strong arguments for temperence, and I can see nothing in that article, but what the "Stalwart" temperence men and women of [Washington] and Chittenden, would endorse, and nothing which they could object to have taught to their children. I ask each man and woman in the county to read this article, which will be found on the 387 page of Appleton's fifth reader, and judge for themselves. I learn that every committeeman on textbooks in the county received a half sheet of the

Argus, with this article marked with a blue pencil. I conclude therefore that a book agent is behind the scenes. I am authorized by Prof Dole to say that he understands that our report was directed to be what I have given it, in this letter
John H. Senter

[*Page 73*]
Mr. Atkins
Dear sir You will oblige me very much, by publishing this article in your next Argus, with my name attached. Yours Truly
John H. Senter

June 3rd 79
G.B. Damon Esq.
Boston.
Dear Sir
Enclosed you will find my idea of the Vermont method of assessing taxes. I told you I believe that I would send it to day, and I have kept my word. I want you get it printed immediately, and send it to me, so that I may criticize it first, then I shall have it submitted to the best lawyers for their criticisms, and we will try and have it correct. You will have to excuse the correction marks I have left on the paper as I have not time to write it over.
Yours tired
John H. Senter

[*Pages 74-77*]

Vermont Method of Assessing Taxes.

The Grand List is the base on which all taxes are assessed; it is 1% of the apprized value of the real estate and personal property, together with the poll list.

The Poll list is $2.00 for every male, from 21 to 70 years of age.

The General Statutes of V$^{t.}$ provide, that the listers in each town, shall make a list of all the real estate and personal property, and the number of taxable polls, in such town; and that the said list shall contain the following particulars.
"First. The name of each taxable person."
"Second. The number of polls and the amount at which the same are set in the list."

"Third. The quantity of real estate owned or occupied by such person."
"Fourth. The value of such real estate."
"Fifth. In the fifth column the full value of all taxable personal estate owned by such person."
"Sixth. In the sixth column shall be set the one per centum on the value of all personal and real estate, together with the amount of the polls, which sum shall be the amount on which all taxes shall be made or assessed."

The State and County Taxes are assessed by the Legislature.

The minimum of the State School and Highway taxes is fixed by law, and a higher rate left optional with the town.

The town tax is assessed by vote of the town. A village tax by vote of the village, and a School district tax by vote of the district.

Examples.

The town of Montpelier voted a town tax of $2.60 on each dollar of the grand list.
The apprized value of the real estate was $702727, and of the personal property $309987, and there were 740 taxable polls. What was the grand list of the town? How much money was raised by this vote. What was John Hammond's tax, who was 30 years of age, and whose property was apprized at $8927.75?
Operation.
$702727 + $309987 = $1012714 assessed value of the property
$1012714 x .01 = $10127.14 1% of the assed value
$2.00 x 740 = $1480 the poll list
$10127.14 + $1480 = $11607.14 The grand list
$11607.14 x $2.60 = $30178.56 amount of mony raised
$8927.75 x .01 = 89.28 1% of assd value of John Hammonds property
$89.28 the property list + $2.00 the poll list = $91.28 John Hammonds grand list
$91.28 x $2.60 ammount raised on each dollar of the grand list gives $237.33 John Hammonds town tax.

2. The apprized value of property both real and personal in the Town of Rutland for the year 1878 was $3415264. The number of taxable polls was 2066. The town voted to raise a tax of $28713.48. What was the tax on a dollar of the grand list Ans. $.75

3. The grand list in the Town of Chelsea was $4403.74, the apprized value of all the property was $368774. How many taxable polls were there in that town? Ans 383

4. The apprized value of the real estate in the City of Burlington was [$25823.73], of the personal property $399937. There were 2040 taxable polls. The City voted to raise [$60305.58] City tax. What was the amount of Henry Cook's tax, who resides in Burlington, who is 73 years of age, and whose real estate is apprized at $750, and his personal property at [$475.50]? Ans. $22.06

5. The estimated cost of schools in School District No. 8 in the Town of Cabot for one year was $765. The amount of public money received from the Town was $6,109. The apprized value of the real estate in the district was $48545, of personal $15428.75. The number of taxable polls in the district 103. How much tax on a dollar of the grand list must the district vote to pay its expences Ans. $1.10

6. James Bell resides in Hardwick he is 44 years of age, his property both real estate and personal is apprized at $8975.50. Hardwick voted a town tax of $1.60 on a dollar of the grand list. The highway tax is $.40 on the dollar. The State tax is $.45. The State School tax is $.09 [as] the School tax is $.86 assd the County tax $.04 on the dollar
What is the amount of his taxes Ans. 315.64

[*Page 79*]
June 4th 79
J.B. [Fassett] Esq.
Moretown.
Dear Sir,

S.I. Goodspeed, now of this town, but recently of Northfield, bought an organ of you, and he says that you were to deliver him a piano stool in the truck free, he has never received it however, and he wants it. Mr. Sargent's leter to him expressly promises one, and you will probably save cost by sending either the stool or its equivalent in money to me or him at your earliest convenience, he has placed this affair in my hands to adjust with you, and a friendly settlement always suits me best, but if that fails I shall try the other course. Awaiting your reply, I remain very respectfully yours John H. Senter

July 7th 79
E.C. McClintock Esq.
Dear Sir

Enclosed you will find an agreement which I want you should sign as agent for [Corofeathers] & Co. and send back to me, and if you want any [writing] from me make out one just as strong as you like and send to me and I will sign for the Town
Yours in haste John H. Senter

[*Page 80*]
June 5th 79
E.C. McClintock Esq.
Dear Sir

Yours of the 4th at hand, in reply I would say that your house is not worth enough to hire me act as agent, while I am on this committee. I will do all I can in convention to morrow because I like your book but farther than that, I cannot go. After your book fight is over in Boston I hope to see you personally, and I can then explain some very interesting things to you. Your book will most likely be accepted in this Town, and I want to arrange terms with you.
Yours in haste
John H. Senter

June 9th 79
M.W. Hazen Esq.
Dear Sir

Please to send me 3 or 4 of Appletons 5th Readers, I think I can place them where they will do good. Yours in haste John H. Senter

[*Pages 81-83*]
June 8th 79
G.B. Damon Esq.
Dear Sir

Enclosed you will find the tax article corrected. Send me as soon as possible a number of the corrected proofs and I will have them subjected to several legal gentlemen for criticism.

We had a big fight in convention. I handled the Arithmetic and Geography question. I know that when the convention was called in the afternoon Greenleafs book had more friends than Fisk, but I went in to win, and I won. I talked two hours on that question. I took your book and Greenleaf, and went through them from begining to end. I think you would have been suprised to find out that Fisk had so many good qualities, then the others spoke their pieces, and some one moved to adopt Greenleaf and it was voted down flat, then I moved to adopt Fisk and it was adopted almost unanimously. I find it makes a difference how a book is shown up. Orange County stood beter for Fisk Friday morning than Washington County did, and yet Washington adopted the book by a large majority while Orange County gave two votes for it. The Geography question then came up and I showed up those books. I went for Harpers book, and when the vote was taken, [Guyatt] had two votes, and the rest were all for the report, [fairly] our report was carried on every point. Smith measured just forteen feet Friday night. Friday morning the air was full of rumors that I was bought for Fisk's Arithmetic. I got the book agents to gather and Ainsworth and Dole, and I spoke my piece. The agents all exonerated Dole and myself, and took back all they had said about us. Ainsworth case looks bad but I think the fellow did not realize what he was doing, it seems had negotations with Allen, Bailey, Haskell, and others. Mr Sanborn and Allen have been very honorable with me, Sanborn although I opposed his book, he has denied point blank any rumors against me. These things are not very pleasant for one who had tried to do his duty [conscientiously.] Well I came out of the fight all right, and [happily] I gave my arithmetics to Miss [Emery] one of the teachers of the Montpelier Graded School who has lately been appointed one of the text book committee for Montpelier, so I want another sett. When you can find time to recreate a little I should be happy to see you, and give you a vivid description of the fight. I am all tired out now but hope now the fight is over to take some peace.

But your fight has just begin, if you want the greater part of this County you will have to fight for it. Each house has got two or three agents apiece in the County, and business will hum for a month. Get your tax article out as soon as you can I made more mistakes in it than I should if I had not had to hurry so much. One thing I want you to remember. If I am alive five years from this time I shant be a text book committee man.
Yours
John H. Senter

[*Page 83*]
July 5th 79

Henry Briggs Esq.
Dear Sir

I have, in my hands for collection, an account for $4.50 against you, in favor of Viola J. Goodno, for [*several words illegible*] immediate settlement will [save costs.]

Yours truly John H. Senter

[*Page 84*]
June 9th 79
E.C. McClintock Esq
Dear Sir

Your Geography was adopted by the Convention Friday. I had a good square fight and won. I found several men in the Convention who had not received your Geographies. I want you to send a geography & Childs history each to Miss Laura [Moxham] and Miss Mary Emery both of Montpelier, they have recently been appointed text book committee for Montpelier, they are teachers in the graded school. I gave my common school Geog to one of the text book committees from E. Montpelier, and I want you should send me three or four I will place them where they will do good

I am just home from the Convention and am tired out. Now you have conquered the enemy in Boston do pay a little attention to this County.

Yours in haste
J.H.Senter

[*Pages 85-87*]
June [9th] 79
F.B. Winnie Esq.
Burlington Vt

Allow me to apologise to you for not answering your kind leter of May 7th, which may have seemed strange to you, but the fact is that I have just received it, how and why it has been so long delayed is more than I know, but I thought perhaps you might like to know why I did not reply

Again you may have thought me over nice in my views, when you received my leter refusing to meet you at Burlington, but My Dear Sir had you known under what difficulties Prof. Dole and myself were placed by the foolish actions of others, you would have seen it in a different light. Well the County fight is over and I am out of it, and I shall never again be fool enough to act on a text book committee. This Town has not adopted any books as yet, and we shall not untill the first day of August. I have never received your price lists which I should like, now if you will accept this explanation of what may have seemed curious to you I shall be much obliged.

I notice some remarks, in your anciently dated, but recently received favor, regarding book agents. I have found them as a class gentlemen, but there are some exceptions to all "general rules." There has been some very strange procedings in this book [contest,] of which, if I ever see you either here or in the great hereafter, I will inform you in detail, but I can never spend time to write it. It would take to much time. I think I could make this tale (not of "two cities") but of book agents and committeemen interesting enough so that you would be willing to sit up untill three o'clock in the morning. By the way who the d—d told you of my little joke on Allen.

Seriously Mr. Winnie, I should like to see you somtime and make your acquaintance. I believe you and I should find something congenial in our natures. I have endeavored in this book business to do my duty conscientiously, and to treat every book agent with respect, to consider their books on their merits, as far as my ability allowed me, and right here let me say that I have been treated handsomely by nearly all the agents even by those whose books I opposed. Mr. Sanborn particularly has done me a great kindness although he knew that I fought for some other book than his

I am not a very "dignified committee man" but I hope I have been an honest one, which is more than they all can say. You asked for my oppinion of your books. I like your geography very much, it has some features better than any other, if your history had a Vermont [apendix] it would be adopted in this town. Your speller I think stands a beter chance with me now than others. The County Comm. [*one word illegible*] to agree on spellers. The greatest objection I have to your readers is that there are six books in the series

Hoping to meet you somtime and to hear from you again soon I remain yours John H. Senter

[*Page 86*]
November [27th] 79
H.H. Moore Esq.
Dear Sir

I have an account against you. Will you please call in and see me about it, the first time your up to the village.Yours John H. Senter

[*Pages 88-89*]
June 9th 79
Benjamin H. Sanborn Esq.
Morrisville Vermont
Dear Sir

Now that I am done with the County Text-Book Committee, permit me to thank you for the kindness you have shown me, in the muddle which my esteemed colleague Mr. Ainsworth made of this book contest. Let me say to you that your action toward me is fully appreciated, and more especially do I appreciate it, as I know you acted toward me from as you did from no selfish motive. You knew that I favored another book more than yours, yet you have not stooped to take an advantage, which you might have taken from the actions of Mr. A. Had it not been for you and Mr. Huse, standing by me and defending the honesty of my motives it would have been very disagreeable to say the least for me. I hope sometime that I may be able to repay you for your kindness in this matter, you did for me what very few men would have done for a stranger, especially when their own interests would have been to blacken my reputation.

I have tried to act conscientiously in this matter, and yet Friday morning it looked to me, as if the whole County had a right to think from what Mr. A. had done, that the whole committee were mixed up with Book agents. I got out if it however and I am happy, but one thing you may remember if you and I are alive when the next book fight comes five years from this time I shall not be on a text book committee

Thanking you again for the honorable course you have taken toward me. I am sincerly your friend John H. Senter

[*Page 89*]
August 5th 79
Agro Simonds Esq.
Roxbury Vermont
Dear Sir

William Martin of this town has requested me to inform you, that you must return his varnish brush immediately, or else he will make you cost. You will therefore do so, or I shall issue a writ against you.
Respectfully yours John H. Senter

[*Pages 90-91*]
June 9th 79
G.B. Damon Esq.
Dear Sir

Yours of the 7th is at hand and contents noted. You will receive to night, a corrected proof of the tax article. Those corrections must be made and be sure and have that comma taken out, where it says, "The minimum of the State School and Highway Taxes is fixed by law, and a higher rate left optional with the Town." State, is an adjective, not two kinds of taxes, as it reads now it means State & School & Highway taxes it should read State School with no comma between State and School. Your arangement of the interest matter is all right. I am not very well pleased with Bro. Demeritt's work in Orange D— on his ministerial soul if he he had had energy enough to run a[quill] – when he could have carried that County for Fisk. I know I had a harder fight on my hands than he did, but I went in to win and he forgot to go in I guess. I was completely [*one word illegible*] out Saturday night and I haven't got over it yet. I will try and send an annual interest table in a day or two but I am not fit to wite a letter now. You can't imagine what a row I found my self in when I got to Montpelier Friday morning.

It was very pleasant to have rumors afloat that I was bought, when, God knows, I had done my duty as I saw it without, a d-d cents interest financially in the matter except out of pocket for my expences, but I knew I had been honest and so I went in. I told the convention when I began on Fisk that the air was full of rumors that my interest in that book was financial not intellectual, but that they must judge of that when I got through. It is my humble oppinion that before I got through that book & speech, they thought I had some reasons for my choice which were not financial any how we got a big majority.

[*Page 91*]
June 24th 79
Messrs. Clark & Maynard,
New York.
Gentlemen

Has T.T. Bailey your N.E. Agent informed you, of the terms, which I told him I must have for my town, for the five years after introduction? Is your Popular History to be published with the map on page 242 as it is, in the copy you sent to me?

Yours truly
John H. Senter

[*Pages 92-93*]
June 10th 79
G.B. Damon Esq.
Dear Sir

I should like to know why in hell you could not wait untill you had received my corrections on that tax article. It will be abused bad enough after my corrections are made, but now you have sent it out, I hope it will catch hell. Why I was so particular about it was because I pitched into Greenleaf's Tax article in the convention, and I wanted yours to be correct, so that the heathen could have nothing to howl about. I have got that annual interest table done but you shan't have it untill I have time to fix it so there can't be a mistake. I would have sent it to-night but now I will keep it untill tomorrow. Seriously I am [*one word illegible*] you did not wait untill you got my correction. I got the first proof at Montpelier Saturday morning. I went and saw several good lawyers, and without telling them who wrote it, asked them to criticise it on the law points, they all said it was right. Then I came home and corrected that proof and sent it you Monday [*several words illegible*] right, and I wanted all the [*one or two words illegible*] punctuation and figures made right. I was so hurried and [worried] when I wrote that article that I wonder I did not make more mistakes than I did. One thing, which perhaps you don't know is I [cant] send a letter to you only once a day and any letter you send to me must be mailed in the morning or else I cant get it untill the next night as I do not live on the R.R. the night mails are of no consequence to me. I will send the annual interest table to morrow night. How does Orange County please you? It don't suit me very well because I think it could have been carried for Fisk, if the book had been shown up. When this book fight is over I should be happy to see you up here in Mad River Valley, we will find some fishing for you and try and make it pleasant. I think now unless some new thing breaks, you will get fifteen of the nineteen towns in this County perhaps this is high but I hope not. Let Orleans County know all about it and Caledonia too. I haven't heard from Smith this week but think he is on the "war path" he was the happiest man in Montpelier [Friday] night Yours [special] and [particular] friend John H. Senter

[*Pages 94-96*]
June 16th 79
My Dear Winnie

Your exceedingly kind favor of the 20th came promptly to hand, and I now hasten to reply. Your very mild request, that I immediately send you by express to you [*one word illegible*] at Burlington, "Monteiths Geogs" Independent Readers, Complete Speller and Barnes Brief History. I should have long since complied with your so delicately expressed command, had it lain in my power, knowing as I did, that of course you were not angry at a poor committee man for not reccomending your books for the instruction of young [readers] in this state, and thinking as I do that it was occasioned by a suden attack of [*one word illegible*] which I believe inflicts you some times, but unfortunately for the finances of A.S. Barnes & Co. those book, which you mention in your pointed epistle, are at present scattered over this town among the different teachers, who are examining their merits and demerits with a practiced and critical eye, and it will take your humble servant some time to collect those treasures of yours together in one compact bundle, when I have accomplished that herculean task I will then endeavor to find the identical wrapping paper with which they were encompassed about, when you so generously sent them to me, with high and fond hopes of their adoption, but perhaps "Allen" may have used some of that paper in his midnight wanderings, in which case an unsupportable loss must accrue to the house of Barnes & Co. I will search diligently however, knowing how much will depend on the result, and if I succeed they shall be sent immediately on a "train," expecting of course that their "expenses will be paid," by the magnanimous Winnie, even if they do get on a train." Permit me to express to you my gratitude for the use of the aforesaid books, and at the same time to express the sorrow and humiation I feel that they are so unavoidably detained feeling as I do the great inconvenience it would be to you if some town should adopt your books, and order that particular sett for introduction, for undoubtedly your house is [*one or two words illegible*] with orders from this state, that this delay will occasion an irremediable loss to the house and may ruin them. The books may have become soiled by their use in looking them over, but you can remedy that by using benzine and cleansing them, and so make a great saving for your house. How cruel it would have been to have allowed you to have made any further expenses in [respect] to my meeting you, as it has turned out. Seriously Mr. Winnie you shall have those books just as soon as I can collect them, but I shall not put myself out much to run after them. I had just one book in my office which came from you when I received your letter. I have taken much pains to show all books sent me to teachers, and have asked their oppinion, and I should ask them to retain them untill they get ready, if you want them before you may come and collect them together, if you would be so kind. I should like to know your wholesale price & disc for five years to towns for Watsons Speller. I don't supose you would object very seriously to our using the book if we want to do so, whether we shall want to or not I cannot say now. Very respectfuly yours John H. Senter

[*Pages 97-98*]
June [17th] 79
Gentlemen

I hereby notify you, that on Tuesday June 3rd 1879, I was riding in my wagon, drawn by two horses, over and upon the highway, leading from the main or river road in said town of Warren, commencing on said river road, near the premises owned by the Ira Richardson Estate and leading to and beyond the premises occupied by Aaron Wheeler. Said highway is known by the name of the Grand Hollow Road, and is a public highway in the said town of Warren, and [*several words illegible*] fifty rods in an Easterly direction from the junction of this above described highway, [*several words illegible*] to the premises owned and occupied by [*several words illegible*] I was about five rods, in a westerly direction from an elm tree [*several words illegible*] on the south side of said highway. I turned my team from [*several words illegible*] in order to pass another team, and [*several words illegible*] wagon wheels striking a stone which was only three feet from the travel of said road, it being within the highway, and also in consequence of the narrowness of the travel of said road it being but of the traveled part of said highway, it being but 10 feet wide at this place, and in consequence of the said highway being [gullied] at this abovedescribed place, and of the general insufficiency and want of repair of said highway, I was violently thrown from my wagon to the ground, and I was severely injured in my shoulders, and back, and left side, and in consequence of which I am now confined to my bed, for which injuries I claim dammage of the Town of Warren

[*Page 98*]
June 24th 79
Clarence H. Pitkin Esq.

Montpelier

Will you have the kindness to inform me what costs are taxable against a delinquent collector, for citation, hearing, witnesses, and extent, under procedings instituted according to the provisions of Chapter 84, Sections 49, 50, 51 and 52 of the General Statutes. I have four such case now in the mill, against school district collectors. They are cited to appear before a justice next Saturday, and I do not know how to tax the cost, and I do not find any rule in the Statute. Business is very brisk with me, for the last two weeks I have worked night and day, hope it will continue. Please answer at once and oblige

Yours John H. Senter

[*Pages 99-100*]

June 17th 79

To the Selectmen of the Town of Warren

Gentlemen,

I hereby notify you, that on Tuesday June 3rd 1879, I was riding in my wagon drawn by two horses, over and upon the highway, commonly known by the name of the Grand Hollow road, said highway commencing near the premises owned by the Ira Richardson Estate in the said town of Warren on the main or river road in said Warren, and leading in a northerly direction to and beyond the premises owned and occupied by Aaron Wheeler in said Town of Warren, and that said highway is a public highway, totally within said town of Warren and open for public travel, and that when I was about fifty rods in an easterly direction from the junction of this abovedescribed road, with the road leading to the premised owned and occupied by E. [Gramby] in said Town of Warren, and about five rods in a westerly direction from an elm tree upon the south side of said highway, and near which is piled some lumber, I turned my horses from the travel of the road, in order to pass another team, and that in consequence of my wagon wheels striking a stone on the north side of the travel of said highway, and within three feet of the travel of said highway, and also in consequence of the narrowness of the travel of said highway at this place, it being only ten feet wide, and in consequence of the general insufficiency and want of repair of said highway I was thrown from my wagon to the ground and severely injured in my shoulders, back and left side for which injuries I claim dammage of the Town of Warren.

[*Pages 100-03*]
June 22nd 79
George B. Damon Esq.
32 Cornhill Boston
Dear Sir

Enclosed you will find the new matter corrected, and altered. I have taken a great amount of pains with it [this] time, and I know it is correct. I have made a very important change in the second paragraph, it will necesitate a different arangement of that page, the heading will have to be placed nearer the top, and the whole page will have to sit closer, if this can't be done then it will be necessary to continue the first page on to the second. I expect you will swear about this, but that won't make any difference, the change will have to be made all the same, and I don't know how in hell you can help yourself. The corrections I have made on those annual interest notes, I ought to have made before as I had discovered them long ago. I am certain they are all right now in the first note on page 1 the printer made a mistake of $100, and I made one of one cent. I think it would be better to have the annual interest table on the fifth page, and the tax article on the last three. If you get very mad at these corrections, I shall ask you why you did not have the articles written before you did so that I could have had time to perfect the original manuscript. I commenced work on that tax article when I was head over [heals] in work doing every thing I could to carry this county for Fisk, and when I was worried and mad because I heard every mail that Ainsworth was slopping over, "The Dam Phool," and I was not in very good time to write arithmetics. Now I have taken three days and have very quietly gone over the whole work. I have received numerous sugestions from people who did not know anything about the subject, and some from those who did. I have considered both for what they are worth, and you now have the result. I presume that you have heard some criticisms on the article and you should have sent them to me. One that I have heard and I presume you have is, "That Firemen are exempt from pool taxes," but this is not so. The Polls of Firemen are set in the list the same as other peoples, but the Town may vote to abate all of their poll tax, except highway taxes now if you hear any one say that Firemen do not pay poll taxes you may very quietly tell the one that tells you so that he is just as much mistaken, as "he would be if he had lost shirt." I think now, and I am speaking advisedly that this tax article is complete. It is as far as I can learn giving excelent satisfaction every where, and of course they all tell me just what they think of it because they don't know who wrote it. I have received from you a large number of books for which please to accept my thanks, they are fully appreciated. In regards to writing books, I think you can give each teacher one of the "Spencerian Keys to Penmanship" and I won't ask for many charts, as I have only "one [pet place]. I know you are giving my town good terms Mr. Damon, and I am well aware that you cannot afford to furnish those charts, but I am not good enough in percentage to figure out what in hell the object is to buy your copy books at the introduction price, which is [80] cts per [copy] less 10% wich makes the nett price 72 cts, when the wholesale price is 84 cts less 1/6 off which makes the nett price 70 cts, possibly you could show me a rule in Fisk that would help me, however if I was to buy many I should prefer the wholesale price. In regard to what books there are in the merchants' hands I don't think I was quite fair with you although I had made all the other agents agree to the same thing, you may exchange your books with him nett price for nett price, not book for book as I told you. I don't know as I had any rather [*three words illegible*] you. I have been down to Waitsfield and have argued Fisk with Mr. Jones and he is now a strong Fisk. I shall keep watch of the [*one word illegible*], however, I put in a word now and then all around here, when it will do good

Smith has been out here, and I like his apperance very much, he wears well, and he is doing good work and when he gets through I think "Sambornum mortuus erat"

Let me know how the status of the book business is
Yours truly John H. Senter

[*Page 101*]
August 19th 78
Melville E. Smilie Esq.
Montpelier, Vt.
Dear Sir,

Set No. 283, S.D. Allen vs. Chas. E. [Keith], for the jury and oblige
Yours truly John H. Senter

[*Page 103*]
June 23rd 79
E.C. McClintock Esq.
Dear Sir

I wish you would send a copy of Warrens Common School Geog. and Munroes Spellers to Josiah Holden of Waitsfield, he is one of the Waitsfield committee & has not received any of your books. I think Waitsfield will take yor Geogs both Common School and Primary, & also the Physical, perhaps Spellers and histories. Send me price lists of your Spellers. Yours truly John H. Senter

[*Page 104*]
June 23rd 79
Messrs. Eldredge & Brother
Philadelphia
Gentlemen

Your circulars relating to school text books are just received. I have long known your [clasical] publications, have used them, and think the best, but I was not aware that you published common school text books or I should have corresponded with you on the subject ere this. By an act of legislature passed at its last session we are to make an entire change of text books in our schools. I have been examining texts-books in reference to the subject some time. I am one of the County committee to recommend text-books, we have made a partial list for adoption already. I am to select and purchase books for my own town, and I have not as yet decided on, Physical Geographies, Grammars or Spellers. In regard to the other books I have as yet taken [no] final standpoint, but so far as I have examined I made up [my mind] which I like best. I should like to examine your books, and prices, both introduction and wholesale
Yours truly John H. Senter Town Superintendent of Warren

[*Page 105*]
June 21st 79
W.W. Ainsworth Esq.
Calais Vermont
Dear Sir

Your favor is at hand, contents noted. In reply I will say that those letters, regarding your negotiations with Whittemore, were sent to me with out my soliciting them, and I do not suspose that that house feel under any obligation to me, as I most heartily opposed their book in convention. I might perhaps obtain them, but I don't see any reason why Huse would give them to me any sooner than to you. I think he will give them to you if you see him. Yes Winnie did send for his books, but I penned him an epistle, in which I endeavored to portray to him the smallness of the thing, and told him I would send them together with the paper that came around them, when I got ready, and not before. Yours truly, John H. Senter

[*Pages 106-07*]
June 23rd 79
M.W. Tewksbury Esq.
No. 8 Hawley Street Boston
Dear Sir

I received your favor sometime ago but have been very busy, and have not found time to answer it until now. I also received the books you sent me for which please accept my thanks. I reccomended your "[Gow's] Manners", to the Convention and it was adopted by the Convention. I gave all the committee men present your adress, so that they could correspond with you if they wished.

Now in regard to my conclusions about that letter from your house in New York, were they not very natural ones under the circumstances?

You say in your letter that you are sorry that committees go to book agents for their oppinions of text books, etc. Well if that was meant for a sly dig at my ribs, I will take it, but if you knew me, perhaps you might form a different oppinion, perhaps you might have meant me, but after what I have seen of the way this book business is carried on, I should not wonder if you had formed such an oppinion.

I have tried, in this business, to do my duty and judge books by their merits, if I have failed, or if I do fail, it will be through my own ignorance, and not any ones else.

I should have been very glad to have made your acquaintance, if I had had an opportunity, but as we have not had an opportunity of a personal acquaintance, we may have formed eroneous oppinions of each other, mine of you by the way has been very favorable, but if you are like a very few of the agents I am glad we never met, most of them however have been gentlemen but "all general rules have exceptions" <u>So do general agents</u>

I wish you would send me your wholesale price list and disc. to towns, of your speller a copy of which I received the other day, this town has not decided on books yet, and I shall not untill the first of August

Hoping to hear from you again

I am Yours truly John H. Senter

[*Page 108*]
June 24th 79
G.B. Damon Esq.
Dear Sir

Enclosed you will find another corrected proof. Either I or the printer made two mistakes in the annual interest table, and some one who figured the seventh note, and I guess it was you, made a two cent mistake on that. I like the arrangement now. It is all O.K.

You have probably swore a blue streak all day since you saw my change in the tax article, which I suspose you got this morning. I wish I could have heard you. I should have enjoyed it much. It would have given me great satisfaction. "Misery likes company." Send me a bundle of the new matter as soon as the corrections are made. I find a good many places where they help the book. I like to compare them with Greenleaf's article. They show well there

Yours in haste
John H. Senter

[*Pages 109-110*]
June 27th 79
Messrs. Clark & Maynard
Gentlemen,

Yours just at hand and contents noted. Some four weeks ago I saw Mr Baily and told him what terms I wanted for my town, he said he was not agent for wholesaling only for introduction, but that he would inform you what I wanted, and that he had no doubt but what you would be satisfied. I told him more explicitly than I can write you, and give him my reasons. What I want is in short as follows. My town instructed me to buy all text-books for the schools, and to sell them to the scholars at cost. Now I want your books after introduction as follows. The town to be responsible for all loss or dammage to the books by fire or otherwise, and to pay for all books that are sold once in thirty days and give you a statement of books on hand, which are to be your property, but if dammaged in any way to be paid for by the town. I have made this arrangement with all publishing houses but yours, and should have written you before but I susposed Baily had. I gave him my reasons and the details, which I have not time now to write, the discount 1/6 is what I expected

I do not observe any answer to my question whether you are to publish the Popular History with that map on page 242 as it now stands. I should like to know.

Yours hastily John H. Senter

[Page 110]
July 14th 79
Hiram Atkins
Montpelier Vermont
Dear Sir

Enclosed you will find ($11.75) eleven dollars and seventy five cents the amount of M.J. Waterman's bill, for which acknowledge the receit. He wants his paper stopped immediately I had a writ served on him, and he was mad for which I suspose you feel as bad as I do
Yours truly John H. Senter

[Pages 111-112]
[date is illegible]
Friend Damon,

Your favors of late dates are all at hand, and I rejoice exceedingly at your happiness, may it continue for ever! I have carefully looked over Prof. [Dance's] work on Note No. 3, and his work is correct if one carries the computation to mills. I have also noted what the author says about the way he computes the interest, that is he calls five mills and over a cent, and drops all under five. He says "it is practical in court and among business men" and I say he is right in that statement, and I further say that he is wrong in his results, on those two notes, and I enclose my solution, which I want you should send to him, and ask him to find the mistake in mine or else own up that he is wrong. I use the mills just as the author does, and I swear he is wrong. It don't make a d-d odds if the mistake is at only 1¢, right is right. Now you send my solution to the author, and tell him that I want that he should find a mistake in my work, or admit the answers right. Well I am very glad indeed you have concluded to put the metric system in to your book. Why in hell did you not say something about it before, that has been the stock argument against the book. Send a circular around d-d quick and let every body know it. I received your specimen's of free [hand drawing] Did you learn that from White? Had a letter from Ainsworth did you? Keeping quiet [eh?] Why in hell didn't he think to practice that before the convention. (The Damn Phool)

Yes I caught those fish the day I got your euphonius epistle and if you will come up into this valley, which you admire so d-d much, you can go with me and do likewise, but bear in mind it must be before the 1st of September, so says the law. I probably should not have considred your request for my final revision as a hint on that definition of the Poll list if I had not been punched on that point untill I got sore and when I got your letter, as I knew you had such a d-d delicate way of suggesting things, I swore I would stop the howl, and so instead of stopping a howl, I got a hell of a growl from you, just my d-d luck! I will tell you some time how those mistakes occurred in the table, I own up solid.
Yours John H. Senter

[*Page 113-114*]
July 1st 79
Messrs. Clark & Maynard
New York
Gentlemen,

Yours received, and in reply I have to say that I have made that, arrangement with D. Appleton & Co., Cowperthwait & Co., [Ivson, Blakeman, & Taylor,] Robert S. Davis & Co., and finaly with every one that I have had any idea of adopting their books, the arrangement is the same as I wrote you.

I wish to make it simply as a matter of convenience. My town is a county town. The town officers are scattered and when one wants to get an order on the treasurer he has got a days work on hand, secondly the money is usaly paid in to the treasurer, in large sums at long intervals, and many times, one cannot get an order cashed just when he wants it, and a bill might not be paid for two or three months over time. I do not purpose to keep a large stock of books on hand but simply what the scholars want. It is not a commission business that I want. The Town is to be responsible for the books, or any loss or dammage which may happen to them, and to pay you once in thirty days for all books sold, and give you a statement of all books on hand. My town is I believe the only town in this County that buy their own books, and I presume the only one in the state.

Perhaps Dr. Anderson is right, but one thing is certain he is also wrong, because the Grammar school History has the map entirely different, now one must be wrong, which is it?

Let me know your decision on terms at your earliest convenience
Yours truly John H. Senter

[*Page 114*]
[July] 5th 79
C.F. Clough Esq.
Waterbury, Vermont.
Dear Sir,

Your favor of the 2nd just at hand, and contents noted, in reply, I would say that I am somewhat in sympathy with the "Green Back movement."

I cannot however meet with you next Wednesday as I have to go Monday morning to Hyde Park on very important business, and shall not be able to return untill week after next

Thanking you for your kind invitation, which I should be very happy to be able to accept, I am yours fraternally John H. Senter

[*Page 115*]
July 5th 79
Dear Damon

I am sory to bother you with all this fuss about those answers, but I suspose you want them right, Don't you? Well with all due defference to Mr. Rowel, I must still insist that the answer to the seventh note should be $393.59. He has changed it to $393.58, I see, and says he "looked it through twice with the same result." I can't help it he is wrong yet, and so I enclose the work and he will see where he made his mistake, which was where he computed the interest on the principal from July 22nd/74 to Dec 28th/78 he makes the interest $79.41 and it is $79.42. I know he feels very sure he is right but nevertheless he is wrong, send him my solution and he will "cave." I should have sent this before but have been away, and have just got back. I am d-d certain that my solution is right, and am ready to fight on this ground, and further more, if you don't send me some of those new proofs I will scalp you. Yours Senter.

[*Page 116*]
July 14th 79
W.C. Maxfield Esq.
Hyde Park Vermont.
Dear Sir

H.W. Lyford of Warren is the owner of the Ober Mill, Eden Vt. He has been informed that the iron works of the mill had been stolen, and that you had bought it, know that it was stolen property, and that it belonged to H.W. Lyford.

Last week I went with Mr. Lyford to Eden and investigated the matter throughly, and I find that we can prove by good reliable men, what I have stated above. You will save yourself trouble, disgrace, and costs by immediately settling this matter.
Yours truly John H. Senter

July 14th 79
W.A. Blake Esq.
Northfield
Dear Sir

I have not as yet secured that note, am waiting to get a surer hold, don't worry I will get it sometime all right, he had a wagon, but sold before I got your note. Yours in haste John H. Senter

[*Page 117*]
July 16th 79
M.W. Hazen Esq.
32 Hawley Street, Boston
Dear Sir

Enclosed you will find an agreement for furnishing books to my town after introduction as you agreed to do with me at the [Pavillion] Hotel Montpelier June 7th. I have sent the same agreement to others, and no one has objected but Clark & Maynard. I do not care whether they agree or not as I had as soon have some other grammar as theirs. Your agent Mr. Ross was here to day, and Mr Benton yesterday. You may send me an agreement to sign for the town and I will sign and return.

Yours truly John H. Senter

July 23rd 79
G.B. Damon Esq.
My Dear Sir

I wish you would send that agreement as we are now ready to adopt your books when that agreement comes along. I was up in Orleans Co. when you was there, and was glad to learn of your success there, answer at once, yours in haste
John H. Senter

[*Pages 118-119*]
[July 23rd] 79
M.W. Hazen Esq.
[6] Hawley Street Boston, Mass.
Dear Sir

Your favor of July 21st is at hand, and I have noted its contents with suprize.

You say that you understood, that I only wanted those terms during the introduction, now sir you must either, think that I am a consumate fool, or you did not so understand it, because you know and I know there is no house but what that is their universal custom during introduction, and further they only ask for a payment in 90 days; but sir I told you that I wanted to make those terms for five years, and I told you my reasons in detail, and you understood that I was making those terms for 5 years. You said that you had never made such terms, with any one, and I told you I had made the same terms, with other houses & you then made a square trade with you, and you then understood it. I presume you had some object in view then, which you have now lost sight of. I am sory Mr. Hazen to find out that you are not a man that I can depend on but on the contrary to find you to be a quibbler. I say this because I know that you understood what terms I wanted for my town, and now I find when the time comes for your signing an agreement to the town, you write me a decidedly thin excuse

However I am glad to find right where you are before I have adopted any of your books. I do not want any connection with any man whose word is not as good as his bond, and I shall not have

Yours John H. Senter.

P.S. You say you will do better than I ask in the agreement, if you read the agreement you will see that it only refers to terms after introduction. I already have your introduction terms in writing J.H.S.

[*Page 119*]
November 21st 79
Watson Fuller Esq.
Dear Sir,

I have in my hands for collection an account against you in favor of William McAllister, for work done [for you] some time ago. Call and settle at once and save further costs

Yours truly, John H. Senter

[*Page 120*]
July 23rd 79
E.C. McClintock Esq.
My Dear Sir,

Your kind favor of July 21st is at hand, and in reply I will say that I am as ignorant of what books will be adopted in this valley as I was a month ago, agents are plenty, and committees change their mind every time one comes along. You will receive an order from this town soon, and we may adopt more of your books than I have talked of. We will do all we can for you. I have heard the same rumor from Montpelier, but I do not know it to be true. I hope it is so, but I doubt it

You may expect our certificate next week. Your friend
John H. Senter

[*Page 121*]
July 24th 79
W.C. Maxfield Esq.
Hyde Park, Vermont.
Sir,
Your favor was duly received, and its contents duly noted. In reply, I have to say, that two things, in your statemet, are, to say the least, very peculiar; the first that you had so carefully kept this iron for three years without informing Mr. Lyford, that you had it in your possession, and second that you now have nothing in your possession but the [bands] of the penstock, of course you would not sell that for old iron, it would sell far better to blacksmiths, but what about the cast iron and shafting, have you got them? Mr. Maxfield it is quite evident to me that you bought that iron knowing that it was stolen, and you had better settle it without further cost
Yours John H. Senter

[*Page 122*]
July 24th 79
W.C. Maxfield Esq. Sir, Your letter in relation to the mill irons is at hand. You say that you had about 75 lbs of bands & other iron. Now Sir there has been much more iron than that taken from the mill, irons that originaly cost more than $75. and I expect to be able to prove that you had them. Also that they were taken from the mill by a nephew of yours instead of the half witted fellow suggested by you in your letter. Now Mr Maxfield I have spent nearly a weeks time and some money in

investigating this matter personally and I propose to get pay for the stolen property if I can get at the responsible parties, which I expect to do.
Yours Truly
H.W. Lyford

[*Page 123*]
July 25th 79
E.C. McClintock Esq.
Dear Sir

I have been finding out, what I could about your prospects in this county for a day or two, and I find it looks very favorable for you. Montpelier, Barre, E. Montpelier, & Berlin are to adopt your readers. In this valley Waitsfield and Fayston will take the Readers and spellers if this town will, and I guess we shall. I had a talk with several committee's yesterday. I think now that this town will adopt Munroe's Readers, Warren's Common School Geog, Berard's History, Goodriches Child's History & Green's Grammars. We shall decide next week and send you our order. I want you to sent a sett of Munroe's readers and Berard's History to E.W. Slayton & Arthur Ralph my associate committee in this town. Send them at once. Sincerly your friend

John H. Senter

[*Pages 124-127*]
July 30th 79
Friend George

I have perused thine epistle which thou wrotest me on the 28th, and it has transformed me into a quaker for want of profane words by which I could express my sentiments.

Firstly I did not understand that our arrangement was to be "confidential," or that it was "a personal one," and I do not hardly see how you could think, it was personal, as I told you, that I was instructed to make those terms by vote of my town, but it seems you did so understand it, and there is where the trouble comes. Had I understood that you was making a confidential personal agreement with me at the Pavillion, I should not have made it, for several reasons, but I did not so understand it, but on the contrary I susposed you were making the agreement by consent of your house, and I judged so from you said in your letter of April 14th from which I copy "circumstances alter cases, and I may have to eat my own words, at least I will have some further correspondence with my house and talk with you when I see you." You was speaking of you

[*page 125 was poorly copied and is completely illegible; page 126 is transcribed below:*]

my town derived from my personal agreements[?]

Well Mr. Damon I believe I always give you credit for being a shrewd, sharp, observer of human nature, and I think so yet, for if you had tried the little game my friend Hazen did, I – well your books would not have been adopted here any how. But Mr. Damon I was very favorably impressed with you at our first meeting, (you certainly will not think I flatter as I have no reasons to do) and I [confided] in you more at our second interview then I ever did to a stranger before, because I believed you to be what so far I have always found you an honorable man, in fact I took a liking to you which I haven't got over

I will return your letter to you if you say so and I will make no copy of it, but just then you say you do not like to put yourself wholly in my power, and then ask me to put my self and my town wholly in your power. You ask me to put more confidence in you than you are willing to put in me. Well your books will be adopted, althought I feel as though I was not do as I ought to do, but I am one of those fellows that you will find where you left them, but in doing this I shall insist that so long as you are agt for I. B. & T. you must furnish these books to this town on consignment and I also shall insist that you furnish a copy, for each school in town, of each book adopted free. I should have insisted on this last clause any way as all house offer the same, and that exchange shall not be confined to grade, and new books shall be exchanged even

I have during this book campaign done all I could for your books, because I thought your books best, and because I liked you, and I am not going back on you now because I think it an honest [misunderstanding,] answer at once & oblige sincerely your friend John H. Senter

[*Page 127*]
Aug 4th 79
Hiram Atkins
Montpelier, Vermont.
Dear Sir

Enclosed you will find note to [ballance] my account. I should have sent it before but, I have been trying to collect money to pay it from people

who owe me, but have not been successfull. I have never heard from you in regard to that [Mitterman] money I sent you. Did you receive it?
Yours respectfully John H. Senter

[*Page 128*]
[*date is illegible*]
E.C. McClintock Esq.
Dear Sir

We have adopted to night, Munroe's Readers & Spellers, Greens Grammars, Warren's Common School & Physical Geography, Berards W.S. and [*one word illegible*] Child's History. I have done all I could for you and I presume more than you expected. I want you should send E.W. Slayton and A.S. Ralph a full set of all the books except Ralph who already has the readers & spellers.

You may send 100 Common School Geographies, 10 Physical, 50 of Berards History, 20 Childs Histories, 25 Munroes [*two words illegible*], 25 first readers, 30 second, 50 third, 70 fourth, 80 fifth, 25 sixth readers, 25 [primary] spellers, 150 practical spellers, 36 Greens Introductory Grammars, 48 Greens New English Grammars, to me as soon as you can, in exchanging books, I shall take a book of a lower grade in exchange for a higher, and I want you to remember we have a great many schools, so give us as many free coppies as you can. I have sent our certificate of adoption to Dole. Now havent we done well for you? Hoping to hear from you soon I am your friend John H. Senter

[*Page is stamped both 129 and 130*]
July [31st] 79
Friend [*one word illegible*]
[*Only a very few words of this letter are legible due to poor copying. The letter appears to refer to a litigation matter.*]

[*Page 131*]
July 31st 79
Friend McClintock

I have been to Waitsfield and Fayston to day and have told them what we have done, and I have done all I could for you. They will adopt your Readers to night and I think the spellers and grammars. Well I think if you had had a good line man to work up your books in this County and State you could have carried a great many towns.

I wish you could find time to spend a few days up here rusticating, if you like fishing we have plenty, and we have mountains to climb &c &c &c.

Did not I suprise you by the number of books we adopted in this town published by your house?

I never mean to promise more than I can fulfill and in this case I fulfilled more than I promised.

Send your books as soon as possible

Your friend John H. Senter

[*Page 132*]
Aug 1st 79
Friend Damon

Send me as soon as you can 100 Fisk Arithmetics Cloth Covers, 50 of the same bound covers, 50 Fisk first Book in arithmetics cloth and 50 of the same bound, 25 of Townsend civil Gov, 12 [Regent] and Strattons Com. School Book [Keeping] & [Blakes] [10] of Swintons Elementary Geographies, 12 setts of Whites drawing Books & [Charts].

I shall exchange all new books I have on hand even, and I shall take a copy of each book for each school in town free. I have already ordered and received the [Spencerian] copy books, and I want one chart for our village school, that will be all the charts I will ask for, but I want you to send 10 keys to the Spencerian Penmanship for each school.
"Who says I'm a hog" Your friend
John H. Senter

Nov. 25th 79
Erbin Bixby Esq.
Dear Sir,

I wish to inquire of you, if you are acquainted with one George Peake, and if so what is his character for truth. [*signature is illegible*]

[*Page 133*]
Aug 1st 79
Prof. Dole
My Dear Sir

I thought I would write what my town had done with the book question. We have adopted Munroes Readers & Spellers, Warren's Common School and Physical Geographies, Greens Grammars, Swinton's Elementary Geography, Fisk's Arithmetics, Spencerian Copy Books,

[Berends] and [Godrich] W.S. Histories, Townsend's Civil Government, Whites Drawing & Gows Good Manners.

I would also say that Waitsfield & Fayston take the same Readers we do. Did you get a card from G.E. Whittemore threatening you on prices? I did and if he had not wrote it his speller would have been retained, but I was not born to be [done] by a book agent. What have you [*one word illegible*]?

Sincerly your friend John H. Senter

Nov. 25th 79
Wm. C. Brookfield Esq.
Dear Sir

I wrote you some time since regarding a note which you bought of George Parker, if you received my letter I should like to know what you intend to do in the matter, as I wish to treat you fairly. [*signature is illegible*]

[*Page 134*]
August 17th 79
Dear Damon

Your books arrived all right, and I found in the box a dictionary not on the bill, for which please accept my thanks.

I now want to know how much four of the largest Webster's Unabridged Dictionaries will cost me apiece. Four of my friends here wish to buy one each, and I told them I thought I could buy them reasonable of you, please to give the best terms and oblige. Truly your friend John H. Senter

P.S. I am more than satisfied with the arithmetics. They look neat and tasty, the metric system is complete, and more than makes up for the loss of those two examples in interest. In fact I am [*one word illegible*] and D-n the man that growls. JHS

November 27th 79
Orvis Whitcomb Esq.
Dear Sir

I have in my hands an account against you in favor of E.G. Hooker. Call and see at once
Yours, John H. Senter

[*Page 135*]
August 79
Mr. Editor

Your correspondent, who reported the particulars, of the burglary committed in this town on the 6th inst, and the arest of Edgar H. Van Deusen, must, most assuredly, have been but little acquainted with the truth of the matter. He made many minor mistakes in his discription, which are of no particular consequence, but one of his statements is entirely untrue, and does injustice to an honest well deserving young man, Eugene Van Deusen the brother of Edgar. Your correspondent says that "suspicion at once rested on Edgar and his brother." It is true that suspicion at once rested upon Edgar but [*one or more words illegible*] [had] the least suspicion of Eugene, in fact he is [*one or more words illegible*] suspicion of that [kind] [*one or more words illegible*] heartfelt [part] of this community for this [*remainder of sentence illegible*]
John H. Senter

[*Page 136*]
August 18th 79
Friend Pitkin

A. sells B. a house, in the house is a sink the frame of which is fastened to the house, the iron sink set in the frame is not fastened to the frame & cannot be a discharge pipe fastened to the sink passes out through the house, no reservation was made of the sink. Qare. Does the sink pass as part of the realty, and a fixture, or is it a chattel?

Please to answer and oblige.
Yours truly John H. Senter

August 21st 79
B. Joy Jeffries, M.D.
Boston, Mass.
Dear Sir,

I write you for information as regards the expense at your Infirmary of opperating on eyes. A young lady of this town has a cataract over each of her eyes, her parents are poor, and as she is estimable young lady several of the people here are willing to help pay the expenses of the opperation and her traveling expenses

You will oblige me very much by giving what information in regard to the matter you can conveniently.

Yours respectfully
John H. Senter

[*Page 137*]
Aug 25th 79
John McGreggor Esq.
Winooski V^{t}
Dear Sir

I must apologize to you, for not answering you esteemed favors sooner, but I have been very busy, and I have also been sick. While I was sick business acumulated on my hands so that I have had to spend all my time to catch up, but I have got around now all right and will try and be a better correspondent. I like your solutions of that problem very much, they are scientific and correct, more so than mine is a great deal. I think your last suggestion a good one, and that it will be a good addition to the problem. I will send you my solution, you will see that I have used different altitudes for the [towers] than you did, but that makes no difference in the principle. I will write you again this week. Yours truly
John H. Senter

[*Page 138*]
Oct. 8th 79
Alfred Lamb Esq.
Dear Sir

Mr. Charles Bragg wants I should issue a writ against you for damage for not delivering cow as per contract. It is so plain a case that I would write you, and give you a chance to settle it and save yourself useless cost please inform me at once which course you will take
Yours
John H. Senter

February 3rd 80
R.H. Mardin Esq.
Bristol, V^{t}.
Dear Sir,

Enclosed you will find an execution against Truman Rockwood. I wish you would give it to your officer, and have him try and secure it if possible. Hewitt has a lien on some cattle which Rockwood has, take them if you can find them for this execution

Do the best you can for me on this and oblige
Yours truly John H. Senter

[*Page 139*]
December 3rd 79
D.D. Hemenway Esq.
Granville, V[t.]
Friend Dan,

If I can sell your mill property here for $600, to a man who will agree to put a mill up on the premises, next year in good shape, and pay the interest annually, and not make any payment for two years, and then pay fifty dollars a year, will the trade be satisfactory to you. The purchase to include all the iron work now on the premises.

You know, you have taken out a water wheel since you gave me your bottom price. Write as soon as you receive this, for I am in hope of closing a trade this time.
Yours truly John H. Senter

[*Page 140*]
January 26th 80
[*two words illegible*] & Williams
Bethel, Vermont.
Gentlemen,
[*Part of the letter was not copied properly and is illegible. Legible words are transcribed below, with illegible portions indicated by ellipses:*]
[Aaron] . . . C.A. Hanks ... which . . . secure the note, . . . is about to run the Statute of limitation, so . . . returns it to you, that you may do what [you] wish with the note. [Gore now lives in Granville] . . . return Mr. Hank's receipt for the note to me and much oblige
Yours very truly John H. Senter

[*Page 141*]
Messrs. [*one or more words illegible*]
[*illegible town name*] V[t.]
Gentlemen
[*This letter is very blurry and faint. It is impossible to read but appears to be a legal matter; the word "negotiations" appears, and a dollar sum may be mentioned.*]

[*Page 142*]
February 16th 80
Hubert Thayer, Esq.
Northfield, Vt.
Dear Sir

I have a school tax against you for School District No. 6, in Warren on grand list of 1879, amounting to [$100] which must be paid immediately, or I shall have to procede against your body.

Yours truly, John H. Senter

February 16th 80
Lucius Cummings Esq.
Dear Sir

John Baird of Waitsfield has a claim against you for extra interest [*two lines illegible*] in 1875 you can save yourself cost by settling with me at once, or I shall bring suit against you for the whole ammount of extra interest he paid you with interest on the same. Please inform me at your earliest convenience [how] you propose to [proceed.]

Yours truly
John H. Senter

[*Page 143*]
February 27th 80
R.H. Mardin Esq.
Bristol, Vermont.
Dear Sir

Enclosed you will find Rockwood's note. The amount now due on this note over and above the execution is ($63.62) Sixty three dollars and sixty two cents. Please to acknowledge the receipt of this and oblige

Yours truly
John H. Senter

[*Pages 144-46*]
October 18th 80
To the Select Men of the Town of Roxbury in County of Washington and State of Vermont,
Gentlemen,

I hereby notify you, that on the 29th day of September A.D. 1880 I was riding in my wagon drawn by my horse, over and upon the highway in the Town of Roxbury in the County of Washington, an open public highway in said Town of Roxbury, leading from the Weston Depot Village in said Town of Roxbury to the Depot Village in the Town of Northfield, and that when near the Rail Road Crossing, which is between the dwelling house of Agro Simonds in the said Town of Roxbury and the dwelling house of Marshall Latham in said Town of Roxbury, and on the easterly side of the said Rail Road Crossing, and between the dwelling house of the said Marshall Latham and about five or six rods from said Rail Road Crossing, my horse and wagon were thrown off the bank on the easterly side of said highway; said highway being insufficient and out of repair at that point, in that there was a steep bank on the easterly side of said highway at that point, and the said highway at that point was not protected by any railing or other guard to prevent teams from going over the said bank, and by said accident solely caused by the said insufficiency of said highway my wagon was broken and injured, both of the shafts were broken the crossbar was broken, the [*one word illegible*] was broken over, and the spokes were broken [out] of both off wheels of said wagon, and the wagon was otherwise scratched and marred, and I was thrown from my wagon, and severely injured in my spine near my shoulder so that I have had no use of my arms since that time, but have been and am now confined to my bed, entirely helpless, and I was otherwise injured in and about my back and spine, and internally, and I was so severely injured that the clothes had to be cut from my back. All of said injuries to my person and wagon were solely caused by the said insufficiency of said highway in said Town of Roxbury, and I shall and do claim damage of said Town of Roxbury for each and all of said injuries to my person and wagon [*The letter ends abruptly here, mid-page.*]

[*Pages 147 and 148 are missing; it is evident that at least one page was torn from the copying book.*]

[*Page 149*]
[*The following two letters were not written by Senter:*]
Warren Vermont August 24th 1881
Davis & Gilson,
Putney,
Vermont.
Gentlemen,

I received your letter by the hand of Mr. J. Waterman. I am sorry to learn that the chestnut mare, I sold to you is lame. I have never known her to take a lame step in her life excepting once, a few days when she cut her leg in the pasture.

I knew but what she was all right, when I sold her to you.

I am intending to be at Chester between now and the middle of September, and I will then drive over to Putney and see you and the mare. I hope before that time, she will be all right
Yours very respectfully
N.N. Robinson

[*Page 150*]
Warren Vermont August 24th 1881
Davis & Gilson,
Putney,
Vermont.
Gentlemen,

I received your letter by the hand of Mr. J. Waterman. I am sorry to learn that the chestnut mare, I sold to you is lame. I have never known her to take a lame step in her life, excepting once a few days when she cut her leg in the pasture.

I never knew but what she was all right when I sold her to you.

I am intending to be at Chester between now and the middle of September, and I will then drive over to Putney and see you and the mare. I hope before that time, she will be all right
Very respectfully yours
N.N. Robinson

[*Page 151 appears to have been torn from the copying book.*]

[*Page 152*]
Aug. 24th 1
Clarence H. Pitkin Esq.,
Montpelier,
Vermont.
Clarence,

The commissioners in the Austin homestead matter met yesterday and set off the whole farm.

Please to have the Probate judge notify you when the report is returned and take an appeal
Yours truly
John H. Senter

Messrs. Plumley & Bates,
Northfield
Vermont
Gentlemen,
Enclosed you will specifications of claims of Cardell & [Bragg] vs. J.M. Hanks & Tr.
Yours truly
John H. Senter

[*Pages 153 & 154 appear to have been torn from the copying book.*]

[*Page 155*]
Aug. 25th 1
H.N. Taplin Jr. Esq.,
Montpelier, Vt.
Dear Sir,
I think I can get $10.00 on D.H. Steel's assessment, which amts. to the sum of $16.95. Shall I take it and surrender his premium note?

I think it the best thing to do, as it will be a very hard matter to force a collection. He says his policy ought to have been canceled.
Yours very truly
John H. Senter

Aug. 25th 1
H.N. Taplin Jr. Esq.,
Montpelier, Vt.
Dear Sir,
I think, I can get $10.00 on D.H. Steel's assessment, which amts. to the sum of $16.95. Shall I take it and surrender his premium note?

I think it the best thing to do, as it will be a very hard matter to force a collection. He says his policy ought to have been canceled.
Yours very truly
John H. Senter

[*Page 156*]
Aug [28th] 1
George A. Sterling Esq.,
Independence, Iowa.
Dear Sir,

I have cited Wheeler to be present at the taking of your and your wife's and Robt. Hoffman's depositions at John Hollett's office Main St. Independence, Iowa before John Hollett Esq. on the 10th day of September A.D. 1881 at 10 o'clock in the forenoon of that day. I want you to be there and to have the others there and give your depositions of all you know of that matter, substantially as you did before have the justice seal up the depositions with the usual forms, and you send them to me at once and send your bill and I will see that you are paid at once [*remainder of letter is illegible*]

[*Page 157 appears to have been torn from the copying book.*]

[*Page 158*]
Aug. 29th 1
George A. Sterling Esq.,
Independence,
Iowa.
Dear Sir,

The case of School District No. 5 vs Aaron Wheeler is settled, and we shall not want your depositions
Yours truly John H. Senter

Aug. 29th 1
John H. Batchelder Esq.,
Waterbury,
Vermont.
Dear Sir,

Enclosed you will check for $3.12. Grand Lodge dues for Mad River Lodge No. 91. Yours truly John H. Senter

Warren Vermont
Sept. 8th, 1881
J.H. Drew Esq.,
Roxbury, V^{t}.

Dear Sir,

I wish you would not come to Warren tomorrow the hearing is adjourned. I will write you soon what day to come, yours truly,

John H. Senter

[*Page 159*]

Aug 31st 1

Daniel H. Steel Esq.

Dear Sir

I have made a very good arrangement with the Company regarding your assessment providing it is paid at once. Call and see me, and we will close up this account so that you will be satisfied.

Yours truly, John H. Senter

Aug. 30th 1

Miss Ella J. Taylor,

Winterset,

Madison County,

Iowa

Your favor of the 23rd inst came to hand last night, and I hasten to comply with your request. Enclosed you will find the testimonial, and, if in any other way I can be of service to you by way of reference or otherwise, you have but to command me,

Your most obedient servant,

John H. Senter

[*Page 160*]

Sept. 1st 1

Elisha Goodspeed Esq.,

E. Warren,

Vermont.

Dear Sir,

I have in my hands, for collection, a demand against you in favor of Franklin Stoddard amounting to the sum of one and 34/100 dollars ($1.34). Please to give this your early attention.

Yours truly

John H. Senter

Aug. 30th 1
Charles Newcomb Esq.,
Waitsfield, Vt.
Dear Sir,

I have, in my hands for collection, an account against you amounting to the sum of five and 96/100 dollars ($5.96); in favor of S.D. Allen. This requires your earliest attention to save you costs. Yours truly
John H. Senter

[*Page is stamped both 161 and 162.*]
Warren Vermont August 31st 1881
To George C. Harlow Esq., overseer of the poor for the Town of Westminister, in the County of Windham, State of Vermont. Sir you are hereby notified that I take an appeal for the town of Warren in the County of Washington and State of Vermont, to the Honorable County Court next to be holden at Newfane within and for the County of Windham on the 2nd Tuesday of September A.D. 1881, from the warrant of and the removal of Franklin R. Baxton together with his family his wife [Susan] Baxton from the said Town of Westminister to the said town of Warren. Said Warrant is signed by Henry [Sarne] and Wm. B. [Cutting] justices of the peace, said warrant of removal was served on the town of Warren on the 10th day of June 1881
Hiram E. Boyce, Overseer of the Poor for the Town of Warren
In the County of Washington State of Vermont

[*Page 162*]
Sept. 1st 1
C. Blakely Esq.,
Montpelier,
Vermont.
Dear Sir,

Please send to me by return mail 1 fluid oz. of Cooper's gelatine, 1 oz. aniline violet (2 R.B. to 3B) and oz of spirit of wine.
Yours truly John H. Senter

Aug 31st 1
Collnis Blakely Esq.,
Montpelier,
Vermont

Please to send me by mail the following articles

6 ¼ oz pure fluid glycerine, 1 fluid oz of coopers gelatine, 1 oz. analine violet (2 R.B. to 3B) and 1 oz spirit of wine
Yours truly John H. Senter

[*Page 163*]
Sept. 1st 1
Hon. L.G. Hinkley,
Chelsea,
Vermont.
Dear Sir,

Will you please to send me a certified copy of the answer of Jackson J. Pratt in the chancery case of Geo. W. Mann vs H.J. Pratt et al. Send me your bill for the same and I will return the money.

I want the copy to use on the 9th of September.
Yours truly
John H. Senter

Sept 1st 1
L.L. Durant, Esq.,
Montpelier,
Vermont.
Brother Durant,

The 9th of September will suit me all right, in fact as far as I now know better than any other day. Yours truly,
John H. Senter

[*Page 164*]
Warren, Vt. Sept. 8th 1881
O.W. Orcutt Esq.
Roxbury, Vt.
Dear Sir,

I wrote you a card yesterday to stop the service of summons on Joseph Drew, but it seems you did not get it, now I want you to tell Drew not to come tomorrow but that I will write to him when to come.

See to this as soon as you get this card and much oblige
Yours truly John H. Senter

Sept. [*date is illegible*] 1
Prof. C.C. Boynton
Townshend,
Vermont.
Dear Sir,

Enclosed you will the questions which we used in Washington County examinations.

Yours truly,
John H. Senter

Sept 2nd 1
J.H. Hunt Esq.,
Baldwin,
Iowa.
Dear Sir

I have neglected answering your last favor, in hopes of getting more information, but I do not get much.

There never has been any money deposited with the Town Clerk, Mr. James Cardell, for you by Blake or any body else. Martin is now making and selling a few machines but I think Durant is not doing anything about. What shall I do with Martin?

Yours truly
John H. Senter

[*Page 165*]
Sept [*date is illegible*] 1
Z.S. Stanton Esq.,
Roxbury, Vt.
Zed,

Your favor of Sept. 2nd is at hand and in reply I will say, that if Edson wishes to deal with reading and deal with methods of teaching it in our common schools I am willing, but I don't want any fine spun theories shot over the heads of the teachers.

I think the subject of the duties of Town Superintendents ought to be treated. Yes I think the ladies should be urged to take a [*one word illegible*] most [certainly].

Yours John H. Senter

Sept 3rd 1
Union Mutual Fire Ins. Co.
Montpelier,
Vermont.

Enclosed you will find policy which Mr. Asahel Young the insured wants canceled, he having sold the premises therein insured

Yours truly,
John H. Senter

Warren
Vermont
Sept. 5th 1881
Harrison Hume Esq.
Dear Sir

Please to send with the books ordered this morning to Slayton & Blair 1 dozs. more of Townshend's Shorter course [in English] Gov't and ½ dozs. [set] [Bayard] & [*one word illegible*] book [Readers]. Thanks, John H. Senter

[*Page 166*]
Sept 5th 1
Hiram Atkins Esq.,
Montpelier
Vermont.
Dear Sir

The Washington County Common School Teachers' and School Officers' Association, will hold their first annual meeting at Middlesex Saturday Sept. 24th. Return checks will be given to those attending, on the R.R. and free entertainment furnished by the citizens of Middlesex to teachers. The program will soon be published, and will consist of practical subjects. I want you to give this meeting an editorial, urging the people to take an interest in this matter.

Yours truly John H. Senter

Sept. 5th 1
E.C. McClintock
Boston, Mass.
Dear Sir,

Please to send Slayton & Blair, Warren Vt. by Express

2 Doz Munroe's Chart Primers				
1	"	"	2nd Readers	
1	"	"	4th	"
½	"	"	5th	"
½	"	"	3rd	"
1	"	Warren's Com. Sch. Geog.		
½	"	Berard's Histories		
½	"	Green's Introduction to Eng. Gr.		
½	"	"	Eng. Grammars	

And oblige
Yours truly
John H. Senter
[*One faint and illegible line of text appears below Senter's signature.*]

[*Page 167*]
Sept. 5th 1
Harrison Hume Esq.,
Boston, Mass.
Dear Sir,

Please to send Slayton and Blair, Warren, V^{t}. 2 Doz each of Nos. 5, 6 & 7 Spencerian Shorter course copy books and ½ Doz Townshend's Shorter Course in civil government.

Please to send this package to No. 15 Bromfield Street to be packed with some books ordered there for the same party
Yours truly
John H. Senter
Supt of Schools
Warren, V^{t}.

Sept. 5th 1
S.P. Kelley Esq.,
Northfield,
Vermont.
Dear Sir,

Mr. William Kelsy of this Town has left a matter in my hands to settle with you. It is for a half bushel, 2 [gold] chizels, a large butter tub, a [two gal jug,] two paint brushes, one pair of compasses, an iron wedge, and a hammer, a two inch [*one word illegible*] and dammage on [*one word illegible*], which articles he left at your place, and which you refused to give when

demanded by him. He claims ($5.95) damage of you, and you must either send that amount to me at once or I shall make you costs
Yours truly
John H. Senter

[*Page 168*]
Sept 7th 1
Vermont Mutual Fire Insurance Company,
Montpelier,
Vermont.

I write to request you to cancel the policy of insurance issued to Stedman C. Tucker. I cannot give you the number of the policy, but its date is February 18th 1881.

Mr. Tucker has gone West and taken the policy with him, the property insured has been sold, and is now insured in the present owner's name, the mortgage has been paid, and that policy is void, only the assessments are running against the surety.

No one else has any interest in the policy and he wishes he had not any

As an act of justice to the surety it should be cancelled.
Yours truly John H. Senter

Sept. 7th 1
A.S. Austin Esq.,
Chelsea,
Vermont.
Dear Sir,

Enclosed you will find fifty cents, your fees for artificial copy of Pratts answer.
Yours truly
John H. Senter

Warren, Vermont
Sept. 7th 1881
O.W. Orcutt Esq.
Roxbury, Vt.
Dear Sir

You will probably see H.J. Pratt over to your place to-morrow, and he will want you to serve a summons on Joe Drew, if he comes I wish you

would tell him for me that the hearing is adj. and not to have it served to-morrow, to arrange with you, and I will write you when to serve it
Yours John H. Senter

[*Page 169*]
Sept. 7th 1
L.L. Durant Esq.,
Montpelier,
Vermont.
Brother Durant,

Your favor of the 6th is just at hand, and in reply I would say that it will be impossible for me to attend to the hearing of Durant v. Pratt on Saturday as I have other business engagements that day which I cannot break, but I will call it Monday or any other day of next week you may select, but send me word by Eldredge as it takes too long by mail and I have this time to notify some parties not to come whom I have summoned
Yours truly
John H. Senter

[*date is illegible*]
Clarence H. Pitkin Esq.,
Montpelier,
Vermont.
Clarence

Enclosed you will find the evidence [we have] in the case James Cardell v. [Austin] [*one or two words illegible*].

I want you to secure [*one word illegible*]and notify [Gibson] of [same by] next week when we will take the testimony at your office.

Let me know what day it is to be and I will be there. Yours truly
John H. Senter

[*Page 170*]
Sept. 9th 1
R.H. Mardin Esq.,
Bristol,
Vermont.
Dear Sir,

Can you secure a bill of fifteen dollars against Wesley E. Dana of your place?

If you can, let me know at once and I will send you a writ. I don't care to dun him, I have done that enough, what I want is to secure it.

If you will inform me I will be much obliged and if you secure it I will pay you for all your trouble

Yours truly John H. Senter

Sept. 12th
E.W. Howe Esq.,
Northfield,
Vermont.
Dear Sir

Enclosed you will find a writ against [S.]P. Kelly, in favor of Wm. Kelsey. You know more about this case, than I do, and I want you to use your own discretion about serving this writ. If Kelly has wronged the old man, serve the writ, and if he has not, put the old man off. If you serve it, charge your fees to Kelsey. I do not have officers fees charged to me.

Yours truly
John H. Senter

[*Page 171*]
Sept 12th 1
Prof. Charles Dole,
Northfield,
Vermont.
Dear Sir,

Your favor of the 10th inst is just at hand, and in reply I will say that Edgerton has gone to Montpelier to school this fall. He talked strongly of going to Lewis College, but the next I knew he had gone to M.

No there are no young men here that would be likely to go this fall. I am very sorry that you are not to have a large class. I am desirous of having that college prosper.

Yours truly John H. Senter

Sept. 14th 1
Charles Newcomb Esq.,
Waitsfield,
Vermont.
Dear Sir,

I find on referrence to my letter book, that I wrote you a letter on the

30th [*one word illegible*], and I have no answer from you as yet. I dislike Charley to make you any cost in this matter, and so I write you again. I have an account against you in favor of S.D. Allen for the sum of \$5.96. This must be paid this week, or I shall have to collect it some other way.
Yours truly,
John H. Senter

[*Page 172*]
October 2nd 1
Clarence H. Pitkin Esq.,
Montpelier,
Vermont.
Friend Clarence,

I have got an allmighty bad cold, and I do not want to come to Montpelier this week unless it be necessary, now will you notify me by mail or telegraph, if the case of McAllister vs. Follett, gets [*one word illegible*] so that I can summon witnesses in season? I do not expect that it will of course, but do not know what may happen
Yours truly
John H. Senter

Sept. [27th] 1
George Brooks Esq.
E. Warren,
Vermont.
Dear Sir

I have in my hands for collection, an account against you of ballace due Dr. Solon Dodge of Lincoln, amounting to (\$18.00).

It must be paid to me at once to save you cost
Yours truly,
John H. Senter

[*Page 173*]
October 24th 1
John W. Gregory Esq.,
Waitsfield,
Vermont.
Brother John,

I have set the case of [*one word illegible*] vs Austin for trial next Friday [the] 28th, when we will endeavor to dispose of it.
Yours fraternally,
John H. Senter

Oct. 23rd 1
George M. Fisk Esq.,
Northfield,
Vermont

The hearing of Durant vs Pratt et al is set for the 26th at Wing's office, be sure and be there
Yours fraternally
John H. Senter

[*Page 174*]
Nov. [1st] 1
Asa Jackman Esq.
Lincoln,
Vermont.
Dear Sir

George Atkins of this town has placed in my hands for collection an account against you amounting to the sum of about ($11.00) eleven dollars for [roofing by] you. [*One or two words illegible*] your earliest attention must be given to this matter to save yourself costs.
Yours truly
John H. Senter

Nov. 3rd 1
Cinton Brackett Esq.,
Roxbury, Vt.
Dear Sir

Thomas Eagan of this Town informs me that he traded horses with you the other day, and that you represented the horse he got all right and that she is [blind] and has the scratches. Thomas is therefore of the oppinion that you ought to make it right with him, and unless you concluded to settle this matter peaceably, I shall be obliged to bring suit against you and make you trouble and costs
Yours truly
John H. Senter

[*Senter mistakenly copied the following letter directly on top of the preceding letter. It is almost entirely illegible except for the following:*]
[Oct. 27th] 1
Solon Dodge, M.D.,
Lincoln,
Vermont.
Friend Solon,
I wrote a letter to George Brooks [*remainder is illegible*]

[*Page 175*]
Nov. 1st 1
E.W. Bisbee Esq.,
Barre,
Vermont.
Friend Ed I will write you before long what time I will be at Montpelier. I am glad you are going in with me
Yours in haste
John H. Senter

November 1st 1
F.J. Green Esq.,
Waitsfield
Vermont.
Dear Sir,
I write you at the request of Miss Louisa Allen, in regard to her claim on the Carroll House. Her claim to day amounts to the sum of ($1249.10) twelve hundred forty nine and 10/100 dollars, and she will take ($1250.00) twelve hundred and fifty dollars for her claim any time this week.
Yours truly John H. Senter

[*Page 176*]
Nov. 7th 1
Clarence H. Pitkin Esq.,
Montpelier,
Vermont
Friend Clarence,
Enclosed you will [*one or two words illegible*] application for an appeal and a bond as you [requested] and advised. I don't [know that] I have drawn the papers right but I have done the best I know, I never [do any]

probate appeals and don't know anything about the business [*one or two words illegible*].
Yours truly
John H. Senter

Nov. 7th 1
James T. Sabin, Esq.,
Secretary Vermont Mutual Fire Insurance Company,
Montpelier,
Vermont
Dear Sir,

Enclosed you will policy of C.E. Billings, which he desires to surrender, he having sold the property therein insured to E.F. Hewitt who pays the mortgage at once.

Yours truly John H. Senter

[*Page 177*]
Nov. 7th 1
George W. Wing Esq.,
Dear Sir

Your favor received and contents noted. I will be ready to have that hearing here the 11th if nothing splits.

Yours truly
John H. Senter

Nov. 7th 1
G.M Fisk Esq.,
Northfield,
Vermont.
Dear Sir

The hearing in the case of Durant vs. Pratt et al will be here on Friday the 11th be sure and be here and bring the testimony and all the papers

Yours in haste
John H. Senter

[*Page 178*]
Nov 7th 1
Received of G.B. Newcomb ($2.00) two dollars it being the money paid [said] G.B. Newcomb, by James McGlaflin [for] Willis McGlaflin on the

29th day of October A.D. 1881. Leaving the matter of the keeping of sheep unsettled, as it was before. I also received ($1.80) one dollar and eighty cents for costs incurred in the suit of McGlaflin vs Newcomb and said suit [was lately] discontinued
John H. Senter
Atty for James McGlaflin

[*The following letter was copied very faintly and is illegible. It appears to be a letter about copies of documents in a legal matter.*]

[*Page 179*]
Nov. [20th] 1
Robert E. Long Esq.,
Waitsfield,
Vermont.
Friend Long,
Dear Sir,
Mr. [Flynn] Caroll of Warren has placed in my hands for collection an account against you for damage done to by your [tree] [*several words illegible*] adjusted at once, or he will [procede against you] for said damage. I shall not be at home for a week to come [*several words illegible*] will be done untill [*remainder is illegible*]

[*Page 180*]
Dec 12th 1
E.P. Barnham Esq.,
Roxbury,
Vermont.
Dear Sir
You will find enclosed your accts, which were placed in my hands for collection. I have done nothing with them. They are not worth the paper they are written on and never were
My charges are nothing.
Yours truly
John H. Senter

Dec. 12
Henry Kew Esq.,
Waitsfield,

Vermont.
Dear Sir

My acct against you for defending Robert [in] his liquor prosecution is long over due. I sent you a [statement] long ago, and I now desire it to be paid soon

Yours truly
John H. Senter

[*Page 181*]
Nov 21st 1
Messrs. Heath & Carlton,
Montpelier,
Vermont.
Gentlemen,

Jackson J. Pratt has this day paid me [$12.46] to settle your note against him. If you will send me the note I will pay the said [due] to your Mr. Heath at Chelsea.

I have sued Thomas [Eagan] on your acct. and if he does not settle I will you the writ. I used Geo. Wing for the justice.

Yours
John H. Senter

April [19th] 2
D.B. Schofield Esq.,
York,
Maine.
Dear Sir,

Having been employed as counsel in the matter of the [*one word illegible*] Factory property in Waitsfield Vermont which you sold to Mr. Stoddard, I am anxious to know the whole circumstance of your trade with Stoddard, so that I can procede understandingly.

Will you kindly give me what information you possess in regard to the matter and very much oblige

Your obed't Servant
John H. Senter

[*Page 182*]
[Apr 17th] 2
[*This letter was copied with too much water and the letters ran, making it almost entirely illegible. It appears to be about someone Senter knows who may owe some money. Senter wrote that the person in question is good for the money: "He will pay."*]

[*This letter was copied on the back of page 182:*]
April 25th 2
Vermont Mutual Fire Insurance Co.,
Montpelier,
Vermont.
Gentlemen,

Enclosed you will find an application for insurance of Asa M. Colby. Also two policies in favor of E.F. Hewitt which he wishes surrendered.

"Vide vale."
John H. Senter.

[*Page 183*]
April 21st 2
C.H. Pitkin, Esq.,
Montpelier
Vermont
Clarence

I have a question, upon which I should like your oppinion. If a school district fails to elect officers at the annual meeting, the old officers still hold their office, as the law provides they shall untill their successors are chosen. Now in such a case can new officers be elected at a called meeting, i.e. does such a vacancy exist as the statute contemplates? Sec 20th Vt Page 487, & 23rd Vt Page 416.

Yours
John H. Senter

[*This letter was copied on the back of page 183:*]
April 28th 2
Russell Flint, Esq.,
West Braintree,
Vermont.
Dear Sir

Levi Liberty of this town has placed in my hands for collection an account against you for ballance due him for labor performed for you, amounting to $9.07. Your immediate attention to this matter will save you costs, and unless I hear from you by the 4th of May I shall make you costs.
Yours truly
John H. Senter

[*Page 184*]
[*These letters were copied on the back of page 184:*]
April 26th 2
Geo. H. Richmond, Esq.,

Please send two [quires] of Justices Criminal Records, and if not ordered, oblige
Yours Truly,
J.H. Senter
for E.H. [Edgar]

April 26th
George Brooks, Esq.,
Warren,
Vermont.
Dear Sir,

Mr. Walter A. Bayly of [this] town has placed in my hands for [collection] an account against you and a Mr. [*name illegible*] which amounted to [$12.50] above one [year ago].

I respectfully request you to give this [your] earliest attention, as it will save you [costs.]
Yours truly
John H. Senter

[*Page 185*]
[*This letter was copied on the back of page 185:*]
April 29 2
K.H. Goodno, Esq.,

Rochester,
Vermont
Dear Sir

You are recognized for the sum of ($10.00) ten dollars in the case of

Goodno vs Cardell and whether you recolect it or not makes no difference. You can ascertain the fact by examining the records of Addison County Court, and you must pay it. If I do not hear from you soon or by the 6th of May, you will hear from me by the way of a writ.

Your attention had better be given to this matter at once, and so save yourself costs

Yours truly
John H. Senter

April [*date is illegible*]
R. Wainwright, Esq.,
Middlebury,
Vermont.
Dear Sir

Will you please send me a certified copy of the record in the case of Goodno vs Cardell, judg rendered at December Term 1880

Yours, John H. Senter
P.S. Send bill

[*Page 186*]
May 4th 2
[*addressee is illegible*]
Gentlemen,

Enclosed you will [find] seventy-five cents for which you will please send the Boston Evening Star.

Resp'y Yours
John H. Senter

May 11th 2
R. Wainwright, Esq.,
Middlebury,
Vermont.
Dear Sir,

Your favor was duly received, and in reply I will say that you may tax costs in the County Court, as that will be more than we can collect, as we have only $10.00 [paid], and then send me a certified copy of the record, but let me say that if Durant has not paid the clerk's bills in that case, as very likely he has not, you may send a bill of them to me, and I will see

about them although I do not agree to pay them myself I will have Cardell settle. Send me a bill of certified copies and I will pay that.
Yours truly
John H. Senter
(re Goodno vs Cardell)

[*Page 187*]
June 12th 2
Joseph A. Wing, Esq.,
Montpelier,
Vermont.
Dear Sir

Your favor of June 5th came to town by due course of mail, but I was out of town and did not return until late Saturday night, and so I will reply now.

I made an answer and copy for you in the case of Downing vs Lyford, and mailed the same to Mr. Clarence H. Pitkin on the last day of May with directions for him to file the answer and to give you the copy on receipt of the same, and I thought of course he had done it, but it seems by a letter he wrote to Lyford last Saturday that he was at Middlebury and did not get the letter on its arrival at Montpelier, had he been in town the answer would have been filed within the ten days you gave me at my request.

Had I been at home when your favor came to town I should have been out there at once and found out what the trouble was. I suppose Mr. Pitkin has now filed the answer and explained the matter to you.

Thanking you for your kindness in notifying me of the want of an answer and hoping everything is now satisfactory I remain your most humble servant
John H. Senter

[*Page 188*]
June 22nd 2
G. H. Whitney, Esq.,
Winchendon,
Mass.
Dear Sir,

Your favor of June 20th is at hand and its contents noted, and in reply I will say that H.J. Pratt of Warren, Washington County Vermont, is the owner of Williams note. It is put into my hands [for] collection, and if collected I am to [pay] the sum received by me to Mr. Pratt's [debt] on my

books he being my debtor. You can bring suit in Pratts name or mine [or] yours as will best suit you
Yours very truly
John H. Senter

[*The following seems to be answers to a series of questions rather than a letter:*]

Yes, [*one word illegible*]
Yes.
A very good country Practice.
Excelent.
Temperate.
Yes so far as known.
Should say that he was
One year and three months,
Should so consider him.
He would.
M.
He is
There are but two, O.D. Greene and E.W. Slayton

There is no Dr. C. Greene in Warren, but have answered these inquiries as though they were asked of Dr. O.D. Greene. In the Vermont Directory of Walton's Register it is entered as C. Greene but it is a mistake his name is O.D. Greene M.D. and is a graduate of the Medical College of Burlington Vermont

[*Page 189*]
June 15th 2
Giles H. Whitney, Esq.,
Winchendon,
Mass.
Dear Sir

I find your name in the list of attornies of the Wilber Mercantile Agency, and so send you the enclosed note for collection. The signor Williams is at work in your town for a farmer by the name of Parks, I believe.

Do not let Williams know that you have the claim untill you can secure it. He does not mean to pay and would be on his guard if he knew that you had the claim.

Please acknowledge receipt.
[*signature is illegible*]

[*This letter was copied on the back of page 189:*]
June 14th 2
Jerrymiah Crane, Esq.,
My Dear Sir,

George A. Atkins of this town has left in my hands for collection an account against you for his son Watson's work, which amounts to a ballance of ($39.65) thirty nine dollars and sixty-five cents.

Your earliest attention must given to this matter, or I shall be obliged to make you costs
Yours truly John H. Senter

[*Page 190*]
June 16th 2
Mr. Charles H. Heath
Montpelier,
Vermont.
Dear Sir,

Your favor of June 14th [is] at hand and in reply I will say [that,] if He who governs this universe [does] not interpose any obstacle, I will [be at] your office on the 20th day of June [*one word illegible*] to procede to the hearing of the [*one word illegible*] for pardon of Nathaniel Blair. [I have] written to C.H. Pitkin the same [as] requested. In regard to the case of [*one word illegible*] vs. Cardell, I will bring the $7.84 to you [I] do not know who is the attorney of record [*last few words and signature illegible*]

June 16th 2
Clarence H. Pitkin, Esq.,
Montpelier,
Vermont.
Dear Sir

I have received a letter from C.H. Heath, Esq., stating that [the] hearing in the matter Nathaniel [Blair's] pardon is to be at Heath & Carlton's [office] on the afternoon or evening of Tuesday June 20th. He also requested [that I] write you and inform you whether [I] could attend to it then or not, [*one word illegible*] and will be there at that time.
Yours truly John H. Senter

[*This letter was copied on the back of page 191:*]
[*Page 191*]
June 22nd 2
Clarence H. Pitkin, Esq.,
Montpelier,
Vermont.
Dear Sir

The Selectmen of Warren have made an application to the Probate Court in this district for a court of inquiry in regard to one Michael Coter of this town an insane person who we think has no settlement in this State, and whom we desire that the state should support at the insane asylum. I have asked the Probate Court to fix the hearing for the 5th day of July 1882. You will have a citation served on you and a copy of the application, and I also for the selectmen of Warren hereby notify you of said application for a court of inquiry, any information I can give you in regard to Coter I shall be glad to communicate to you at any time. I notify you personally and also by citation so that there can be no question of sufficiency of notice.

Yours truly
John H. Senter

[*The next page was stamped with the numbers 192 and 193. The letter was copied on the back of the page.*]

[*Page 192*]
June 22nd 2
Hon. Harvey N. Tilden
Montpelier
Vermont
Dear Sir

Enclosed you will find an application by the selectmen of this town for a court of inquiry in the matter of the insanity Michael Coter of this town. Will you be so kind as to fix the earliest date possible for the hearing, sign the citation and hand the same to Sheriff D.W. [Duffy] to serve on Mr. C.H. Pitkin. I should be glad if you could fix the date of hearing for the 5th day of July, 1882

If you will be so kind as to inform me by [postal] and of the time you fix upon you will greatly oblige me. I have left the date of hearing

blank so that will fix the date in the same, accordingly [as] you can have the hearing. There must be at least ten days notice to Mr. Pitkin or I would ask for an earlier date as the man Coter is dangerously insane and should be sent to Brattleboro at once
Very truly yours
John H. Senter

[*Page 193*]
June 26th 2
[George] A. Wheeler, Esq.,
Warren,
Vermont.
Dear Sir,

Mr. H.W. Lyford informs me that you have paid, Mr. C.H. Clay the note he left with me for collection. And I hereby notify you that the case of C.H. Clay vs you is discontinued. Mr. Clay ought to have informed that he had settled with you.
Yours truly
John H. Senter

[*There appears to be a second letter copied very faintly behind the following letter:*]

July 1st 2
Reuben B. Miller, Esq.,
Warren,
Vermont
Dear Sir,

I have an acct against you of [$8.00] in favor of C.A. Hanks. I have written you once before about and if you do not attend to this at once I shall send a writ
Yours truly
John H. Senter

[*Page 194*]
July 3rd 2
Daniel Barnard, Esq.,
Franklin,

N.H.
Dear Sir;-

I find your name on the list as attorney for the Wilber Mercantile Agency, and so I adress you in regard to one Wells Blake who lives in Franklin. I have in my hands for collection a note against him which amounts to the sum of $22.00. Now if you can collect the same or any part thereof sufficient to pay costs by attachment or trustee, I will send the note to you.

Unless he has changed very much from what he was when he left here, it will be better not to let him know that you have the note untill you can secure it.

If you can find any chance to secure this debt I will send this note at once, as the owner is very anxious to secure and cares very much more to make Blake pay it than he does for the money

Please to answer as soon as convenient and oblige yours truly
John H. Senter

[*Page 195*]
July 6th 2
Hon. Charles Heath
Montpelier,
Vermont.
Dear Sir;

James McGlaflin of this town received a letter from you recently about a matter left in your hands by one Merill, and desires me to say to you that while he denies all legal liability to Mr. Merill, he was missinformed about the [chair] and is willing to make that right, he has left with me five dollars which I will send you if you desire it, in full settlement, and if this does not satisfy you we will pay nothing, but fight. (44°40' or fight) let me know at once your determination, John H. Senter

July 6th 2
Clarence H. Pitkin Esq.,
Montpelier,
Vermont.
Dear Sir:-

Enclosed you will [find the] amended prayer to bill James [*one word illegible*] Austin et al. If it is all [right] file it, if not make one [to] file and oblige yours truly
John H. Senter

[*Page 196*]
July 6th 2
Reuben B. Miller, Esq.,
Warren,
Vermont.
Dear Sir;-

I have in my hands, for collection a note against you in favor of Rev. Mr. Walbridge. This must be paid at once to save you costs

Yours truly
John H. Senter

July 6th 2
John Cardell Esq.,
Warren,
Vermont
Dear Sir;-

Alonzo Parsons has left in my hands for collection an acct against you for shingles, amounting to $5.00 without interest

Please attend to this at once and save yourself costs

Yours truly
John H. Senter

[*Page 197*]
July 8th 2
E.W. Bisbee, Esq.,
Barre,
Vermont.
Brother Bisbee;-

Will you do me a favor? D.H. Steel of this town bought last season a wagon of Jackson & Townshend of your place, now I want to know if he bought it in his own name, and if not in whose name did he buy it? If you will find out for me I will endeavor to reciprocate sometime

Yours truly John H. Senter

July 11th 2
Hon. L.G. Hinkley
Chelsea,
Vermont
Dear Sir:-

Enclosed you will find ($7.84) seven dollars and eighty [four] cents. This money is amount of costs which the defendant was ordered to pay the plaintiff, in the case of John Colby vs Edwin Cardell, at the June Term A.D. 1882. I do not know the name of the attorney for the plaintiff since Judge Rowell retired from the [court] so I pay it into [court]
Yours truly
John H. Senter

[*Page 198*]
July 13th 2
Giles H. Whitney, Esq.,
Winchendon,
Mass.
Dear Sir;-

Your favor is just received, by reason of my being away from home, when it arrived.

Ten dollars is rather a small [amt.] to take for that note after deducting costs. I have not seen Mr. Pratt but I [think] as you do that perhaps it is the [*one word illegible*] thing to do, and so I will instruct [him] to settle at that rate if you can't do [better], but make him pay the cost [*one word illegible*].
Yours truly
John H. Senter

July 13th 2
Hiram Atkins,
Montpelier,
Vermont.
Dear Sir;-

I can and will see that Waitsfield, Warren, Fayston, and Roxbury are represented at the District Convention at Wells River July 27th, if you wish, I shall of course be there. What it is up any way? Is our friend! Davenport on the war path or what is in the air? Let me know at once if you want I should start those delegates.
Yours truly
John H. Senter
P.S. I am glad to see, that you are combing out Davenport. He is nothing but a demagogue.

[*Page 199*]
[*This page was detached from the copying book and placed in the Index just before the "IK" tab.*]
July 12th 2
Hon. W.H.H. Bingham,
Montpelier, Vermont.
Dear Sir;-

Yesterday I called on Mr. Charles T. McArty of Fayston in regard to the Margret Bittis notes. He told me at first that he had a sett-off, but when I asked what it was, he related the following tale, which does not amount to much of a sett-off.

He says he took some cattle of Bettis to sell, that he sold some of them to his father-in-law for \$85.00, and some or rather the remainder to another man for \$80.00, that he agreed to give Bettis what he got for the cattle, after paying him for his trouble, he gave Bettis his notes for [\$140], and he now says his father-in-law went into bankruptcy and he did not get much out of it and the other man had not paid him as yet, and he thought he ought not to be obliged to pay Bettis for that reason. Will you send me at once some blank writs signed by a Morristown Justice and I will see if he will pay, but this must be done at once. [He] is good now but slipping and may shift his property, and leave me in the cold unless I move at once

Yours truly
John H. Senter

[*Page 200*]
[*This page was torn loose but was inserted in the correct place in the copying book. The letters were copied on the back of the page.*]
July 19th 2
Hon. W.H.H. Bingham,
Stowe,
Vermont.
Dear Sir;-

Your favor was duly received and I acted at once; the debt is well secured by the attachment, and it was the only way he would secure it.

He says he will fight but I don't see what he is to fight about, but undoubtedly he will be up there before, the return day [of] the writ and make some arrangement.

I am sorry to learn of your illness, but [glad] to hear that you are better. I hope [*last line and signature are too faint to read*]

July 22nd 2
H.N. Taplin, Jr.,
Treasurer of Vermont Mutual F.I. Co.,
Montpelier,
Vermont.
Dear Sir;-

Enclosed you will find check for fifty dollars, which please to pass to my credit.

Send me premium notes as per inclosed cards. I believe they are already charged to me, if not charge them. Also send me a writ against Whitney of Granville, leave court day blank.

I will try and get something down there soon
Yours very truly
John H. Senter

[*Page 201*]
Aug 17th 2
Hon. Wm. P. Dillingham
Waterbury,
Vermont
Friend Will;-

I have brought suit against Bucklin, and have also learned that when G.N. Hanks deeded these same premises to Banister he made a stipulation with Mr. B. that the proceeds of the same when sold should be applied to the payment of his debt to his father the plaintiff in our suit. So we have an equitable consideration for the contract, which originated from G.N. Hanks and Banister acted simply as an agent in taking that contract.

I have examined the records in regard to the [Way] mortgage, and find that the mortgage was made Oct 6th 1879, was placed on file in the Clerk's office Oct. 16th 1879, and was recorded April 25th 1882. I give below a verbatim copy of the condition of said mortgage which is rather awkward in the wording but I guess it good. "The conditions of this deed are such that if "I shall well and truly pay or cause to be paid all [moneys] heretofore loaned or may hereafter loan of said Cardell, L.E. Hanks or either of them and in case I shall [see] them collectively or individually harmless from all papers, notes or obligations that they E. Cardell & L.E.

Hanks [have] heretofore signed, or may hereafter sign or in any way become holden for me and I shall see them harmless of all liability to me".

You see that the scribe who drew the mortgage was not a master of the English language but he got in enough such as it is.

Yours truly
John H. Senter

[*Page 202*]
Aug. 17th 2
M. J. Francisco, Esq.,
Secretary Vermont Accident Association
Rutland,
Vermont.
Dear Sir;-

H.W. Lyford of this place was accidentally injured so as to disable him for a few days, about a fortnight ago, and he immediately wrote informing you of his accident the fourth of August, and has received no answer from you as yet. Also Mr. Milford Bayley received a receipt from you for his claim about ten days ago, and immediately returned the same to you, and has not as yet received any answer from you. What is the matter? Do you receive the communications? And if you do receive them, why do you not answer? Or have they been miscarried? Please to inform me at your earliest convenience. Yours truly John H. Senter

[*This letter was copied on the back of page 202:*]
Aug 22nd 2
Josiah Holden, Esq.,
Waitsfield,
Vermont
My Dear Sir;-

Enclosed you will find blank for a copy of record in the case of State vs Stoddard. I have filled it out so far as I can without the original papers to save you the trouble will you kindly fill out the rest sign it and return to me, so that I can enter it at County Court

Yours very truly
John H. Senter

[*Page 203*]
[*These letters were copied on the back of page 203.*]

Aug 23rd 2
Mrs. Margaret Baird
Fayston,
Vermont.
Dear Madam;-

I send to you in this letter a bond for costs in your case against Charles Clay for trespass. I want you should sign it and get a good responsible man to sign it with you and bring it out to me. Your case will come to trial this fall and I want to see you and the boys about it

Yours truly
John H. Senter

Aug 23rd 2
Fred C. Richardson,
E. Montpelier,
Vermont
Dear Fred;-

Enclosed you will find bond for costs in your case against James. I want you to get a good responsible man to sign it with you and return it to me so that I can be ready for trial. Your [case] is set for the jury and will probably be this fall.

Yours truly
John H. Senter

[*Page 204*]
[*These letters were copied on the back of page 204:*]
Aug. 25th 2
O.W. Orcutt, Esq.,
Roxbury,
Vermont.
Dear Sir;-

I saw Fred Cardell the other day in regard to your notes and mortgage and he refused to sign the same.

He says that he wrote to you about this matter.

He very evidently wants to <u>back</u> <u>out</u>. I await your further orders.

Yours very respectfully,
John H. Senter

Aug [25th 2]
Boston Weekly Globe
Boston,
Mass.
Gentlemen;-

Please to send a copy [of] the Weekly Globe 14 months to each of [the] following addresses.

Dr. O. D. Greene Warren, V^{t}.
George W. Drew Warren V^{t}.
and William S. Martin East Warren, V^{t}.

You will find check for [\$2.^{25}] enclosed

Yours truly
John H. Senter

[*Page 205*]
[*This letter was copied on the back of page 205:*]
Aug. 25th 2
Clarence H. Pitkin, Esq.,
Montpelier,
Vermont.
Friend Clarence;-

Our man Coter, that I made application to the probate court for an investigation concerning, and who I afterward told you had become sane, is now raving crazy, and must be seen to at once.

Please to inform me of the earliest possible moment that you can attend to the investigation, and also be kind enough to speak to the Judge so that he will be at Montpelier.

Yours very truly,
John H. Senter

[*Pages 206-07*]
June 4th 3
M. J. Francisco, Esq.,
Rutland,
Vermont.
Dear Sir:

Hiram Wood of E. Warren, Vermont, on the 15th day of August, A.D. 1883 took out an insurance certificate, No. 2640, in the Vermont Accident Association of Rutland Vermont. About the middle of

November 1882, while engaged at his work as a wood chopper, he was thrown backwards over a [log], and was injured in his spine just below his shoulder blade on his right side. The place injured became very much discolored and swollen, but he is an ambitious hard working man, and he thought he would not stop work, although very lame and stiff, after two or three days he was obliged to, and did stop work, on the 22nd of Nov. [a] medical examiner here, Dr. O.D. Greene [was] called, as Mr. Wood continued to grow worse. Soon after this Dr. Halett of Moretown was called, both of these M.Ds. examined Mr. Wood and both were satisfied that his disability was occasioned by the fall and injury above mentioned.

He had neglected notifying you untill after this examination, as I understand because he was in hopes to be able to work, and did not wish to make any call on the [association] if he could avoid it.

He has not done an hours work since he tried those two days, after his injury, and has been ever since, and is now entirely helpless. All of these statements can be proven to your satisfaction. He has written to you or had others several times about the matter, but for some, to him, unknown reason, you seem to entirely ignore him. What he wants is that you should thouroughly examine this matter and satisfy yourself [about it] and if you find it an honest claim to settle honestly with him, if not an honest claim, or if you are not satisfied that it is, he wants nothing, but you will either fairly hear and investigate this claim [or] the courts will. I don't intend this as a threat, as I have always found you square [and] upright, I expect to now.

This man is an honest, hard working man and I do not think the Vermont Accident Association, cares to [*three or four words illegible*] settling an honest claim with such a man for a technical quibble, if they do it shall be made known.

I request you to lay this matter before the directors, and to at least treat [him] with consideration enough to answer [this] letter, and not remain as you [have] with Mr. Wood entirely dumb.

Yours truly
John H. Senter

[*Page 208*]
June 4th 3
Selectmen of Hancock,
Gentlemen;-

Mr Charles Stone informs me that undertook to play a sort of hocus-pocus settlement with him about his injury which happened to him by reason of the insufficiency of a bridge in your town.

Gentlemen perhaps you can make yourselves believe that you have accomplished a shrewd financial stroke in what you have done with this poor simple man, but you cannot make anybody else think so. The kind of settlement you [have tried] to force onto Charley will not stand [as] long in law as you were in making it. You must either make an honest settlement with him, paying what is just and square or I shall procede to bring suit against your town and give you a chance [to] explain your so called "Settlement" in court.

Yours truly
John H. Senter
P.S. Write me your determination what you will do, and I will give you untill June 16th to answer this letter, after that costs will be made if I do not hear from you.
John H. Senter

[*Page 209*]
June 12th 3
Hon. Charles H. Heath,
Montpelier,
Vermont.
Dear Sir;-

In accordance with your request per your Mr. Fay, the case of E.R. Long vs. William John Maxwell will be continued untill June 29th 9 a.m. same place, at which time and place I am desirous of cleaning you out.

Yours truly,
John H. Senter

[*This letter was copied with too much water and is almost completely illegible. It appears to be similar to the previous letter.*]
June 12th 2
Hon. C.H. Heath
Montpelier,
Vermont.
Dear Sir;-
[*remainder is illegible except for occasional words*]

[*Page 210*]
June 13th 3
Osmand D. Clark, Esq.,
Montpelier,
Vermont.
Friend Osmand;-

Your favor is just received, and contents duly noted. In reply I will say that Mrs. Wallace has a farm, or rather William L. Wallace has, here in Warren. I don't know how many acres, enough any how, for the more land such as that is one owns the worse off they are. There is an old house on the place, and a large part of it has been overgrown with bushes. There is quite a part of it timbered land, but it is hard wood timber, and hard wood timber in this town is not worth anything. The place is dear at $300.00, don't think you will be liable to find a customer.
[*signature was cut off at the bottom of the page*]

June 12th 3
Geo. W. Wing, Esq.,
Montpelier,
Vermont.
Dear Sir;-

Your favor of June 10th is at hand, and contents noted, in reply I will say that we have had some consultation with Mr. Lyford, and can now say that we will not accept of either Mr. Plumley or Ferrin.

We will accept either W.P. Dillingham, C.H. Heath, M.E. Smilie or S.C. Shurtleff alone. I believe you have never given us a choice, but your man [Downing] [hangs round] a man a while and [sounds] him then proposes him as master that wont go down. Yours fraternally
John H. Senter

[*Page 211*]
February [12th] 4
Charles W. Bragg, Esq.,
E. Warren,
Vermont.
Friend Bragg;-

S. Banister has placed in my hands for immediate collection an account against you in his favor. Call and see me at your earliest convenience.

Yours truly
John H. Senter

Warren, V^{t}. Feb. 14th 84
47.^{00}
F.E. Donahue
Forty-Seven ——————————————————— which if
Nathan [Treater] delivers one 2 ½ cords of wood as agreed the present winter, is to be in full of all acct and [matter] between us to date
John H. Senter

[*Page 212*]
Feb. 15th 4
Lervis Story, Esq.,
Fairfax
Vermont
Dear Sir:

I have in my hands for collection a note payable to G.W. Cardell which today amounts to the sum of twelve dollars. This must be paid at once to save you costs.

Yours truly
John H. Senter

Feb. 15th 4
Daniel Tarbell, Esq.,
E. Granville,
Vermont.
Dear Sir:

By reason of the thaw I am unable to come to your place Thursday but if you desire I will come on the 21st of this month. If that day will suit you write me, and I will come.

Yours truly
John H. Senter

[*Page 213*]
Feb. 17th 4
Hon. W.H.H. Bingham,
Montpelier
Vermont.

Dear Sir;-

Enclosed I send application of O.H. Richardson for insurance on mill. This is the one I told you of sometime since. You may think I am stradling my agency out when I get as far as Middlesex village, but Mr. R. is an old acquaintance of mine. The rate you will observe I leave blank. I think the risk an exceptionally safe one, and my judgment would be 43%, but if you do not [coinside] with my judgment you can put it at 50%. If you do not wish to take it at 50% reject it. Yours fraternally

John H. Senter

Feb. 26th 4

Lervis Story, Esq.,

Fairfax,

V^{t}.

Dear Sir:-

Your favor enclosing twelve dollars came promptly to hand, and I [return] your note, which amounts to $11.52, writing letter 50. = $12.00.

Yours fraternally

John H. Senter

[*Page 214*]

Feb. 17th 4

C.M. Wilds, Esq.,

Middlebury

Vermont.

Friend Charles:-

Will you please to send me from the clerk's office the copy [of] appeal and the specifications in the case [of] Briggs vs Ralphs, as we are to try the case before the referees at Granville Feb. [29th]. You will thus oblige very much

Yours truly John H. Senter

Feb. 17th 4

F.N. Holman, Esq.,

W. Randolph,

Vermont.

Dear Sir:-

I suppose you have been informed by Mr. Huse that our case Briggs vs. Ralph is to be heard Feb. 29th

Of course you understand that we ought to have a rule issued, and that as you are the appealing party it belongs to you to procure the same under the rule of court. I did not know but you might have forgotten it, so I mention that you may be sure to have it on time.

Yours truly

[*signature was cut off at the bottom of the page*]

[*Page 215*]

Feb. 27th 4

James [Minehan], Esq.,

Lincoln,

Vermont.

Dear Sir:-

I have in my hands for collection an account against you amounting to the sum of $9.08 which together with fifty cents for this letter making $9.58 must be paid at once or I shall make you costs.

Unless I hear from you by March 8th I shall bring suit.

Yours truly,

John H. Senter,

P.S. The account is in favor of Dr. J.S. Dodge of Lincoln.

Feb. 27th 4

Marshall Chaffee, Esq.,

Roxbury

Vermont

Dear Sir:-

I have in my hands for collection an account against you in favor of J.S. Dodge M.D. of Lincoln it amounts to the sum of $34.58, including interest to date.

Please attend to this at once

Yours truly

John H. Senter

[*Page 216*]

March 8th 4

Mrs Lizzie Griffith

Waitsfield

Vermont

Dear Madam:

Your favor of the 4th inst is at hand and its contents duly noted. In reply I will say that I do not exactly understand what you mean, or how you expect I or any one else can get your papers served until we find out where your husband is I have writen several letters [to] find out where he is and so far have been unable to find him, if you want to be to the [expense] advertizing the bill by publication [in] some newspaper, all right – but it will [cost] you some twenty dollars extra, or if you [*entire line illegible due to faint copying*] satisfy you, you had better employ [some other] lawyer, as I do not care to be found [failing] when I am doing all that is possible.

I have explained this matter to you when I have seen you the best I could. I do not understand what you [blame me] for, and as I have done my duty by you [in] the matter I do not care.

Yours truly
John H. Senter

[*Page 217*]
Mar 9th 4
[C.] Hubbard Esq., Selectman of Granville
Dear Sir:-

On examination, I think [the] town Agent, or an attorney for the town [should] make the disclosure of the town. [It is] more usual for an attorney for the [town] to make the disclosure in writing, [but] if you prefer to manage your case with-[out an] attorney I have written out a disclosure for your town so far as I could [with] the facts at hand, and I have written [*one or two words illegible*] where you must fill in the [*one or two words illegible*] and amount. It will be necessary [for the] town officers who know about the [*several words illegible*] to testify as to the [*entire line illegible*]. If after hearing the justice should decide that the town is chargeable [I] should advise an appeal as you [can] surely win in County Court, but if [you] do have to take an appeal, be sure [to] do it right pay the justice twenty-five cents and furnish bail. If you [should] want any thing of me I shall be [at] Montpelier House, Montpelier [for] all of this week but shall come to Warren Saturday night, shall be [at] Roxbury Saturday afternoon.

Yours truly
John H. Senter

[*Pages 218-19*]
[*The beginning of a long letter on these two pages was copied with too much water*

and is largely illegible. Fortunately, a nearly identical letter was recopied in its entirety on pages 220-225, so the legible fragments of the letter on these two pages have been omitted here.]

[*Pages 220-25*]
March 30th 4
Hon. B.B. Smalley,
Burlington,
Vermont.
Dear Sir:-

Your kind favor of the 22nd was only received by me Saturday night on my return from Montpelier, or I should have replied ere this.

You say, that of course you will see me at our State convention, that is not at all probable as you will observe from what follows. In regard to my opinion of your bring[ing] a delegate to the National Convention, I have this to say. I did not, and do not think that there was or is one democrat in Vermont, but what expects and desires your election. If a man in Vermont that can command the respect and exert the influence in our National Councils, that you can, I do not know of him, of course you will go to Chicago at the head of our delegation, and go to as the unanimous choice of your party. I don't believe Davenport himself would have it otherwise. The whole party has not as yet gone raving mad, as they must be not to send you.

As to the personnel of the delegation, I quite agree with you, that they should be "cool level-headed men," and I would add one or two other to me quite as essential qualifications, i.e. they should also be clean and respectable men, with brains, men who will honor the office, and not be a reproach and disgrace to the party. If we can't do anything else here in Vermont, let us so conduct our party, that it shall be entitled to the respect even of our opponents. I for one do not wish the democracy of Vermont represented at Chicago with any such timber as our Republican friends used four years ago when the sent L. Bart Cross, perhaps they can afford to be sneered at but we can't. Undoubtedly Bart contributed liberally to their campaign fund, the same as no doubt Bascom has to ours, but if that is to be the criterion of fitness, why not set the office up at auction and knock it down to the highest bidder and not go through the formula of a convention?

John C. Burke, Esq., of Albany is the right man for the place, I think, he is cool level-headed clean, able, and respectable. I most cordially [approve of his selection] and would were I to take any part in the convention heartily support him for that position. With [Amos Aldrich] I am not personally acquainted, but from what I hear of him, think he would be all right. I should also be pleased to see the Hon. W.H.H. Bingham a delegate. We might well be proud of such a delegation which would have both character and brains.

Then so far you and I agree, but now there comes a trifling difference of opinion, which [I] must express though with great hesitancy and diffidence. In the first place I will state my position in regard to, and my relations with the chairman of our State Committee.

Of Hiram Atkins I have the greatest respect and esteem. He has always been very friendly to me both personally and politically, and I fully appreciate his kindness to me, he has conferred many favors upon me which have been far beyond my power to reciprocate, but I have in return done the best I could. I have stood by him through thick and thin, but there is a Rubicon over which my regard and respect for him will not ferry me, and so if I do cross it I must <u>wade</u>.

I have always worked with him in our state politics, and while I remain in the party [I] shall never go into any fight against him, although in this matter of delegates, I cannot work with him. So much for my relations with him. Now Mr. Atkins has <u>mentioned</u> the name of Frank Haven Bascom to me as <u>his</u> <u>choice</u> for a delegate from this County and I have very frankly expressed my opinion to him about the matter, he has expostulated with me but to no avail, he has tried to convince me, but I have, as he well knows, remained unconvinced. Now I am struck with the to me wonderful <u>coincidence</u> of your solicitude for Bascom, and it has occurred to me, however strange and chimerical it may seem to you, that Hiram has been the moving [cause] of your favor to me in regard to Bascom. I am well aware with what [pertenasity] he sticks to those whom [he] thinks to be his friends, which is very commendable in him, so long as personal friendship does not produce party dishonor. I may be and probably am wrong in this surmise, but I answer your letter on that hypothesis.

Personally I am on good terms with Mr. Bascom and wish well, but that has nothing to do with his fitness as a delegate. In my opinion (since you flatter me by asking it) his selection as a delegate would be a very unwise move. I hardly think Mr. Atkins appreciates the position he will place the party of this County in by such a course, if he were to canvass even Montpelier with a purpose of finding how the matter was he would be astonished to find that the better class of democrats were disgusted with the idea, and throughout the county he would find that no other man than himself could pull Bascom through. I think Mr. Atkins has asked several leading democrats this question, "Which do you prefer Bascom or G.B. Evans of Moretown, and of course they have said Bascom, but that is not exactly fair, as one man of considerable influence said to me, "Who in hell wants either of them"? They do not think and I do not think we are driven to that alternative yet, if we are God help the party!

The selection of such men for delegates [and] the nomination of such men generally is one great reason why our party remains so weak in this state. Many young men of liberal ideas are deterred from voting with us by such a course, and such a course [persisted] in will drive others out of the party.

You will think I am putting this strong but could you or Mr. Atkins hear what I do about the matter you would see things different. Very likely Atkins has told you that I am influenced by Henry Oviatt in this matter, as he intimated that to me, but he is mistaken, for I did not even know how Oviatt stood untill Atkins told me. Mr. Smalley I have no personal feelings in this matter & have "no axes to grind." I am not a sore head [for I] have always had in the party every position *[one or two words illegible]* accept, but I must and do emphatically protest against Bascom's election.

Frank has interviewed me lately, sent as I thought by Hiram, and I told him I did not feel at liberty to support him, he asked me as between himself and Evans if I would not support him and I said yes, but what in hell has Evans to do with the matter? Why not say S.C. Shurtleff, B.P. White, W.H.H. Bingman, Homer W. Heaton, Hiram Atkins or some man of that stump? Are we so d—d hard up that it must be either Bascom or Evans, if so good bye for me, I will step down and out.

However I do not wish to make any disturbance in the party, if I could, nor to try to force my opinions against the wishes or the policy of either you or Mr. Atkins, and I shall not, for two reasons, the first, because I am not, so egotistical as to think it would amount to any thing, if I should, and secondly, because I will not under any circumstances go in to any fight with a man who has placed me under [as] many obligations to him as has Mr. Atkins, and as I am convinced from your letter that he is bound to push Bascom at all hazards and I can't prevent it by peacfull means, I will take a back seat.

Therefore I think that I will not attend the State convention, as under the circumstances [I] think it would not be best, for I certainly [should] kick if Bascom's name was proposed, [as] I never will be an abettor of my party's dishonor, so I will as gracefully as possible retire from the battle and the party and [let] those wiser than I run the machine [*one or two words illegible*] themselves, I do not mean that I shall ever be anything else but a democrat, but simply that I will take my foolish head out of politics as far as any active service is concerned.

Please to excuse this long letter as you asked me for my honest opinion and I have given it squarely and bluntly. I should very much rather talk than write, and if I knew when you were at Burlington any time this week or the first of next, I would come down, as I shall be at Montpelier, if you write to me during that time direct to Montpelier, Montpelier House.

I want you to accept the nomination for Governor and so allow us to have a candidate for that office we shant be ashamed of.

Yours sincerely
John H. Senter

[*Page 226*]
April 21st 4
George Berry, Esq.,
Waitsfield, Vermont.
Dear Sir:- On my return from Montpelier I received a letter from you, in which you say you expect some trouble with Godfrey Sumner about a cow and that you shall want my services, if you do. I shall be happy to assist you, but perhaps you do not understand my terms. If a client wishes to retain me against a prospective lawsuit, I charge five dollars retainer. If you want me on those terms, I will charge you five dollars whether I do any thing or not. If you do not wish me to do that, I shall feel at liberty to act for Mr. Sumner should he desire.

Let me hear from you at once

Yours truly
John H. Senter

April 21st 4
J.S. Dodge M.D.,
Lincoln,
Vermont.

Friend Solon:-

I learned from Mr. Gore that you had returned to Lincoln, and now I can go to work for you. I will sue Chaffee at once. Your Mr. Minehan has been over here to see me but I was gone, if he has not paid you I will bring suit against him, as he is clearly liable.

Yours

John H. Senter

[Page 227]

April 21st 4

H.B. Cady, Esq.,

Waitsfield,

Vermont.

My Dear Sir:

Enclosed I send you bill of services [for] Parker's case, and I will say right here [that] this bill must now be paid or fixed up [some] way or I shall bring suit against you. The services were rendered for you and at your request and are very reasonable, and must [be] paid. I do not desire to hurry anyone [but] it is time this matter was closed up and unless I hear from you by May 1st I shall send an officer.

Yours very respectfully

John H. Senter

[*Senter copied Cady's bill on this page:*]

H.B. Cady on account with

John H. Senter.

1879							Dr.
June 18	To 1 day defending Parker Cady						5.00
Sept Term	" Term & Atty fees. State vs. Cady (two cases)						10.00
1880							
March Term		"	""""	"	("	")	10.00
Sept	"	"	"	"	("	")	10.00
		" Int on above					8.00
							$43.00

I suspose you [have] a charge against me for pictures, and I have not figured the interest very fine on you, but if you wish to settle now, and I make this offer only for the purpose of settling with out costs or trouble, send me $30.00 and I will square accts with you, otherwise I shall seek to recover for the last cent my due.

[*Page 228*]
April 21st 4
C.H. Clay, Esq.,
Waitsfield,
Vermont.
Dear Sir:-

Enclosed you find bill of your account with me. You will remember that you gave me a note to collect against one George Wheeler for collection, and afterwards settled with him yourself, and did not notify me. I brought suit as you instructed and then found your receipt cutting off the note, so I paid the officer, and withdrew the suit, now I want my [pay]
Yours
John H. Senter

[*Copy of the bill for C.H. Clay:*]
C.H. Clay in account with
John H. Senter

1882			Dr.
June 17	To writ you vs Wheeler		1.00
"	"	" Cash Pd Officer	1.50
"	"	" Intr	.30
			2.80

[*Page 229*]
Ellen Mahuron
Warren,
Vermont.
Dear Madam:-

I enclose bill of my services rendered for you. It has run sometime and I should like to have it closed up. So please to remit at once and oblige
Yours very truly, John H. Senter

[*Copy of the bill for Ellen Mahuron:*]
Ellen Mahuron
In account with
John H. Senter

1881		Dr.
November 26	To writ You vs. Joseph P. Tucker	$1.00
December 19	" One Day Trial of Your Case vs. Tucker	3.00
"	"""" Execution " " " "	.25
"	" " Interest on Same	.75
		$5.00

April 21st 4
Mrs. Arvilla Hanks,
Warren,
Vermont.
Dear Madam:-

I have an account left in my hands for collection against you amounting to some ($8.00) that together with fifty cents for this letter must be paid at once to save you costs.

Yours very truly
John H. Senter

[*Page 230*]
April 21st 4
Michael Moriarty, Esq.,
Waitsfield
Vermont.
My Dear Sir:-

I have in my hands for collection an account against you of ($2.25) in favor of Daniel Austin of this place.

Please attend to this at once and oblige,

Yours very truly
John H. Senter

April 21st 4
O.W. Orcutt, Esq.,
Roxbury,
Vermont.
Dear Sir:-

I enclose writ vs. Marshall Chaffee which I want secured, do your best, if you know of any body owing Chaffee enough to trustee have his name inserted as trustee. Yours truly
John H. Senter

[*Pages 231-32*]
April 21st 4
William Strong, Esq.,
Waitsfield,
Vermont.
Dear Sir:-

Sometime last winter as you will remember, I and one Mr. Joslyn made a bet of five dollars which was deposited in your hands. The bet was as follows. I said I had a cow that would come in in April that was giving eleven quarts of milk per day. Mr. Joslyn turned up his nose at the statement of 11 qts per day for any cow, and I said that I had a five dollar bill in my pocket that said my cow would give 11 qts that day or the next day he immediately put up the money and I did the same. Well sir I did not bet that my cow would calve in April, or any thing of that kind, I bet she would give 11 qts of milk that day or the next. I measured her milk carefully for a week and she gave 82 qts that next week, and I can prove it, she gave 12 ½ qts. the next day which was the day I bet on but I took her average for week so Joslyn would not say there was any hocus pocus about one day. I now understand that he claims the money on the ground that she will not calve this April, and has sent a man to see her, to find out, well I don't myself think she will calve this April, but I do claim that when she would calve is no part of my bet, but if he insists that it was, one thing is sure no particular April was named and I will endeavor to accomodate the gentleman and have her go to bull in [summer] so that she will calve next April, any how.

But joking aside I claim that bet, and I hereby notify you not to pay my money to any one but myself. If Mr. Joslyn claims his of course I cannot collect it but I claim I have fairly won it; and by all the wager rules it is mine, but if he demands his money I have nothing to say but you must not pay him or anybody else my money, the five dollars I put in your hands to any one but me. If you do I shall hold you responsible,
Yours
J.H. Senter

[*Page 232*]
[*Bill for Fred Parker:*]
Warren Vermont April 22nd 1884
Fred Parker
In account with

John H. Senter

1883		Dr.
Sept. Term Wash. Co. Ct.	To Term and Atty fees Grundy vs. You	7.00
" " "	" " Cash Paid Clerk's bills	1.48
March " "	" Term and Atty fees Grundy vs. You	7.00
		$15.48

Fred I do not send this to dun you or any thing of the kind but I have adopted a rule to send a statement of acct. to each of my clients at the close of each term of court so that they may know just how big my bill is as they go along, and not think I am bleeding them.
Yours truly
John H. Senter

[*Page 233*]
April 22nd 4
W.G. McAllister, Esq.,
Waitsfield,
Vermont.
My Dear Sir:

I enclose cost bond which I want you to sign and get some other responsible man to sign, and return to me, so that I can file it in your case in compliance with the rules of court. I also enclose bill of my service rendered in your case. Not as a dun, but I have adopted a rule to send a bill of my services to each client after each term so that they may know just what I am charging them, and then they cannot say that I have been unfair. After this I shall send a bill after each term of court.

Please to understand I do not mean to dun [*last line is faint and illegible*]
Yours truly, [*signature illegible*]

[*Bill for W.G. McAllister:*]
Warren Vermont April 22nd 1884
W.G. McAllister,
In account with
John H. Senter

1884	Statement of Account	Dr.
Jun 17	To Writ you vs Josiah Smith	1.00

" 29	" 1 Day on trial of you vs. Josiah Smith	5.00
Feb. 14	" Replevin Writ You vs Patrick and Josiah Smith	2.00
" "	" " Bond " "	1.00
March Term	" Term and Attorney fee you vs Smiths	7.00
" "	" Cash Pd Clerks bill	1.48
		$17.48

[*Page 234*]
April 22nd 4
Franklin Stoddard, Esq.,
Warren,
Vermont.
Dear Sir:-

I enclose a bill of my services in Hill vs. Hewitt. This is not a dun or any thing of the kind, but simply a statement so you may know just how the account stands. I have adopted the rule of making a statement of acct to each client after each term of court, so they will all know exactly how the charges stand. I also enclose cost bond for you to sign and return to me so you can be ready for trial, the case is referred to M.E. Smilie and H.W. Kemp [*one or two words illegible*] men, and the case is to be tried in June.

[*several words illegible*] [call] and see me, and we will [*last one or two lines and signature illegible*]

[*Bill for Franklin Stoddard:*]
Warren Vermont [*one word illegible*]
Franklin Stoddard
In account with John H. Senter

1883		Dr.
June 11	To Co. Ct writ (Special declaration) Hill vs. Hewitt	$3.00
Sept Term	" Term and Atty fees Hill vs Hewitt	7.00
" "	" Cash Pd Clerk's Bills	1.38
1884		
March Term	" Term and Atty fees Hill vs Hewitt	7.00
" "	" Clerk's Bills	.48
[1882]		
Nov 14	" Collection and writing letter to Ralph	.50
		$19.36

1883		
Nov 14	By Cash from Ralph	$2.00
		$17.36

[*Page 235*]
[*Bill for George A. Atkins:*]
George A. Atkins
In account with
John H. Senter

Statement		Dr.
[*illegible*] 7th	Writ Robinson vs. Miller	1.00
[*illegible*] 3	To Letter to [Hartshorn]	.50
	" Retainer	5.00
	" Letter to Sherbino	.50
[*illegible*]	" Writ you to Sherbino	1.00
Feb 2	" 1 Day trial You vs Sherbino	5.00
March Term of Washington Co. Ct.	To Term and Atty fees You vs Sherbino	7.00
		$20.00

George this is not a dun, but I have made a rule to send a statement of account to every client at the close of each term of court so they may know just [how] their bill stands, and so they wont be disappointed when they come to settle at last, as under the new fee bill, no discount is made.
John H. Senter

[*Page 236*]
[*Bill for F.A. Allen:*]
Warren, Vermont April 25th, 1884
F.A. Allen,
In account with,
John H. Senter

Statement		Dr.
1880		
Oct 15	To Services for you in the mater of the Ralph Bank Note	2.00
"	" Mortgage to " from Ralph	1.00
1883		
Oct 8th	" Writ You vs Howard	1.00

Nov. 2nd " Services in case You vs Howard	3.00
March Term 1884 " Term and Attorney fees You vs Howard	7.00
	$14.00

[Asbury] this is no dun but I have adopted a rule of sending a statement of account to each client at the end of each term of Court, so that they may know exactly how my account stands twice each year, and then no will be disappointed with my charges
Yours truly John H. Senter

April 25th 4
George W. Wing, Esq.,
Montpelier,
Vermont.
Friend George:-

Since my return from County Court I have been mousing around my library hunting for law to fit my views and wishes in divers and sundry cases in which I am anxious to thrash the other party, and as one of the results of my labor I have found the case of Pinnock vs Clough reported in the 16th Vt 500, and if that case is not a clinker in the case of which you have heard in which one Hicks vs Groton and one L. Stoddard as defendant, then I am at sea. Look at it and see what you [*one word illegible*] "H. Pinnock" does not notice it to any [*last one or two lines and signature illegible*]

[*Page 237*]
April 23rd 4
Hon. Frank Plumley,
Northfield,
Vermont.
Dear Frank:-

Cardell is raving [around] me about that ten dollars in the matter of Bishop vs Cardell, recognisance, and I said you would pay it and stop his howling.

I have got heartily sick of it and you would if you had it for breakfast, dinner, supper and for lunch.

Please to close it out. This town is for Nichols further deponent sayeth and knoweth not.

Yours truly and fraternally
John H. Senter

[*Bill for Dan Tarbell:*]
Warren, Vermont, April 23rd 1884
Dan Tarbell,
In account with,
John H. Senter

1884		{Statement}	Dr.
March Term of Washington County Court			
"	"	To Term and Atty. Fees J.W. Brock vs. You	$7.00
"	"	" Trial of your case in County Court	10.00
"	"	" Retainer, Making and Filing Pleas, and hearing before Clerk on Costs and assessments of damages	5.00
			$22.00

Mr. Tarbell, I send you bill of my services as I have adopted a rule to send to each of my clients at the close of each term of Court, so that every man may know just what I am charging him as I go along, a detailed statement
Yours very truly
John H. Senter

[*Page 238*]
April 24th 4
J.S. Dodge, M.D.
Lincoln, Vermont.
Dear Solon:

I have brought suit against Marshal Chafee, and the court will be at Lincoln May 31st. I also enclose writ against Minehan which you will please get signed by your justice, and then have your officer serve. I also enclose blank which please have signed and return to me at once as I want to bring suit against Chaffee and wife. You old physic probably thought I sue both accts. in one writ, but that kind of medicine won't work on the wife's acct. I set the courts all on one day, and I will come over and [raise ruin] with the victims.
Yours, John H. Senter

[*Pages 238-40*]
April 25th 4
W.M. Strong, Esq.,
Waitsfield,
Vermont.

Dear Sir:-

I have the honor to acknowledge your very effusive favor of the 23rd inst. And in reply I will say that for a disinterested party who has very little to say, it is quite an interesting document.

In reply to query why I had not called for the Stakes, I must say that perhaps I am less ravenous then you thought, but my main reason has been that I have had no opportunity without putting myself out, and I thought the money quite safe in your hands, and I should not have written you when I did, but that I was informed that Mr. Joslyn and the [*one line illegible*] ground of the April [clause].

[Well] sir, I should have been a little astonished at your fervor in the matter had I not heard some talking you had done about the matter before I received your favor signed with the additional title of stake holder, which I concluded was done so I should not infer that an interested party was the author.

I made the bet that my cow would give 11 qts. of milk that day or the next. I did not bet she would calve in April.

I did make the statement that she would calve in April, and she shall if she lives another year.

Now as to your very plainly expressed determination to pay Messrs. Joslyn and Reed ten dollars, I have this to say, you can pay [*one word illegible*] or anybody else, whatsoever you see fit and as for me I want no revenge out of you or the old cow either, but I have already notified you that I claim my money, and now I demand it, and I mean exactly what I say. I have no quarrell with you and want none, or with anyone else. But if you choose to have one why that is all right have one. Now if you pay the money you do so with full notice, and assume your own responsibility.

If you should stop to think just what my statement was when I made the bet perhaps you would not be as sanguine to shout ["Prank"] whatever that be. I said when I bet that my cow would give 11 qts. of milk that day [or] the next day and that I had a five dollar bill in my pocket that said so. I said nothing about when she would calve when I made the bet, although I did say before that [she was] was [calving] in April, or rather that she [would] calve in April. Now by your theory Messrs. Joslyn and Reed must have bet that I [*one word illegible*] such cow, instead of betting as I say [*one word illegible*] that she would not give 11 qts of milk [*one to three words illegible*]. Now there were others present [who understand] this just as I do, and I think William you yourself will have to own [that I] state the case just as it is, however [it may] be that it is the way I understand it, and [*one to three words illegible*] right there untill I am otherwise [*one word illegible*], and loud talk about ["Prank"] or any [*one or two words illegible*] won't have but little effect.

Don't for a moment my dear sir think I care very much for five dollars, for [while] I am poor enough, I can manage [to] [*one line illegible*]

[If] Mr. Joslyn and Reed will [agree to it] you may pay that money (I mean the $10) to the most needy family in your village and you may be the judge who it is. So please don't howl about that.

Hoping you are serene and contented in the office of stake holder.

I remain as ever, yours truly

John H. Senter

[*Page 241*]
April 28th 4
H.H. Hall, Esq.,
Chelsea,
Vermont.
Dear Sir:-

I am looking around [to] find a place to build a house, and [I have] been looking at your place here [now] occupied by M.S. Sterling, what [is your] price, and when could you give [possession] of the premises?

Please answer at once, and oblige

Yours truly
John H. Senter

April 30th 4
E.F. Briggs, Esq.,
Granville,
Vermont.
Friend Briggs:

To convince yourself that I stated the law as it was in the case of Bowen vs. Clark, and that I did not lie to you, will you look at the case of Hodges vs. Green, 28th Vermont Reports Page 358. That case will I take it sustain me in my position, both as to whether that was a contract within the statute of frauds, and as to the count in general assumpsit [*remainder of letter is missing or illegible*]

[*Page 242*]
May 1st 4
Fred Parker, Esq.,
Waitsfield,
Vermont.
Dear Sir:-

I am in receipt of the enclosed card from Mr. Palmer, which you see requires an answer at once.

When will you prefer to have the hearing? Write me at once.

Yours truly
John H. Senter

May 1st 4
Hon. E.F. Palmer,
Waterbury,
Vermont.
Dear Sir:-

Your favor of today is at hand, and in reply I will say that I will write to Mr. Parker to-night, and on receipt of his reply will fix on day and write you.

Yours truly
John H. Senter

[*Page 243*]
May 3rd 4
O.W. Orcutt, Esq.,
Roxbury,
Vermont.
Dear Sir:-

I enclose writ against Marshall Chaffee and wife, which you will secure at once. If Mr. Chaffee wants to settle this matter he can with me or you.

His own bill which was the one the other writ was brought on amounts to-day with interest to the sum of $40.00. His wife's bill the one issued to-day amounts with interest to the sum of $19.00. The two writs are $2.00 so that if he will pay you $60.00 and also so pay your costs at once it will stop costs, otherwise it will be otherwise

Yours truly
John H. Senter

May 5th 4
Charles W. Porter, Esq.,
Montpelier,
Vermont.
Dear Sir:-

Enclosed I send you a copy of Pltff's specifications in Allen vs. Howard please to acknowledge the receipt of same on enclosed card and oblige

Yours very truly
John H. Senter

[*Page 244*]
May 4th 4
Messrs. Pitkin & Huse,
Montpelier,
Vermont.
Gentlemen:-

Your favor of the 30th [last] was only received last evening on my return from Granville, where I had been for three days, and engaged in the trial of seven cases (It [wasn't] much of a time for cases there either) I should have replied ere this had I been at home.

I am perfectly satisfied to have you lead as I think you have the longest suit of trumps. Go ahead and all will be correct.

Ask Charles W. Porter's lieutenant, Tom whether, Great Johnny Wing and Little [Tony Elwood,] are match for Great Hiram Atkins and Little John Senter. Yours truly John H. Senter

[*date is illegible*]
Hiram Atkins,
Montpelier,
Vermont.
Dear Sir:-

I enclose copy for notice I wish 100 copies printed and sent to me. I also send copy for some cards. I want printed in script type all but the Granville notice on the bottom which [may] be in fine type. I want 250 of the cards.

Yours truly
John H. Senter

[*Page 245*]
May 7th 4
E.G. Farnham, Esq.,
Shoreham,
Vermont.
Dear Sir:-

S.D. Allen of this [town] is now away from home, and I have the charge of such of his business as needs attention when he is absent; and among other things is an account or rather a claim against the estate of Ashley Wolcott.

Mr. Allen desired me to write you in a friendly business way about the matter.

I understand from him that the estate is considered solvent, if this be so we will send our account for ninety dollars and accrued interest for a horse sold to deceased, but if the estate is not perfectly good beyond doubt [*one line illegible*] horse was disposed of before Mr. Wolcott's death, as the horse was only sold conditionally as can be established by his letters to us. Of course if the horse was sold by Mr. Wolcott we should be unable to hold the horse as the claim was not recorded. Will you have the kindness to write if the estate is solvent and if so when the commissioners will meet, but if not solvent whether Mr. Wolcott's estate now own said horse?

Yours very respectfully
John H. Senter

[*Page 246*]
May 5th 4
George W. Wing, Esq.,
Montpelier,
Vermont.
Dear Sir:-

I write to inquire what day prior to the June Term of the Orange County Court, will be most convenient for you to attend to making the disclosure of the trustee in Bank vs. Parkers and Trustee.

If you will name a day I and Mr. [Plyner] Parker will come out and we will attend to the matter.

Thine Fraternally,
John H. Senter

May 6th 4
Hon. Homer W. Heaton,
Montpelier,
Vermont.
Dear Sir:-

Nathaniel Stockwell is dead and buried, and of course I cannot make any purchase of the premises now until after the action of the Probate Court. Now I should like the place but I cannot hang up on a [pinhook] until doomsday waiting for it, and as I cannot buy now, can I rent it? I will pay forty dollars rent for it this year if I can have it at once, and will buy it just as soon as it can be sold. What do you say? Let me know at once what can be done as I am about to do something.

Yours truly
John H. Senter

[*Page 247*]
May 7th 4
Hon. Frank Plumley
Northfield,
Vermont.
Friend Frank:

Your favor of yesterday enclosing check for ten dollars in payment of costs in the matter of Bishop et ux vs Cardell is duly received. Frank don't think I should have hurried you about this matter if it had been my business, but it was not, and I was punched until I got sore. As for interest you may put that in your eye.

Yours fraternally
John H. Senter

May 7th 4
Amos Pierce, Esq.,
Warren,
Vermont.
Dear Sir:-

Mr. Geo. A. Wheeler has put in my hands for adjustment a little matter about a [chair] of his which you took from his premises yesterday without leave. Now sir you must bring that [chair] to this office and pay for this letter at once or I shall issue a writ and make you costs.

Yours truly John H. Senter

[*Page 248*]
May 7th 4
L.D. Tilottson, Esq.,
Washington,
Vermont.
Dear Sir:-

On the 31st day of March I received a letter from you enclosing a note against Orrin S. Clough of this place, and also containing directions for me to bring suit.

Upon the same day I received your letter I made inquiries of Mr. [Plyner] Parker a clapboard manufacturer of this place for whom Clough was at work and found he would be [paying] him enough in about a week to cover your debt so I waited and then had a writ served. Mr. Clough was quite indignant that [he] should be sued upon the note saying he [left] the money for you at Washington with [*one line illegible*] there last, well he settled the matter by giving me an order on Mr. Parker, for the amount of the note and the costs, which Mr. Parker accepted, and will pay when he receives returns from lumber, when I will remit to you. I write so that you may know what has become of your note.

Yours truly
John H. Senter

[*Page 249*]
May 8th 4
George W. Brooks, Esq.,
Warren,
Vermont.
Dear Sir:-

I have in my hands for collection an account against you, which must be paid at once to save your further costs. Call and settle with me before Monday night. Yours truly
John H. Senter

May 10th 4
Hiram Atkins, Esq.,
Montpelier,
Vermont.
Dear Sir:-

Enclosed you will find one dollar for which send Argus and Patriot

six months to H.J. Pratt Warren V^{t}.
Yours truly
John H. Senter

[*Page 250*]
May 8th 4
C.F. Camp, M.D.,
Waitsfield,
Vermont.
Dear Sir:-

I have placed in my hands for collection an account against you which requires your earliest attention.

Please attend to this at once and oblige
Yours respectfully
John H. Senter

May 8th 4
Charles Pike, Esq.,
E. Warren,
Vermont.
Dear Sir:-

There are two cases set for trial at my office May 13th one at 9. a.m. and one at 10 a.m. in which you are the court, also one here May 15th at 9. a.m. The writs are returned to me, so I write to notify you. Please to be [hand] and oblige, Yours truly
John H. Senter

[*Page 251*]
May 10th 4
Charles M. Wilds, Esq.,
Middlebury,
Vermont.
Friend Charles:-

I send you, enclosed specifications in Atkins vs. Sherbino, also I return notice in Lycoming case. I shall be over at Middlebury [at] the June Term of Court and we will talk of a [reference] in the Sherbino case. Clarence and I had [it] left with the court so that an entry can be made at any time.
Yours fraternally
John H. Senter

May 10th 4
Messrs. Pitkin and Huse,
Montpelier,
Vermont.
Gentlemen:-

Enclosed I send you copy of plaintiff's specifications in Atkins vs. Sherbino. I have sent a copy also to Messrs. Stewart and Wilds.

Please to acknowledge receipt of specifications on enclosed card.

Yours truly
John H. Senter

[*Page 252*]
May 10th 4
Charles W. Porter, Esq.,
Montpelier,
Vermont.
Dear Sir:-

What do you say to a reference in the case of Allen vs. Howard?

I like that way of trying causes which are of the kind of this case. Let me know at once what you say to this proposition.

Yours truly
John H. Senter

May 10th 4
Harlan W. Kemp, Esq.,
Montpelier,
Vermont.
Friend Harlan:-

I should have answered your letter long ago only I expected to have come to Montpelier ere this, but have been very busy. I have had more business this spring than usual. I don't think of any thing to add to our pleas in the Lycoming case, so you may as well file them any time.

Yours fraternally
John H. Senter

[*Pages 253-54*]
May 11th 4
My Dear Zed:-

Thou art violently carried away from grace; there is a devil haunts thee in the likeness of a fat, lazy man; a tun of man is thy companion; thou [bolting-hutch] of beastliness; thou swolen parcel of dropsies; thou huge bombard of beer; thou stuffed [cloak] bag of guts; thou, my sweet creature of bombast, how long ago is't since thou sawest thine own knee? Thou has more flesh than another man, therefore more frailty.

Out upon thee for a sordid wretch t'would beat his doctor of his physic. Away, you starveling, you bull's pizzle, you vile [paunch] of sin. O, for breath to utter what is like thee! I am accursed to rob in such a thief's company, ye fat-kidneyed rascal, you [*illegible*-presser], you horse back-breaker; you huge hill of flesh.

Thou art so fat-witted, with drinking Gotham's beer, and unbuttoning thee after supper and [*one line illegible*] to demand that truly which thou wouldst truly know.

Has not my worthy client who handles the [*one word illegible*] and pestle called thine to a reckoning many [*one word illegible*] and oft, without avail? Did he not relieve his aches and pains with many a lotion and soothing drop, where now would his dear Julia's bones been [laid] er'st she had made her bed to him, had not his [*one word illegible*] skill and infinite wisdom snatched her from the [*one word illegible*] grave? Fight wilt thou, thou lizzard livered poltroon; and that too by the "Bellowing Bulls of [*one word illegible*]" now doubt thou wouldst bellow loud enough [*one word illegible*] all mercy but as for fight that were the greatest [*one word illegible*] of all. But by the Lord [if ye] are glad ye have the money and out of that great store I will demand only sixty silver buzzards, besides which you shall fully recompense that faithfull minion of the law, i.e. Orcutt for his well done labor in behalf of [*remainder of line illegible*]

I'll have my debt, speak not against my debt;
I have sworn an oath that I will have my debt;
Thou callest me pelican; before thou had'st a cause;
But since I am a pelican beware my beak;
For the justice with his fat round belly shall grant me my most
 righteous cause.
I'll not be a soft and dull eyed fool;
To shake the head, relent and sigh and yield
I'll have my debt.

Have I not interceded by letter with your stony hearted client all to no purpose? And now because I have him in my power by the strong arm of the law shall I relent? Shall I throw away my physic on such a craven dog as he, because thou [threw the better] fight. Why if fight is what you want

"[Pile] on McDuff and damned is he who first cries hold enough." Hads't thou cried for mercy you would have had it, but that mercy would have been tempered with justice.

Well Zed, Julia's acct. amounts to	$18.83
Marshalls acct. amounts to	37.00
Two writs amount to	2.00
Orcutt's officer fees amount to	5.70
Total	$63.53

Sixty three and 53/100 dollars will be [required to liquidate]

Verily I say unto thee thou parody on justice it must be [63.50] or fight, fight, fight.

Thine fraternally
John H. Senter

[*Page 255*]
May 12th 4
Hon. E.F. Palmer
Waterbury,
Vermont.
Dear Sir:-

Excuse the delay, but I write as soon as possible. I can attend to that case any day from the 26th to the 30th of May both inclusive, and I cannot before as I am fixing for Supreme Court

Yours truly
John H. Senter

[*Page 256*]
May 17th 4
H.H. Van Deusen, Esq.,
E. Warren,
Vermont
Dear Sir:-

Mr. Goodspeed has been to see me today in relation to his rights about the water conduit which heretofore has supplied your house and his. He presents some different phases of the matter than you did. It seems there is a deed from Childs to him [for] the surplus water, also a reservation of the same rights for Goodspeed, in Childs' deed to Powers he also claims that he has always been ready and willing to do, and always has done his equitable share of repairs on the aquaduct. This makes a different [object] than the one you presented to me, and under the circumstances I advise you as I do him [*several words illegible*] you have neither of you any idea [*one line illegible*] litigate it in the courts, and when you get through very likely you will neither of you be any better for your experience.

If you and Goodspeed cannot agree and most likely you cannot, I would suggest that you refer the whole matter to som disinterested man whom you both can agree upon and let him decide, and then abide by his decission. This will be by far the least expensive and I presume more satisfactory in its results to both of you, than a chancery lawsuit costing from two to five hundred dollars.

Of course I do not pretend to dictate to either [of you] but you have neither of you any money [to pay] fighting about those water rights. I [have sent] this letter to Goodspeed and sent it by [*one or two words illegible*] hope it will accomplish its [*last one or two lines and signature illegible*]

[*Page 257*]
June 18th 4
Milo Bucklin, Esq.,
Warren,
Vermont.
Dear Sir:-

D.C. Geer has placed in my hands for adjustment a small matter relating to a work bench which he bought of George A. Hanks, and which you sold to B.F. Shaw. You will give this your earliest attention and save costs
Yours very truly
John H. Senter

June 17 4
George Wilkins, Esq.,
Stowe,
Vermont.
Dear Sir:

The school tax assessed on the farm known as the Wheeler farm by school district No. 5 in Warren amounts to ($13.30) thirteen & 30/100 dollars, and said tax must be paid at once, or the collector will have to sell the land. Will you please attend to this matter at once and see that the sum is paid, as I understand you manage the [farm for] the recent [mortgagee.]

Yours
John H. Senter

[*Page 258*]
June 18th 4
Robert Riley, Esq.,
Granville,
Vermont.
Dear Sir:-

I have in my hands for collection, an account against you in favor of L.R. Joslyn of Waitsfield, to the amount of ($4.70) four dollars and seventy cents. Please attend to this at once
Yours truly
John H. Senter

[*Pages 258-59*]
June 20 4
Geo. W. Wing, Esq.,
Dear Sir:

In re Denslow Upham's last will and testament of which I spoke to you this morning I will so far as I can give you an outline of the matter. The testor was a man of 84 years, he had two children, to wit, Dr. E.F. Upham [of] Randolph and Susan M. Gleason of Warren, wife of John C. Gleason. John C. Gleason is the executor of the will.

For the last six or eight years Mrs. Upham wife of the testator has been entirely helpless and confined to her bed, and the testator has been feeble requiring constant care, and they have lived in the family of Mr Gleason. Sometime last September, Upham made a will in which he willed his grand children, two hundred dollars each and willed [to Dr. Upham] his safe, part of his silver ware, part of his [books], and part of the family pictures and nothing more, the remainder of his property in trust for his wifes support, and after her death to John C. Gleason & Wife. Early in January of this year, Mrs. Upham died, and in due course of [time] the testator sent for J.H. [Hastings] and made a new will the one now in controversy for which will he devised, the same articles in detail as in former will to Dr. E.F. Upham and also in addition the sum of $1000.^{00}, he willed $100.^{00} to each of his grand children, and [all] of the remainder to John C. Gleason and Wife. [Dr.] E.F. Upham contests the will claiming I suppose undue influence, and want of capacity [to] dispose. I think we

can establish the [*one word illegible*] by a large preponderance of testimony. [Of course] we do not know that, Upham will contest the will, and I hardly know what we ought to do about witnesses, he may not appear and so of course I don't wish to put the [proponent] to any more expense than is necessary. Write what you think will be absolutely necessary under the circumstances, we not having been notified of a contest.
Yours
John H. Senter

[*Pages 260-61*]
June 23rd 4
F.N. Holman, Esq.,
Randolph,
Vermont.
Bro. Holman:-

Your favor of the 20th is hand and contents noted, in reply I will say that as to the matter of costs, the referees taxed the witnesses costs and reported it. I took no copy and have no idea of the amount the other costs are regulated by statute and the clerk can tax them. As for the judgment of J.D. Mitchel against Ralphs as trustees, I have a lien on the judgment which is a prior lien by force of my being the attorney of record for my fees and disbursements which amounts to over one hundred dollars. I shall insist on that and according to all the decisions, I think it clear my attorneys lien will hold. If you think otherwise, we shall have to fight for I do not propose to let up a hare on my lien. I have filed notice of my lien in clerks office on the docket and shall strive to maintain the same.
Yours
John H. Senter

[*Page 261*]
June 23 4
Charles M. Wilds, Esq.,
Middlebury
Vermont.
Friend Charles:-

I enclose bill of my services in No. 60 Briggs vs Ralph. I have filed notice of attorney's lien. You will see there is a trustee judgment in case filed as offsett. I maintain my lien is entitled to be [paid first]; of course there will have to be added to my bill, the amount of the clerk's bill for judgment fees yet to come

I enclose Holmans letter, you see by that he expects judgment against him on the report

Will you look at the papers and have the matter passed upon for me, it will greatly oblige and I will pay you your just proportion of the [sum.]
Yours John H. Senter

[*Page 262*]
June 25th 4
C.W. Porter, Esq.,
Montpelier,
Vermont.
Dear Sir:

Have you considered the matter of referring the case of Allen vs. Howard? I am anxious to dispose of that case and shall expect to try it in Sept. Term of Wash. Co. Ct. if not referred, so that [if] we refer it, I want it tried and judgment [reported] at Sept. Term.
Yours
John H. Senter
P.S. I congratulate you on your nomination. You noticed that the Warren delegates [*last line illegible*]

June 25th 4
E.G. Farnham, Esq.,
West Cornwall,
Vermont.
Dear Sir:-

As I have not heard from you since your favor of May 10th I thought I would write and ask you if the commissioners on the estate of Ashley Wolcott had fixed a days for examining claims against the estate also whether, the real estate was sold so as to make the estate solvent.
Yours truly
John H. Senter

[*Page 263*]
June 30th 4
C.O. Graves, Esq.,
Washington,
Kansas.

Dear Sir:-

Your favor of June 24th came to hand last night, and I hasten to reply. I should have informed you how matters stood long ago, if I had had any knowledge of your address, but I did not.

On the day set for the trial of your case Mr. A.S. Ralph appeared and gave judgment on the note, and took an appeal to the next term of Washington Co. Ct., as he said for time to pay the demand. L.M. Heath recognized for [costs.] Ralph will probably pay it before court time, if not I shall press a trial and get execution at the earliest moment.

Yours truly
John H. Senter

June 30th [4]
H.N. Taplin, Esq.,
Montpelier
Vermont.
Dear Sir:-

I return uncollected assessment receipts, except that I retain D.H. Stut's receipts for the sum of $16.95 which I am in the way of working up by fare on the stage, he agreed to let me [ride] out part of it; by making a discount and as that is the only way to get it I accepted the proposition. When I have rode all I can on that account I will divide with the company.

Yours truly
John H. Senter

[*Pages 264-65*]
May 17th 4
S.D. Allen, Esq.,
Warren, Vermont.
Dear Sir:-

I have investigated the matter of your claim for a horse, which you sold to Ashly Wolcott during his life, and which horse by the terms of the sale was to be and remain your property until paid for, although no record was made of the lien in the town Clerks office, and although the said Ashly Wolcott has since deceased and the horse has come into the possession of the administrator of his, Wolcott's, estate.

The law of conditional sale is well settled in this State, the purchase money having become due and being unpaid, you are the absolute owner of the horse in question, and entitled to possession on demand which right of possession can only be defeated by the payment of the purchase money

See West vs. Bolton 4 V^t^. 558.

Buckmaster vs. Smith 22 V^t^. 203

Burnell vs Marvin 44 V^t^. 277 & cases therein cited.

Such was the law of this state, settled by repeated decisions prior to the enactment of a statute relating to "Liens on Property Sold," passed in 1870 and amended in 1872 now found in the Revised Laws Sec 1992, and such is now the law of this state except where it is abridged or qualified by this statute. This statute was enacted solely to prevent fraud against those who bought property ignorant [by] notice either actual or constructive, of any [reserved] lien by the vendor. This statute did not limit, abridge, or disapprove of oral or nonrecorded liens or conditional sales as between [the] parties thereto. To all the world excepting <u>attaching</u> creditors and <u>bona</u> <u>fide</u> purchasers <u>without</u> <u>notice</u> the law remains the same as before the enactment of this statute.

The administrator of Ashly Wolcott's has the same and only the same rights and interest in said horse as Ashly Wolcott had with he died, he stands simply as the legal representative of Ashly Wolcott.

There is and can be no fraud against the creditors of Ashly Wolcott. Wolcott had no <u>vested</u> interest in this horse, his was only an inchoate interest which could only become vested by payment of the purchase money, untill that is paid the horse is yours. This statute which requires a record names the classes it seeks to protect, and leaves all others to their rights at common law.

See, Kelsey vs. Kendall 48 V^t^. 24 and also see Burnham vs Marshall to be reported in 56 V^t^., which case was exactly like this one, and was heard at the last [General] Term of Supreme Court, it was held in that case that the rights of a conditional vendor, where the lien [reserved] was oral and of course non-recorded, attached to the property in the hands of the vendee's administrator, and that the administrator was liable in trover for a conversion of the property.

Your course then Mr. Allen is to demand of the Administrator the horse in question and if he neglects to either pay the sum due upon the horse or to deliver him to you he is liable in trover for the value of the horse

Yours truly

John H. Senter

[*Page 266*]

Aug. 4th 4

H.C. Backus, Esq.,
Middlesex,
Vermont.
Dear Sir:-

I have in my hands for collection an account against you in favor of Richardson & Fullerton of Waterbury, which I enclose. I also enclose blank order on H.W. Lyford for the amount and trust you will sign and return same to me at once

Yours truly
John H. Senter

Aug. 5th 4
Geo. W. Wing, Esq.,
Montpelier,
Vermont.
Bro. Geo. W. Wing:-

I tellephoned you the other day, but have received no answer, and to-day I cannot find you. Harlan is here and is growing impatient about this case and that to with good reason. Can you not see Judge Rudfield and get some order so that progress can be made in his case.

He has a right to be impatient and if any thing can be done, Do it

Yours truly
John H. Senter

[*Page 267*]
Aug. 6th 4
Richardson and Fullerton,
Waterbury,
Vermont.
Gentlemen:

Your favor of the first inst. was duly received. I have looked up White, and find that he has no attachable property, but he earns good wages and leaves chances to muster sometimes.

If I were you, I should get judgment against him, and that will bring the amount above ten dollars and then when he leaves the bars down muster his wages. If you would like to do so, have some of your Waterbury Justices sign the enclosed blank writ and return to me at once. I do this as it will [*three words illegible*] to attend to the case at Waterbury than here, and as it is book account one of your firm would [have] to make

[oath] to the acct.
Yours truly
John H. Senter

[*Page 268*]
October 22nd 4
J.D. Hanks, Esq.,
Lincoln,
Vermont.
Dear Sir:

H. W. Lyford of this place asked me to write you a line regarding the bill incurred for [keeping] the Lincoln [Bank] on the night of Oct. 3rd which amounts to $12.50 he thought perhaps as I had heard nothing since then relating to the matter it might have been forgotten

Please attend to it at once
Yours Truly
John H. Senter

[*Page 269*]
[*Bill for George Atkins:*]
Warren, Vermont October 22nd 1884
George A. Atkins,
In acct with
John H. Senter
1884

			Dr.
Amount of bill recorded Apr. 22d, 1884			20.00
May 10	To Specifications You vs Sherbino		2.00
"	"	" 2 copies of same for Deft.	2.00
"	"	" Postage on same	.15
"	"	" Cost bond	1.00
Aug		To 1 day Trial You vs. Sherbino before Referees	7.00
Sept Term		Term & Atty fees " " "	7.00
			$39.15

[*Bill for Daniel Tarbell:*]
Warren, Vermont Oct. 22nd 1884
Daniel Tarbell
In account with John H. Senter

	Dr.
To 1 Day at your Place in [sawdust] case	5.00
" Retainer in Chancery case Andrews vs You	5.00
" Term fees Andrews vs You & Tewksbury	8.00
Chancery	$18.00

[*Page 270*]
[*Bill for Fred Parker:*]
Warren, Vermont October 23rd 1884
Fred Parker,
In account with
John H. Senter.

Statement						Dr.
1883						
Sept Term	Washington	Co.	Court	Term and atty fees	Grundy vs. You	7.00
"	"	"	"	" Cash Paid Clerk's Bill	"	1.48
1884						
March Term		"	"	" Term and atty fees "	"	7.00
"	"	"	"	" Cash Paid Clerk's Bill	"	.66
May 31	To 1 Day at Waterbury on trial of Grundy vs You					7.00
Sept Term	Washington Co. Court Term & atty fees					7.00
						$29.94

Fred this will come very handy to me at this time if you can pay it.

[*Bill for Frank Stoddard:*]
Warren, Vermont, October 23rd 1884
Frank Stoddard
In acct with
John H. Senter.

	Dr.	Cr.
To amount of bill rendered Apr. 22d 1884	$19.36	$2.11
September Term Washington County Court Term fees	7.00	
Cash Pd Clerk's Bill	2.00	
	28.36	2.11
Bill Due	$25.25	

[*Page 271*]
Oct. 23rd
Boston Globe,
Boston,
Mass
Gentlemen:-

Enclosed I send you 75 cts for which send Christopher Moore Warren Vt the weekly Globe till Jun 1st 1886.

I sent you sometime in the latter part of last July $2.25, seventy five cents for a weekly Globe, and $1.50 for the daily for myself for 3 months. I received the daily directed to T.N. Senter for one month only, and although I have written you twice about this matter, [*one word illegible*] have not as yet heard from you

Will you send that daily along? and if not why?
Yours
John H. Senter

[*Page 272*]
[*Bill for W.G. McAllister:*]
Warren, October 23rd 1884
W.G. McAllister
In acct. with
John H. Senter

		Dr.
	To amount of bill rendered April 22nd 1884	$17.48
September	Term 1884 Washington County Court.	
	Term and attorney fees You vs Smith	7.00
		$24.48

Oct. 23rd 4
Charles Pike, Esq.,
E. Warren,
Vermont
Dear Sir:-

In the matter of Graves vs Ralphs which was appealed from your judgment, to County Court as the appeal was not entered, I am now entitled to execution, will you now make it out and send it to me
Yours John H. Senter

[*Page 273*]
Nov. 11th 4
George W. Wing, Esq.,
Montpelier,
Vermont.
Bro. George:-

Recognizing the fact that in the Downing case we are beaten, we are now anxious to close it up, and I write this so you may confer with your client and then I ask you to make us a proposition of settlement.

Yours truly
John H. Senter

November 12th 4
Asa M. Colby, Esq.,
Warren,
Vermont.
Dear Sir:-

Alonso S. Ralph has a claim against the estate of his mother, which is unpaid, and he desires me to inform you, that unless you arrange for its settlement at once, he shall cause administration to be taken upon her estate. You will therefore take notice and act as you may think best [in] the matter.

Yours very truly
John H. Senter

[*Page 274*]
Nov. 28 4
Rev. George S. Gurnsey
Rochester,
Vermont.
Dear Sir:-

Several communications have been received from you by the Selectmen of Warren, regarding a lien record or want of such record in Warren Town Clerk's Office for a certain horse, sold by Norman Robinson and which horse came into the possession of D.H. Steel. Now Sir as I am the attorney of both the Town of Warren and Mr. James Cardell they have referred the subject to me and requested me to inform you how the matter stands. Well Sir 1st as regards the Town, they have no interest whatever in the matter, as Mr. Cardell is perfectly responsible to answer to all damages which you may recover against him. So the Town will take no steps in the matter but will let you and Cardell settle your own affairs.

Now as to Mr. Cardell, he acknowledges [no] liability to you whatever in the matter, but claims and can show that your [previous] claim to the horse is and was nothing but fraud, and further can show that even if [you] owned the horse you never owned the claim or note [conditional,] but the same was [paid] to Robinson, was cancelled and is void and [of] no effect. Now my dear sir do not waste more valuable time or stationery writing [more] letters about this, but if you have a good case go ahead and we will endeavor to meet [you.] "But look before you leap" and remember that we do not intend to give one cent but at the [*one word illegible*] of the law.
Yours John H. Senter

[*Page 275*]
Dec 2nd 4
C.F. Camp, M.D.
Barre,
Vermont.
Dear Sir:-

Your bill to Bixby & Co. amounted to $24.09. [Disc] on thermometer 2.50 left $21.59. You paid me $5, left due $16.59. Will you not at once send me check for that amount. I discount the whole price of the thermometer and charge no interest although B. & Co. say they are not to blame for the breakage. Please to close this up.
Yours
John H. Senter

Nov. 29 4
W.H. Bradley, Esq.,
Dear Sir:-

Your note secured by mortgage on Store building in Warren, which note was made payable to E.F. Hewitt or [town] and now held and owned by John C. Gleason is in my hands, and it will amount on the 1st day of January A.D. 1885 to $91.50. I am instructed by Mr. Gleason to inform you that said note must be paid by that time or else foreclosure proceedings will be commenced. So much for business now I wish to congratulate you upon the election of Cleveland & Hendricks. We have got them this time certain
Yours truly John H. Senter

[*Page 276*]
[*The following bill was copied into this book, but appears to have nothing to do with John Senter:*]
L.L. Durant
In account with
S. Banister

			Dr.	Cr.
1883				
July		To 5 Bush Oats	3.25	
1884				
April		" Grinding	.30	
"	29	" do	.15	
May	6	" 100" Meal	1.60	
"	10	" 100" do.	1.68	
"	21	" 55" do.	.88	
"	24	" 100" do.	1.60	
"	31	" 85" Feed	1.41	
June	5	" 100" do	1.70	
		" Sack of Flour	1.88	
Aug	14	" Feed	1.25	
Sept.		" 75" Feed	1.28	
			16.98	16.98
[*one number illegible*] By Cash				3.38
		Bill due	13.60	$13.60

[*Page 277*]
Dec 1st 4
Messrs. Hendee and Fisk,
Morrisville,
Vermont.
Gentlemen;-

Can you collect note of $35.00 of E.C. Butterfield of your town if so bring suit at once in your own name and I will send note, or if you think you can collect at any time I will send note.

Yours truly
John H. Senter

Dec 11th 4
Hon. William P. Dillingham,
Waterbury,

Vermont
Bro. Will:-

In the case of McAllister vs. Smith, [replevin], you will rember I asked you as regards to [a reference] sometime ago. Have you [connected] with your clients and Brother Clough so you can give me a proper answer? I should like very much to refer it as I am [*last three lines and signature illegible*]

[*Page 278*]
Dec 9th 4
[*first name illegible*] Howard, Esq.,
West Hartford,
Vermont.
Dear Sir:-

In the case of Allen vs. You in Washington County Court, you paid Mr. Allen [damages] sometime ago, and were to pay [costs] at once. I informed Mr. Porter [*one word illegible*] attorney in September what the amount [of cost] I have never received any answer [*one word illegible*] about it.

The costs are as follows

$1.50
12.70
[*several figures below this are illegible*]

So you see the whole [amount] was $24.98. So send [*one to three words illegible*] for $25.00 or I shall be obliged [to make] execution and make [you costs.] When you send check [I will send] a discharge in full of [all] costs. Send check to me [*one or two words illegible*]
Yours John H. Senter

[*Page 279*]
Dec. 15th 4
Edwin Martin, Esq.,
Granville,
Vermont.
Dear Sir;-

I have in my hands for collection an account against you in favor of Dr. O.D. Greene amounting to the sum of Seven dollars ($7.00). I shall be at Granville next Saturday, and you can leave it at D.D. Hemenways for me any time before then.

Yours truly
John H. Senter

Dec 15th 4
Hon. Caroll S. Page
Hyde Park,
Vermont.
Dear Sir:-

If you will send me at once an execution or if time has run a writ against Grant I can secure it. If it was here now I could secure it certain, and if no change is made I can when it comes.

Yours truly
John H. Senter

[*Page 280*]
[*The following two letters appear to have been copied on top of each other, making them almost completely illegible.*]
Dec. 16th 4
Boston Weekly Globe
Boston,
Mass.

Enclosed find postal note for [(.70) seventy] cents for which send Weekly Globe [14 months] [Julian Severy Warren Vermont.]

Yours truly
John H. Senter

Dec. 18th 4
W. Prescott Esq.,
Montpelier
Vermont.
Dear Sir:-

George W. Drew has a horse and wagon which are worth some two hundred dollars but she [*one or more words illegible*] chattel mortgage of \$60.^{00} [*one or more words illegible*] them and secure your debt, but [*one or more words illegible*] tender the fifty [*one or more words illegible*] due on the mortgage. What do you say?

Yours truly
John H. Senter

Dec 22nd 4
Rufus Wainwright, Esq.,
Middlebury

Vermont.
Dear Sir:

Will you tax the costs in the case of Briggs vs Ralphs and send me a copy so that I can submit it at once to the other side, as I want execution within 30 days from adjournment of court [*three words illegible*] my lien on property attached. I believe the masters [retained] the witnesses travel and time on their report

Yours truly
John H. Senter

Index of People and Places Mentioned in John Henry Senter's Letters

Note: References are to the page of John Henry Senter's letterpress copying book on which the name appears. If a letter spans more than one page, only the first page of the letter is given; thus, a person or place may be mentioned on page 18 of a letter spanning pages 17-19, and the reference in the index will be to page 17. A person or place may be mentioned more than once on a single page, but the page reference is given only once.

Because nearly all of the letters were written by Senter while he lived in the town of Warren, Vermont, no mention of either Senter or Warren is made in the Index, unless the town of Warren is specifically mentioned in the letter.

As in the section containing transcriptions of Senter's letters, square brackets are used for two purposes: for editorial comments or to indicate that the enclosed text is partially or completely illegible.